THE
ARGENTINE RIGHT

Its History and Intellectual Origins, 1910 to the Present

THE
ARGENTINE RIGHT

Its History and Intellectual Origins, 1910 to the Present

Edited by
Sandra McGee Deutsch and Ronald H. Dolkart

SR
BOOKS

A Scholarly Resources Inc. Imprint
Wilmington, Delaware

The paper used in this publication meets the minimum requirements of the American National Standard for permanence of paper for printed library materials, Z39.48, 1984.

Scholarly Resources Inc.
104 Greenhill Avenue
Wilmington, DE 19805-1897

Library of Congress Cataloging-in-Publication Data

The Argentine right : its history and intellectual origins, 1910 to the present /
   edited by Sandra McGee Deutsch and Ronald H. Dolkart.
       p.   cm. — (Latin American silhouettes)
   Includes bibliographical references and index.
   ISBN 0-8420-2418-2 (alk. paper). — ISBN 0-8420-2419-0 (pbk.)
   1. Argentina—Politics and government—1910–   2. Right and left
(Political science) I. Deutsch, Sandra McGee, 1950– . II. Dolkart, Ronald H.,
1933– . III. Series.
F2848.A74 1993
320.982—dc20
                                              92-20368
                                                CIP

Contents

About the Contributors, **vii**
Preface, **ix**
Argentine Presidents since 1910, **xi**
Introduction, **xiii**

Antecedents of the Argentine Right, **1**
David Rock

The Right under Radicalism, 1916–1930, **35**
Sandra McGee Deutsch

The Right in the Década Infame, 1930–1943, **65**
Ronald H. Dolkart

The Right and the Peronists, 1943–1955, **99**
Richard J. Walter

The Right and Civilian Regimes, 1955–1976, **119**
Leonardo Senkman

The Right and Military Rule, 1955–1983, **147**
Paul Lewis

Conclusion, **181**
Glossary, **189**
Index, **193**

About the Contributors

Sandra McGee Deutsch teaches history at the University of Texas at El Paso. She is the author of *Counterrevolution in Argentina, 1900–1932: The Argentine Patriotic League* (1986). She is currently working on a study of the right in Latin America.

Ronald H. Dolkart is a member of the history faculty of California State University, Bakersfield. He is the coeditor of *Prologue to Perón: Argentina in Depression and War, 1930–1943* (1975).

Paul Lewis teaches political science at Tulane University, New Orleans. His book, *The Crisis of Argentine Capitalism*, was published by the University of North Carolina Press in 1990.

David Rock is a member of the history faculty at the University of California at Santa Barbara. His publications include *Argentina, 1516–1987: From Spanish Colonization to Alfonsín* (1987, 2d ed.).

Leonardo Senkman teaches in the Institute of Contemporary Jewry at Hebrew University, Jerusalem. His publications include *El antisemitismo en la Argentina*, 3 vols. (1986).

Richard J. Walter is a member of the history department at Washington University, St. Louis. His most recent book is *Buenos Aires and Argentine Politics, 1912–1943* (1985).

Preface

The editors have shared for many years an interest in the history of the Argentine right. Our initial joint effort was a panel at the 1985 meeting of the American Historical Association. The enthusiasm of the participants, most of whom are included here, inspired us to plan this collection of essays, with the addition of other colleagues. The editors' primary appreciation is directed to the contributors to this volume for their patience and cooperation. Dr. Margaret Rose read portions of the manuscript and made many valuable suggestions. We are particularly grateful to Rainelle Sica for her superior word-processing skills through several revisions. We wish to acknowledge the funding provided for the translation of Dr. Leonardo Senkman's article by the Center for Inter-American and Border Studies, University of Texas at El Paso, and by the deans of Arts and Sciences and of Graduate Study and Research at California State University, Bakersfield. Finally, we want to thank Richard M. Hopper, editorial director at Scholarly Resources, for his interest and support and Dr. William H. Beezley and Dr. Judith Ewell for their enthusiastic encouragement of this work.

Argentine Presidents since 1910

Roque Sáenz Peña	1910–1914
Victorino de la Plaza	1914–1916
Hipólito Yrigoyen	1916–1922
Marcelo T. de Alvear	1922–1928
Hipólito Yrigoyen	1928–1930
José F. Uriburu	1930–1932
Agustín P. Justo	1932–1938
Roberto M. Ortiz	1938–1942
Ramón S. Castillo	1942–1943
Arturo Rawson	1943
Pedro Ramírez	1943–1944
Edelmiro J. Farrell	1944–1946
Juan Domingo Perón	1946–1952, 1952–1955
Eduardo A. Lonardi	1955
Pedro E. Aramburu	1955–1958
Arturo Frondizi	1958–1962
José María Guido	1962–1963
Arturo Illia	1963–1966
Juan Carlos Onganía	1966–1970
Roberto M. Levingston	1970–1971
Alejandro A. Lanusse	1971–1973
Héctor J. Cámpora	1973
Raúl A. Lastiri	1973
Juan Domingo Perón	1973–1974
María Estela (Isabel) Martínez de Perón	1974–1976
Jorge R. Videla	1976–1981
Roberto Viola	1981
Leopoldo F. Galtieri	1981–1982
Reynaldo Bignone	1982–1983
Raúl Alfonsín	1983–1989
Carlos Saúl Menem	1989–

Introduction

To many readers of the popular press outside (and perhaps even inside) Latin America, the term "Argentine right" seems redundant. The public often views Argentina as the successor to European fascism since World War II, the place where war criminals went for refuge and received a hearty welcome from indigenous Nazi sympathizers. The right, in the form of apparently totalitarian governments, such as Juan D. Perón's first and second administrations (1946–1955), or in the form of repressive anti-Semitic dictatorships, such as the reign of the generals (1976–1983), appears to epitomize Argentine politics. Of all the nations in the postwar world, none seems so identified with the extreme right as Argentina.

This viewpoint fails to account for the facts that Jewish and other refugees also made their way to Argentine shores in the 1930s and 1940s and that ideologies besides fascism influenced Perón and the generals. Nevertheless, despite its oversimplifications, this image has affected academic scholarship as well as popular perception. Argentina has been a favored locus for studies of fascistlike groups. Yet this literature has been limited in its scope to one sector of the right, that is, to those groups known collectively as the "nationalists," or Nacionalistas. The most visible and extreme of rightists, they embody the heritage of European fascism of the 1930s, and their authority and symbols pervade Argentine society. The Argentine right's ability to appropriate and maintain for itself the designation "nationalist" in contrast to elsewhere in Latin America, where the left is synonymous with nationalism, indicates its importance.

Although possessing an influence far beyond their limited numbers and squabbling groups, the Nacionalistas represent only a part of the Argentine right. Moreover, although the Nacionalistas have figured prominently in works on twentieth-century Argentine political history, such studies usually have been partisan, written either by Nacionalistas or by their die-hard opponents. The presentations also have tended to concentrate on ideology as expressed by Nacionalista intellectuals in a variety of books and journals and have devoted little attention either to the Nacionalistas' social origins or to the historical context in which the Nacionalistas operated. Finally, most works have been narrowly chronological and have focused on the decade of the 1930s, which represented a high point of Nacionalista activity. A scholarly analysis of the entire spectrum of the Argentine right, from its inception to the present, is the objective of this volume.

Considering the Argentine context, it would be useful to define some terms. In this volume, the word "ideology" refers simply to the world view of a particular social group or set of groups. It does not mean "distorted or selected ideas in defense of the status quo of a social system," as Karl Marx used it,[1] although the Nacionalistas' distortions of Argentine realities are a theme of the book.

Another vital term to define is, obviously, the "right." From the beginning of its political usage during the French Revolution, the right has stood for resistance to progressive political and social change. In each context, this resistance has assumed different forms. The right has encompassed a wide range of movements, from conservatism, whose pragmatic support for monarchy and church did not exclude adjustment to modernization, to the more rigid counterrevolutionary activism, which refused to compromise with any threat to a hierarchical social structure. During the nineteenth century, these factions of the European right cooperated in their opposition to most aspects of classical liberalism, to greater democratic participation, and to the rising middle classes. By the early decades of the twentieth century the right had attracted new adherents from the ranks of former liberals frightened by the specter of the working class. Their extreme hostility to Marxism and to the complexities of industrial society led some sectors of the right to formulate sinister doctrines of social Darwinism, anti-Semitism, and antimodernism. Although these issues often were divisive, the right formed alliances that included groups with positions ranging from moderate conservatism to military authoritarianism to aristocratic reaction to ultranationalistic fascism.[2]

With its overwhelmingly Spanish and Italian population, Argentina is linked to Europe more closely than other Latin American nations are. Therefore, that many Argentines received European rightist doctrines, particularly in their Mediterranean forms, with enthusiasm and joined rightist groups was not surprising. These organizations, however, were not mere imitations of movements from across the Atlantic; the Argentine right grew in response to indigenous political, economic, social, and regional circumstances, and the divisions that arose within it, from moderate to extreme, reflected local conditions. Thus, one cannot study the components of the right in isolation or solely in terms of an often abstract philosophy. The interaction between and among the various factions of the right and the relationship of the right, particularly its extremist members, to the larger course of Argentine history constitute the genuine significance of this political force.

The authors of these articles generally use the term "right" in its broadest sense, to denote the full spectrum of opinion included in this category. They attach modifiers, such as "old" or "new" or "liberal," to define different persuasions or descriptions of the right. And they designate component groups by titles, such as conservative, fascist, or Nacionalista. The editors also have adopted the lowercase spelling of, for example, "right," "conservative," and "fascist" when these terms are employed in a generic sense but have capitalized "Nacionalista" and kept the Spanish form because it refers to a specific Argentine classification and because it avoids any confusion that the term "nationalist" might cause.

As in Europe, the roots of the right in Argentina can be found in the revolt against classical liberalism, which had inspired the modernization of the nation in the last half of the nineteenth century. Liberal policies not only had created a prosperous export-based economy but also had fostered inequality. Criticism of economic and political liberalism had coalesced into a rightist persuasion by the turn of the century. The more immediate cause of the formation of a rightist movement was the labor unrest of the second decade of the twentieth century. The right organized in response to lower-class demands for a more equitable distribution of wealth and power. From its inception, then, fear of a left that would upset the hierarchical arrangement of Argentine society bound the right together.

By the 1930s, after a decade of activity, a clear division between two major rightist factions had emerged, and this difference would persist over time. On the one hand, the conservatives represented an "old right" of the upper classes, which was tied to the export economy, and their main objective was to maintain their privileges through the exercise of political fraud. On the other hand, the Nacionalistas formed a "new right" of varied social origins, including leaders from the wealthy oligarchy and a growing middle-class constituency. Their principal goal was sweeping: to purify Argentina of leftist and liberal corruption (a demand that often included conservative politicians), thereby creating a powerfully independent *patria*. Much of the history of the right to the present time lies in the interaction between these two persuasions, old and new. The constant crises that have afflicted twentieth-century Argentina have influenced this relationship.

The division between conservatives and Nacionalistas was only the first to trouble the right. Other fissures have opened, with a "new" right emerging in each decade to challenge the former militants. Thus, the question of whether to support Perón during his first presidency split the right. After 1955 some sectors of Peronism moved to the left and entered into conflict with the right, but others joined forces with the right, further entangling an already intricate political web and in turn provoking the military interventions and dictatorships of recent years.

The evolution of this broadly defined Argentine right, and its internal and external dynamics, is the subject of this book. Each contributor has focused on a significant period of Argentine history and interpreted the way in which the changes of that time influenced and were influenced by the right. The study begins with David Rock's inquiry into the foundations of the right in political philosophy and Argentine events. In "Antecedents of the Argentine Right," Rock notes the authoritarian threads that tied the juntas of the most recent military regimes to their late nineteenth-century forebears. The tenets of European counterrevolutionary doctrine filtered into Argentina and eventually became the core beliefs of Nacionalismo—the love of order, hierarchy, corporativism, militant Catholicism, landed estates, and other particularisms; and the hatred of liberalism, leftism, feminism, Freemasonry, and Jews and other "foreigners." Had it not been for local conditions, however, these ideas would have had little resonance. A clericalist movement in the late 1800s criticized secular marriage and education and, gradually, other liberal institutions. The turn of the century witnessed a more widespread questioning of the economic ramifications of liberalism, despite the apparent affluence it had promoted. Secular opponents of the liberal model of economic development, and of the foreign immigration, the materialist order, and, particularly, the labor movement that had accompanied it, began to align themselves with the elements of the Catholic church who hoped to tame the poor. Thus, from its inception, the Argentine right united its forces around the issue of co-opting and repressing the working class.

Bourgeois fear of unions, anarchism, and Marxism in the early twentieth century supplied the impetus for converting philosophical concepts into action. Sandra McGee Deutsch examines these events in "The Right under Radicalism, 1916–1930." In response to serious labor disturbances in 1919, the first prominent rightist group, the Liga Patriótica Argentina, arose. Similarly distressed by post-World War I worker militancy, the earliest circles of Nacionalistas coalesced in the late 1920s. The birth of these groups also was related to the decay of the old conservative parties that had governed Argentina since 1880. The vacuum in the "old right" encouraged the formation of a new, more extreme, right. The two organizations reacted against Argentina's short-lived experience with democratic rule under the Unión Cívica Radical (UCR), or Radical party. The Liga, the Nacionalistas, and the upper classes from which came the leaders of these groups concluded that democracy would not protect their interests against the lower class and, erroneously, that the Radical party was allied with that class. Although both the Liga and the Nacionalistas recruited from and were tied to the old right, tensions and ambiguities marred relationships among these three groups. Indeed, Nacionalismo itself represented an alliance of forces, some of which viewed the former elite more favorably than did others. During these years, 1919–1930, the right, despite the growing divisions within it, managed, with military support, to weaken the foundations both of civilian rule and of what had been the strongest labor movement in Latin America.

The revolution of September 6, 1930, opened the Década Infame, a period synonymous with rightist dominance in Argentina. The tension between the resurgent conservatives of the old right and the Nacionalistas of the new right forms the theme of Ronald H. Dolkart's chapter, "The Right in the Década Infame, 1930–1943." The groups united to oust the Radicals and bring to power the military under General José F. Uriburu, but the Nacionalistas' hopes for a corporativist state soon were dashed under the succeeding regimes, all of which were dominated by conservative landowners. The 1930s witnessed a dramatic national debate that revolved around the precepts and activities of the right. The organization of numerous paramilitary groups resulted in repeated acts of violence against perceived enemies on the left and in the publication of scores of newspapers, pamphlets, and books that denounced its adversaries—Communists and Jews—and exalted its causes—the church and the army. In place of policies that only sought to suppress labor unions, the right now attempted to put forward its own answers to class divisions through programs of authoritarian control, notably in Buenos Aires province under its governor, Manuel Fresco. What most strongly shaped the right in this period, and proved to be the most divisive issue, was the intrusion of European concerns. The questions of Great Britain's dominance over Argentina, the course of the Spanish civil war, and, above all, the rise of Italian Fascism and German Nazism separated not only left from right but often conservatives from Nacionalistas. The international pressures on Argentina increased with the outbreak of the Second World War, which the right hoped it could use to solidify its power over the nation.

With the coup of 1943, many Nacionalistas assumed that their moment had come. In "The Right and the Peronists, 1943–1955," Richard J. Walter demonstrates that they were mistaken. Members of this rightist sector had assumed prominent roles in the military government, but as Perón rose to power he replaced some of them. Despite their reservations, the Nacionalistas decided to support Perón for the presidency in 1945; they were swayed by his military-authoritarian image, antileftism, advocacy of religious education, and criticism of the oligarchy and foreign capital. They soon realized, however, that Perón had co-opted them for his own ends and for a program that deviated from their own orthodoxy. Although some Nacionalistas remained his supporters, most turned against him, citing his personalism, his courting of the masses, his wife, his concessions to foreign oil companies, his corruption, and the high cost of his social welfare and nationalization measures. The main reason for their opposition, however, was that Perón, not the Nacionalistas themselves, held power. Nevertheless, the Nacionalistas' critique increasingly coincided with that of other influential Argentines. The final break came with Perón's attack on the Catholic church, a move that impelled Nacionalistas and other rightists into a conspiracy that culminated in a successful coup. Once again the right had united against a workers' movement, although Peronism was hardly left-wing. Although Perón's ideological orientation remains a matter of debate, his appropriation of Nacionalista ideas indicated the links between him and the right.

The extent to which Peronism became a problematical issue for the right is the theme of the chapter by Leonardo Senkman, "The Right and Civilian Regimes, 1955–1976." The old right had split during Perón's administrations, and many of its adherents turned to Peronism. With a declining base of support, the remaining conservative parties, or the "liberal right," alternated between supporting civilian and military rule, depending on which seemed more likely to maintain economic privilege and keep Peronism out of power. As in 1919, the vacuum on the right enabled extremists, such as the Nacionalistas, to gain influence. An indicator of their extremism was the factor that Senkman particularly emphasizes, that is, anti-Semitism. As other writers in this volume also show, hatred toward Jews appeared early in the twentieth century and remained a rightist credo, scarcely diminished in Argentina even after the European Holocaust. Yet anti-Semitism could not bring unity to the Nacionalistas, who were divided between die-hard anti-Peronists, or "Gorillas," and those who favored a rapprochement with the Peronist masses. To further complicate the picture, the Peronists splintered into left and right, and the latter allied themselves with some Nacionalista groups. Despite its fragmentation the right managed to unite its forces against the threat from below—the Peronist left and other popular groups. In doing so, once again the right undermined civilian rule and strengthened the military's propensity to rebel.

As Paul Lewis points out in "The Right and Military Rule, 1955–1983," the military has proved itself no more able to rule than civilians have in the years since 1955, partly due to the division of the right. He elucidates the confusing overlap between liberal and Nacionalista rightist influences on the military and painstakingly examines the composition of military governments. The armed forces selected members of both factions to serve in its administrations; because liberal rightists confined their liberalism to the economic realm, they did not object strenuously to the curtailment of political freedoms. Nevertheless, the liberal right subdivided into the "ultras," who viewed military rule as essential in repressing Peronism, and the "moderates," who preferred civilian administrations provided that they excluded Peronists and radical leftists from participation. The military also maintained ties with another rightist faction, the violent "underworld." Nacionalistas inside and outside the military despised liberal rightists for what they saw as the latter's submissiveness to foreign influence, whereas the liberal right considered Nacionalistas anachronistic. These divisions paralyzed successive military regimes, enabling civilians to return to power. Still, although they may have disagreed over tactics, all factions of the military and civilian right believed in the need to suppress the left, a task that the military carried out ruthlessly in the Dirty War of 1976 to 1983.

In 1983 it seemed as though Argentina had entered a new phase. The war over the Malvinas and the revelations of the Dirty War and of administrative ineptitude had discredited the military and its allies. Moreover, for the first time Argentines had spurned the Peronist party in a free election, choosing Raúl Alfonsín, a Radical, as president. Observers speculated that both the right and Peronism had lost their influence. By 1989, however, economic and political crises had served to restore Peronist fortunes with the election of

Carlos Saúl Menem (scarcely an orthodox Peronist), as well as the right's role as "spoiler." The right continues both to rally diverse supporters against the specter of the left and in its attempts to weaken democracy, yet its divisiveness impedes its quest for power.

Notes

1. Harry M. Johnson, "Ideology and the Social System," *International Encyclopedia of the Social Sciences*, 18 vols. (reprint ed.; New York, 1972), 8:77. There is a voluminous literature on the nature of ideology. Two excellent works are Jorge Larrain, *The Concept of Ideology* (Athens, GA, 1979); and Paul Ricoeur, in *Lectures on Ideology and Utopia*, ed. George H. Taylor (New York, 1986).

2. On divisions within the right see especially Hans Rogger and Eugen Weber, eds., *The European Right: A Historical Profile* (Berkeley, 1965); and Arno J. Mayer, *Dynamics of Counterrevolution in Europe, 1870–1956: An Analytic Framework* (New York, 1971), 48–55. On the relationship between French conservatives and fascists, see Robert Soucy, *French Fascism: The First Wave, 1924–1933* (New Haven, 1986).

Antecedents of the Argentine Right

David Rock

The "demented generalized repression"[1] in Argentina during the late 1970s erupted from political tensions that had been brewing for at least a generation.[2] Less fully understood than these conditions are the Manichaean ideological drives of the military juntas that led the repression, the "culture of fear" that they inspired, their "cult of death," and the "semantic delirium" by which they identified their enemies. Tulio Halperín may be right to propose that Argentina is "a country that was born liberal,"[3] and the military regimes of 1976 to 1983 bear many traces of this liberal tradition. Even so, the events of these years highlight the nonliberal, authoritarian threads in Argentine politics, and they have refocused attention upon the right—its historical origins and development, its entrenchment among power groups led by the military, and the sources of its strikingly archaic mission in effect to save western Christian civilization. "A terrorist is not just someone with a gun or a bomb," General Jorge Videla declared, "but also someone who spreads ideas that are contrary to western and Christian civilization."[4]

In 1976 the military junta proclaimed itself responsible not to the law but to "God and History." "We are heirs to a millenary civilization grounded on Christian revelation, Greek philosophy and Roman order," trumpeted *Cabildo*, the militant right-wing periodical.[5] Addressing the troops who had captured the Islas Malvinas from Great Britain in 1982, a priest saluted "the Argentine people, who are Catholic, Hispanic and Roman, [and who have] fought for the defense of our Nation and for Jesus Christ."[6]

These authoritarians dismissed both liberals and democrats as "pseudo-heroes who embody the French Revolution in our country."[7] Raúl Alfonsín, who was elected president in 1983, personified "leftist ethics, modernist culture, Anglo-Saxon 'Atlanticism,' " and his foreign minister, Dante Caputo, "international Judaism and Masonry."[8] Other pronouncements evoked the discourse of medieval scholasticism. For example, in 1976 the junta's first foreign minister, Admiral César Guzzetti, compared his government's bloody assaults on rebels and dissenters with the human body's reaction to disease or infection: "When the social body of the country has been contaminated by a disease that corrodes its entrails, it forms antibodies."[9] The infamous General Ramón J. Camps, who boasted of his complicity in the deaths of five thousand "subversives" during the late 1970s, defined his victims as "terrorists or pacifists [*sic*] who supported changing the existing institutions to impose a political system contrary to humanity [*antihumanista*], contrary to Christianity, and dependent on the foreigner." Camps denied suggestions that he was a Nazi. "I consider myself a man of the right, a conservative, an extreme defender of humanity," he declared.[10]

In examining these strange but deadly ideological encrustations, we are immediately reminded of the distinction drawn by Hugh Trevor-Roper between "traditional clerical conservatism" and "dynamic fascism," which were as different as "the divinely consecrated absolutism of the Stuart kings and the naked unconsecrated absolutism of Hobbes."[11] Perhaps, in a very general way, the rise of the Argentine junta in 1976 resembled the rise of Benito Mussolini in 1922 or of Adolf Hitler in 1933 in signaling the conquest of power by Joseph Burckhardt's "*terribles simplificateurs*," or those who would "rule with utter brutality."[12] In its moribund phases under General Leopoldo Galtieri in 1982, the military regime sought to fashion a dynamic fascistlike movement by attempting external expansion reminiscent of Germany or Italy before the Second World War. But as Carlos Waisman has remarked, the dominant currents of the military regime, and of the Argentine right in general, differed from those in fascism in being "purely authoritarian and anti-mobilizational."[13]

Less than in fascism, the main roots of the Argentine right lay in the European Reaction. The right survives today in Argentina, as it does elsewhere in Latin America, as a curious relic of the clerical and antiliberal counterrevolution that erupted alongside the French Revolution and the rise of Napoleon. As such, the right's closest modern European analogues are Portuguese *integralismo* and Spanish right-wing nationalism led by General Francisco Franco. Like its Portuguese and Spanish counterparts the Argentine right often has betrayed incipiently fascist features, but it has done so without developing true fascism's pagan cult of the totalitarian state.[14] In a similar way, Argentina's "Dirty War" of the 1970s resembled the Spanish civil war much more closely than it resembled the wars of conquest initiated by Nazi Germany or Fascist Italy. "The fields of Spain have become God's witnesses in the blood of its martyrs and its heroes. In community of faith and inspired by Spain's example, we shall embark upon our own struggle," declared a right-wing Argentine militant in 1936.[15] Forty years later the right in Argentina seized its opportunity to follow Franco's example and to fulfill Heinrich von Treitschke's dictum, "War is the only remedy for an ailing nation."

European Influences on the Right

This essay relates the Argentine right to the broader currents of the European counterrevolution as that movement developed after the French Revolution.

The first section summarizes the basic tenets of the counter-revolutionary right, drawing on both their European and Argentine sources. The second section discusses some of the European writers who influenced the Argentine right. The essay's third section outlines the right's main features during its earliest years before 1914.

The term "right" refers to the brand of ultraconservatism whose starting point lay in an organicist conception of society and in antiliberalism, that is, in opposition to the "natural righteousness" of human beings proclaimed by Jean-Jacques Rousseau, to the "rights of man" as enunciated by the French Revolution, to the theories of popular sovereignty that began with John Locke, and to the economics based on Adam Smith that centered upon competition, specialization, and unfettered individualism. However, before 1914 antiliberalism in Argentina was more latent than articulate, and what existed of a "right" up to that time contained numerous liberal remnants. "Before the war," declared the right-wing poet Leopoldo Lugones, "it was possible . . . to believe in liberty, democracy, equality" even while simultaneously condemning some of their manifestations and consequences.[16] Before the war the radical right was primarily a literary movement, largely prepolitical and unorganized—little more than a set of disconnected impulses. At this point, the leaders of the right were "simple aesthetes" who believed in the "supremacy of intelligence and spirit" but whose political stance was "anaesthetized by prosperity." These precursors contrasted with the young militants of the early 1930s who "no longer smiled, . . . [they] lifted their fists, and prepared for combat."[17]

"Counterrevolution" is used here in its common European sense, to denote the archaic, reactionary, and mostly clerical antiliberalism that sprang from the French Revolution. The term "Nacionalismo" in Argentina refers to the antiliberal counterrevolutionary movement that emerged during the late 1920s and 1930s, so that at least until the late 1930s "nationalist" in Argentina, as in Franco's Spain, usually meant an affiliation with the extreme right.[18] Counterrevolutionaries and Nacionalistas alike were often distinguished less by what they proposed than by "the vigour of their negations" and by their attempts to weave "a futurism of the past," that is, to reconstruct a conservative authoritarian government and restore the temporal power of the church, particularly in education, which the anticlerical liberals had taken away.[19]

"Fascism," by contrast, had socialist origins, a mass appeal, and a lower-middle-class base. In fascism reactionary and revolutionary impulses collided dialectically. In Argentina by the 1930s we often encounter language characteristic of fascism as opposed to counterrevolution. For example, some Nacionalistas favored a dictatorship to "impel action; [dictatorship] will silence dissent; it will do constructive things."[20] Similarly reminiscent of fascism were pronouncements such as "the best proclaim themselves" or "prophets do not reason, they announce; they hear and interpret the sentiments of the popular classes."[21] Fascistlike concepts of education appeared also in the aspiration for a system that was "expressive, affirmative, goal-directed [*finalista*], active, constructive."[22]

For the most part, however, the fascist features of the right in Argentina amounted to little more than superficial additions to a counterrevolutionary base. To an Italian Fascist observer, for example, the Argentine right in the 1930s was merely "patriotic," was "insufficiently social revolutionary," and was too circumscribed by historical nostalgia and retrospectiveness to be considered a genuine offshoot of Mussolini's original movement.[23] In Argentina the fascist revolution had its greatest impact on early Peronism rather than on Nacionalismo.

Nacionalismo lacked the cult of instinct, will, and force inherent in true Fascism as well as the movement's commitment to forging a mass organization. Nacionalistas and fascists were divided most deeply in their respective attitudes toward the church and religion, with the former constantly objecting to the latter's "bureaucratizing," or "using," religion. To many Nacionalistas, fascism had the same liberal rationalist parentage as socialism and Marxism, which all differed fundamentally from Nacionalismo in having abandoned Christian metaphysics. Whereas Nacionalismo embodied "the old hispanic cult of personality," fascism grew from the "socialist-totalitarian and the lay-social sperm of the nineteenth century," and Mussolini and Hitler were "neo-socialists." These were typical dismissive remarks heard during the early 1930s.[24]

In Argentina the right displayed far greater sympathy toward the Italian than the German brand of fascism. For example, Manuel Gálvez, the right-wing novelist, found the Argentine Radicals to be "not very far from fascism: nationalist, believing in working for the people, in sympathy with rapid and even violent procedures. . . . Like Italian fascism, the Radical Party wants to work on the People's behalf within a framework of order, respecting religious, family and social traditions."[25] Nazism, in contrast, represented "the exaggerated nationalism condemned by the church." Leading Nacionalistas often condemned totalitarian Nazism as a by-product of the Reformation, which embodied "four hundred years of apostasy," and sought to restore the "religion of Valhalla." Franco, however, symbolized a "heroic mission of authentic Christianity," and the Spanish civil war posed the choice between "the highest religious and cultural values of the west and Marxist barbarism."[26]

These distinctions and attempts at definition often are made more easily than they are applied strictly. The Argentine right always has drawn eclectically from many different, often incompatible, sources, its notions "bundled together or left in a liquid state, so that anyone could extract a twig or take a sip and believe that he had discovered the truth."[27] In practice the terminology of counterrevolution coexisted with traces of other traditions, and the distinctions between them remained unperceived.

Typical of the right's ideological promiscuity and blurred referents was a statement made in 1933 by the young Argentine Nacionalista Julio Irazusta, who proposed the following "principles" as a means of "salvation" from the depression: "traditional political doctrine . . . the restoration of order . . . renewing the eternal tradition of humanity, innovate conserving and conserve innovating, reestablish the primacy of the political over the economic, restore destroyed or subverted spiritual hierarchies."[28] Irazusta derived his vocabulary of "salvation" and "subverted spiritual hierarchies" from the Catholic ultramontane movement. His expression "traditional political doctrine" evokes Edmund Burke or Joseph de Maistre. The curiously self-contradictory phrase "renewing the eternal tradition" is a borrowing from the Spanish and French right that originated in German idealism and in the writings of Hippolyte-Adolphe Taine. "Innovate conserving and conserve innovating" possibly echoes the commitment to pragmatic reform in Franklin D. Roosevelt's inaugural speech in 1933, and "the primacy of the political over the economic" imitates Charles Maurras's *politique d'abord.*

As this example highlights, foreign influences heavily marked the Argentine right despite its claim to be uniquely "nationalist." The "cosmopolitanism" that the right ostensibly decried constantly obtruded in its vocabulary and concepts, and the movement often appeared as little more than a highly derivative offshoot of a Franco-Spanish and Roman trunk. Like its early French counterpart the Argentine right could be defined as "a synthesis of antirationalism, antipositivism, racism and nationalism."[29] Like Portuguese Integralismo, the Argentine right began as "traditionalism," as an aesthetic cult of history, before it evolved into a political movement.[30] At first verbally (but ultimately, during the 1970s, in practice) the right often emulated the fanatical militants among the Spanish nationalists, as it also enshrined Catholic dogmas that were rooted in the philosophy of ancient Greece.

The right absorbed these influences unevenly and asynchronically, sometimes in highly distorted forms, and subject to the political conditions that prevailed in Argentina. The messages from Europe that were the fastest to penetrate came from Rome and were disseminated by highly educated priests who worked as journalists and political activists. Priests such as Gustavo Franceschi, Julio Meinvielle, and Leonardo Castellani played a vital role in the expansion of the Argentine right, occupying much the same position in the movement as the "liberation theologians" did in the Latin American left of the 1960s and 1970s.

Several of the leading members of the Argentine right in the 1930s were university-trained classicists, and their political writings contained numerous classical allusions. A flourishing trade in books with Spain kept the right-wing intelligentsia in Argentina abreast of current Spanish fashions. French influences, by contrast, often arrived more slowly, and sometimes indirectly by way of Spanish or other Latin American writers. The works of the Spaniard Angel Ganivet, for example, became well-known in Argentina soon after their publication. Argentines grew familiar with Taine through Ganivet and others, and with the French conservative writer Ernest Renan through José Enrique

Rodó's *Ariel,* which was first published in 1900 and was based on Renan's essay *Caliban, suite de la conquête.* Similarly, there were few references to Maurras in Argentina until the 1920s, although he had been active politically since the Dreyfus affair of the 1890s. The influence of non-Latin European writers in Argentina often was narrowly circumscribed by the availability of their writings in Spanish or French translation, although by the 1920s a few members of the right could read English. Sinclair Lewis's novel *Babbitt* (1922), for example, provided abundant ammunition for the right's anti-American campaigns.

The early (pre-1914) right adopted relatively few European authors and often took those they did adopt rather lightly. The mature right of the 1930s, by contrast, maintained contact with a much broader intellectual network. In part the difference between the two periods bore witness to the expansion of publishing and communications during the 1920s. But this deepening of intellectual linkages was due above all to the crisis of liberal Argentina after 1918, which launched a deliberate quest for alternatives to the liberal order and to liberal institutions.

The Dogma of Counterrevolution

The central propositions of the counterrevolutionary right emerged during the nineteenth century. The right led a quest for "order" whose emphasis on balance and due proportion was inspired by ancient Greece. The right's conception of a national "tradition" embodied the Aristotelian idea that "a thing contains what is necessary to fulfilling its purpose." Therefore, "each People, like each man, has through history a charge, a mission," and "history has the end of promoting civilization." The right resurrected Saint Augustine's idea that humans belonged as citizens to two commonwealths and owed their allegiance to both the church and the state. The universe, Saint Augustine and his medieval successors held, constituted a hierarchy under God, in which the higher ruled the lower; likewise, the earthly city, they declared, should be "an ordered concord" of its members in rule and obedience.[31]

In this vein the Argentine Nacionalista Jordán B. Genta described his militant counterrevolutionary teachings as a "humanist pedagogy, with a classical content."[32] When he was appointed to head one of Argentina's universities in the early 1940s, Genta adopted the slogan *Hay que aristotelizar la universidad* (literally, we must "aristotelize" the university).[33] In Argentina, "Nacionalismo rejects all the modern errors: materialism, positivism, pantheism, and that false, gross philosophical movement that began with Descartes and culminated in Kant. On the other hand we sustain Aristotle and Saint Thomas Aquinas: great and glorious thinkers . . . rooted in ancient Greece."[34]

For the right, authoritarian government and an organic society based on corporate institutions were "natural" to humanity, part of the divine ordination. The legitimacy of authoritarian government stemmed from the proposition of the medieval and early modern scholastics that people in a community "form a single mystical body . . . a necessary whole, which therefore needs one single head."[35] The Latin American, and Argentine, version of this idea found expression in a remark by Simón Bolívar that members of the right sometimes quoted. "The new states of America," Bolívar had said, "require kings with the title of presidents." Equally, "the head of state concentrates in himself complete sovereignty, and does so by God's grant, Lord of all power," because "power is a being, and God is the source of all being; power is dominion, and God is Lord. . . . Power is a right, and in God is to be found the origin of all rights."[36]

For European counterrevolutionaries the ancien régime represented the nearest approximation to the classical ideal. In this state, local and corporate rights and the ruler's obligation to serve the "common good" prevented arbitrary or tyrannical abuse of power. Thus although each society could possess only one sovereign "head," in practice power was diffuse and decentralized, an idea that found expression in the maxim *à l'état le simple contrôle*. Society itself was constituted so that "the principal cell of the nation has to be the municipality and the family; the nucleus is the province; and the vertebrae which give shape to the whole system is the state."[37]

This type of multilayered decentralized structure remained completely incompatible with popular democracy, which required the surrender of all rights to a sovereign people and, therefore, the extinction of all traditional limits to the exercise of power. The right argued against democrats that inequalities were also "natural," because society comprised the same rank order of intelligences and abilities as it did of corporations. Freedom was a right intrinsic to humans that derived from God, as opposed to a birthright derived from some imaginary Rousseauistic state of nature; still less could freedom exist as the juridical concession of a temporal power.

The right denounced the French Revolution as a "rebellion against God," which destroyed the "natural order" of the ancien régime and "corrupted the blood of the Christian world . . . with the poison of liberalism."[38] Revolutionary liberalism brought tyranny because it extinguished, in Burke's words, the "historic, peculiar institutions" and the "intermediate authorities" that formed a necessary link between the individual and the state.[39] By destroying the corporations, liberalism attacked the "social nature" of human beings originally defined by Aristotle.

In the profane ethics of liberalism, morality no longer stemmed, as it should, from natural law or from divine revelation, but from the rational intuitions of a self-conscious person. Liberalism sponsored a vision of each individual as "the center of all," and inflated one's "unbridled feeling of selfhood," ideas that embodied what the right called "the Judaeo-Protestant (and Kantian) God of the inward conscience."[40] Erroneously following Rousseau and "believing man good," the liberals "had cast aside all his constraints in favor of laissez-faire," and in doing so induced chronic moral anarchy.[41] The liberal precept of "freedom before the law" again assumed the false definition of a person as an individual, as an "unsocial" being deprived of the necessary bonds of society and therefore, as scarcely a person at all.

One Argentine writer expressed his opinion that a "liberal democracy . . . has destroyed social solidarity and exalted the isolated individual, the modern specimen of the rootless man; the inhabitant of the great world cities, egotistical, atheistic, destructive. . . . With the liberal revolution appears the naked citizen, the perpetual climber, grasping, dominated by his appetite, unruly."[42] Liberalism, therefore, had destroyed the society "natural" to a person based on the old corporations and had produced "the unmanning of man." The Argentine Nacionalista Enrique Osés found liberalism "not equitable but tyrannical," and, he added, it "does not enhance human personality, but cheapens and degrades it."[43] In Argentina, moreover, liberalism stood at variance with national tradition—it was a "bastard," the result of a "foreign Masonic weed," "a malignant heresy."[44] Indoctrination in liberal ideas produced the odious "international type," the mere "machine for production and consumption," "social depersonalization," and the "dehumanization of culture."[45] Liberal universities were the centers of "subversive ideas, which have infected the whole [national] organism."[46]

Liberal democracy, as exemplified in universal suffrage and the secret ballot, conferred an "unconditional and irresponsible liberty," and it falsely assumed "everyone's capacity to govern, with no other restriction than having reached the age of eighteen."[47] Democracy's false egalitarian dogmas induced a "flattening of hierarchies at the caprice of the multitude."[48] Among democracy's other odious manifestations stood feminism, whose origins, the Argentine right contended, lay in "the United States, which has encouraged [feminism] in order to spread pacificism" and to weaken resistance to American imperialism.[49] "Women were not born for public life. . . . This feminism is opening yet another door to revolution and anarchy. . . . Outside the home the woman is much more likely than the man to lapse into moral disorder."[50]

Counterrevolution in Argentina thus meant resurrecting the virtues of the preliberal and predemocratic past—reconstructing its absolute rule, its hierarchies, its corporations, and its particularisms, which formed the constituent parts of an overarching organic unity.[51] "Let us organize the Counterrevolution," proclaimed *La Nueva República* in 1927, "we have on our backs more than a half-century of intellectual disorientation: the sophistries of Romanticism and the French Revolution."[52]

In this quest the right led another onslaught against capitalism and "materialism," as it dismissed the nineteenth century, the age of progress, as "the stupid century," in the words of the French fascist Léon Daudet.[53] Capitalism was a source of "moral perversion," an enthronement of avarice and envy. *Querer ser otro es ya querer no ser* (To wish to be someone else, is to wish not to be) declared the nineteenth-century Spanish proverb. Capitalism represented "anonymous and vagabond wealth"; under its influence, according to one Argentine writer, his country had become "a foreign degeneration of liberalism."[54]

The right viewed socialist and Marxist ideas as corrupt offshoots of liberalism, products of the profane Promethean myth of human perfectibility that emerged in the sixteenth century. This idea was particularly common in Argentina, where leftism of every hue represented "the summit of the rationalist deviation," the consequence of the "pagan Renaissance,"[55] "the false Protestant Reformation."[56] What had begun in the sixteenth century, the Nacionalistas commonly argued, reached its final abysmal expressions in the late eighteenth and early nineteenth centuries in Rousseau and Karl Marx. "Luther became the precursor of Thomas Münzer, the ideologue of [sixteenth-century] Anabaptist Communism, and of René Descartes, the father of all the forms of modern Idealism, including the mechanicism [*sic*] of Rousseau and the historical materialism of Marx."[57] The similarities between liberalism and socialism stemmed from the fact that "the principle of the equality of all born from liberalism is the same principle as the levelling of all."[58] "Communist theory and practice," declared Genta, "are no more than modern liberalism carried to its final conclusion as the negation of western Christian order."[59]

As internationalist and universalist movements, liberalism and Marxism alike embodied "humanity without a country."[60] Thus misfit immigrants, "sinister looking mulattoes, *gallego* taxi-drivers, Basque milk-men, and fanatical women" stood out among those attending a Communist party rally in Buenos Aires in 1934.[61] Whereas liberalism destroyed society through the concept of humans-as-individuals, the leftist movements, as doctrines of class struggle and international community, "split" each nation's organic structure. The right commonly expressed approval for Lenin's remark in 1914 that "Marxism cannot be reconciled with nationalism, be it even the most just, purest, most refined, civilized breed."[62]

Militant nationalism in Argentina as in Europe dragged the right into the "stinking marshes" of anti-Semitism, as Jews became identified with the hidden instigators of the various movements and ideas that the right rejected.[63] In the anti-Semitic eschatology of the right, Jews continually were depicted as creeping along "in darkness with a dagger in one hand and dynamite in the other."[64] To the Argentine as well as the European right, Jews became "the deadly enemies of the nation and of the Catholic faith of the people," and "Jewish materialism" stood in irreconcilable opposition to the "spiritual character" of the Latin peoples. Jews were considered the occult sources of the spirit of skepticism, tolerance, and relativism that began during the Renaissance and then dominated the Enlightenment, the French Revolution, and the liberal revolutions of 1848. Jews, said the right, led the liberal or socialist quests for a world order that they intended to dominate. According to the right, in offering a false earthly paradise and earthly salvation, socialism and communism represented secularized versions of the Jewish messianic prophecy.[65] "The Russian soviet," declared a Nacionalista in 1931, "is nothing more than the same institution as the Jewish Kahal." A few months earlier, as the world depression deepened, the same writer had argued that "the present state of the world, with its profound illness, its universal disorientation, its enormous unemployment, . . . has a hidden cause, which manipulates, intensifies and coordinates the other more visible causes, with incredible and tenacious intelligence: this is the Jewish war against the Christian world."[66]

In this kind of extreme anti-Semitic propaganda, most of it originating in mythical Jewish plots such as described in the fraudulent *Protocols of the Elders of Zion*, Jews were scheming to inoculate "Christian governments" with "liberalism" and thus kill them, to destroy the aristocracies by taxation, to form great industrial monopolies, and to seize world supremacy by controlling gold supplies.[67] "Nine hundred years before Christ," declared a Jew caricatured in Hugo Wast's "El Kahal," "the conquest of the world by our race began. . . . The Serpent departed from Jerusalem. Five centuries later it reached Greece. . . . In 1940 we shall control Tokyo, in 1950 Buenos Aires, and sixteen years later the Serpent's head will meet the tail in the plains of Moab."[68]

Standing alongside anti-Semitism in the ideology of the right was anti-Freemasonry. In Europe, Catholic opposition to Freemasonry began in the early eighteenth century, manifesting itself in the conflict between "the true faith" that Catholics claimed to represent and the deist orientation of the Freemasons, who proclaimed humankind's "natural righteousness."[69] The right conventionally depicted the "world league" of Freemasonry as yet another instrument of the Jews that "aims at the destruction of the Christian faith and its replacement by an ancient paganism; and since Freemasonry too does not acknowledge a Fatherland, it becomes the natural ally of the Jews against church and state."[70]

Extreme opposition to Freemasonry became prevalent in Spain, where it assumed particular virulence following the Abbé Agustín Barruel's treatise of 1812, *Compendio de las memorias para servir a la historia del jacobinismo*. In this work, Barruel depicted the French Revolution as a Jewish and Masonic plot.[71] Later, Freemasonry allegedly was "mixed up in nearly every anti-religious and political disorder which has divided and bloodied [the country]."[72] In this vein the Spanish right blamed the abdication of Alfonso XIII in 1931 on "Masonry . . . bribed with Soviet gold."[73] In Argentina anti-Free-masonry had the same general features as it had in Spain. To the Nacionalistas, "Jewry, Masonry and Communism are the three ideological manifestations of the same negation of and hatred towards the Divine Redeemer."[74] In 1934 the Argentine Nacionalista priest, Juan Sepich, dismissed the incumbent liberal president, General Agustín P. Justo, as "that fat Mason."[75]

In Argentina, however, antagonism toward foreigners at large usually overshadowed both anti-Semitism and anti-Freemasonry. Here "foreigners," often regardless of their background, contaminated the "national essence" and polluted national tradition: "Let us clean out of the country all the whining dross who are the failures from abroad," urged Leopoldo Lugones. "Our prisons," he continued, "are full of foreigners. . . . The beggars, those who abandon or exploit children, drug traffickers, pornography merchants, alcoholics, tramps, professional agitators: all foreigners."[76] In the 1930s the Argentine right led campaigns to slow new immigration, to arrest the flood of the "thousands of Czechs, Poles, Armenians, Bulgarians and Russians who have invaded our shores." The right wanted a total ban on non-European immigrants: "The yellow races [*amarillos*], Mohammedans, Syrians."[77]

Jews, Masons, or simply "foreigners" were thought by the right to pose other threats because of their economic power. Toward the end of the nineteenth century the French right, closely followed by the right in Spain and elsewhere, embarked on campaigns against finance capitalism and industrial monopolies, denouncing international finance as another component of the Jewish conspiracy. In France, for example, Jews were attacked as the "masters of finance, industry and commerce. . . . The Parasite! There's the enemy."[78] In Argentina versions of the same idea took root during the 1920s, and became one of the leading features of Nacionalismo in the 1930s and 1940s. Throughout this period the Nacionalistas attacked the Jewish families that controlled the grain-exporting houses in Buenos Aires and the Bemberg consortium, which dominated the local beer industry.

During this period the conspiracy theories that were rooted in antiSemitism became assimilated into the anti-imperialist campaigns led by the Nacionalistas against Britain and the United States. In 1933 the Nacionalistas made a biting attack upon Sir Arthur Samuel, a British minister of Jewish family, for the insulting suggestion that Argentina join the British Empire. In 1935 a right-wing journalist attacked criticisms of the Nazis that had appeared in the *Buenos Aires Herald*, the local English-language newspaper. "Either the *Herald* receives money from the Jews to attack Germany," he declared, "or the *Herald* is a Jewish newspaper, edited by Jews and written by Englishmen."[79] The English and the Jews, who were alleged to be in league in a campaign for world domination, are "Siamese twins,"[80] said another commentator in 1940. Simultaneously, the Nacionalistas expressed their hatred toward the "Jewish-Yankee plutocracy in Wall Street"[81] and toward "the Yankee film, a weapon of social corruption controlled by the nationless Jews, which poisons the souls of our boys."[82]

Not only the right in Argentina adopted this conspiratorial vision of the imperialists with its origins in European anti-Semitism. The same vision also found its way into the analysis made by the left. The leftist Raúl Scalabrini Ortiz, for example, defined British influences in Argentina in a way that clearly echoed the tirades of the right against Jews and liberals:

> We have before us an enemy whose techniques of world domination have the following features: astuteness, cunning, indirect maneuvers, ill-faith, constant lies, the subtle manipulation of its local agents. And let us not forget that this enemy has been here for the past hundred years. Let us not forget that we are

victims of an educational system [created by this enemy] designed to lead us aside from an awareness of reality.[83]

European Ideologues of the Argentine Right

Before 1914 conservative Catholics, Latin American antipositivists, and the writings of the Spanish "Generation of 1898" supplied the main sources of inspiration to the Argentine right. French influences—the "romantic manifestations of anti-romanticism"—led by Charles Maurras, took a leading role in the 1920s.[84] By the 1930s and 1940s the Nacionalistas were drawing ecumenically from classical and modern European conservative writers. These authorities ranged from Plato and Thucydides to Hilaire Belloc and the Russian mystic, Nikolay Berdyayev, whose book *The New Middle Ages* for a time commanded enormous popularity.[85]

From its beginnings the Argentine right was the slave of fashion, continually embracing and discarding its intellectual mentors.This mentorship took several different forms. The right-wing periodicals often reproduced extensive fragments from foreign works they admired, using them as sources of authority and propaganda. Frequently, the influence of European writers becomes difficult to document or prove because it consisted of unattributed practical applications of ideas or concepts from abroad, which were heavily edited and adapted to local needs. The works of the European philosophers or classical authors admired by the right often were ingested slowly, over long periods of time, in university classes or other organized study groups. Federico Ibarguren, for example, as a young man had his first contact with the writings of the medieval scholastics in classes offered by the lay religious association Acción Católica. He and many of his classmates were, he admitted, "lazy adolescents, [and] ill-prepared." However, these classes gradually induced in Ibarguren not only a "second religious conversion" but also a lifelong commitment to conservative Catholic philosophy.[86]

Two principal intellectual traditions dominated the Argentine right: the clerical counterrevolution of the early nineteenth century and the "new right," rooted in German idealism and Darwinism, which appeared in France after 1870. Leonardo Castellani, a leading member of the clerical wing of Nacionalismo between the 1930s and the 1960s, listed the following nineteenth-century French and Spanish writers as the movement's principal sources of inspiration: French counterrevolutionaries, led by de Maistre and the Vicomte de Bonald, and Spaniards such as Juan Donoso Cortés, Jaime Balmes, and Marcelino Menéndez Pelayo.[87] References abound to these five writers in all the major Nacionalista literature, ranging from the periodical *La Nueva República* in the late 1920s to Enrique Zuleta Alvarez's two-volume study of Nacionalismo published in 1975.[88]

The Savoyard Joseph de Maistre led the attack against the French Revolution. De Maistre rejected all written constitutions: "The rights of peoples are

never written, [or if they are they amount to no more than] declaratory
enunciations of prior [unwritten] rights." De Maistre argued that the rights of
a people proceeded from concessions by a sovereign, and he attacked the
French *parlements* as perennial sources of subversion: "Protestant in the
sixteenth century, *'frondeur'* and Jansenist in the seventeenth, Enlightenment-
contaminated [*philosophe*] and republican in the eighteenth." Furthermore,
"among all monarchs, the harshest, the most despotic and intolerable is the
People-Monarch."

Rousseau and the doctrine of the social contract represented de Maistre's
other principal targets. "It is a capital error," de Maistre contended, "to
represent the State as the consequence of a choice based on the consent of
men, upon a deliberation, and upon a primitive contract." Rousseau had
"constructed his whole philosophical edifice on an anti-Christian proposition
that Man is good." Instead, argued de Maistre, human nature was depraved
and required an absolute monarchy, supported by the church, to subdue and
contain it. De Maistre's writings displayed other strong influences of the
Catholic natural law tradition: constitutions expressed the "nature" of peoples;
constitutions produced peace when rulers observed the "fundamental law";
the basis of each nation was the family and the corporations.[89]

Louis Gabriel Ambroise de Bonald's writings pursued many of the same
themes. Anti-imperialists among the Argentine Nacionalistas recalled Bonald's
warning that the great danger of representative government was the opportunity it "offered for foreigners to intervene in [national] affairs with their gold."
"The men of the [revolutionary] party," according to Bonald, "do not belong
to their own country. . . . The Revolution is their homeland [*patrie*]. . . .
[Moreover, the Revolution shows] a profound hatred for Catholicism, whose
destruction is the single aim of its policy."[90]

Bonald attacked the doctrine of popular sovereignty with arguments
identical to de Maistre's. Political power was independent of people."[Power]
resides in natural law. . . . It is divine, because God is the author of all the
natural laws of the states." As an apologist of the ancien régime, Bonald
viewed absolutism as sanctioned by natural law and, therefore, as fully legitimate. He contrasted absolute power with the arbitrary, and therefore lawless,
power he saw as having arisen during the French Revolution. "Absolute
power," he declared, "is power independent of the subject, but arbitrary power
[is] independent of the law. And when you erect the people as the power, you
necessarily confer upon it an arbitrary power, that is, a power independent of
the law."[91]

"Spanish philosophy," declared Gustavo Franceschi, the Catholic priest
who was a leading ideologue of the Argentine right, "from Seneca to Balmes,
will be a perennial source of wisdom, an art of living, a limitless land of vital
experience, of practical discipline, of intimate creations."[92] Among the Spanish philosophers most widely quoted by the right in Argentina, Juan Donoso
Cortés was remembered as both an eloquent opponent of liberalism during the

1848 revolutions and an early proponent of the violent defense of public order through military dictatorship.[93] "When legality can save society, uphold legality; when it cannot, embrace dictatorship," advised Donoso Cortés.[94] He was also an early prophet of the impending ideological war between Catholicism and socialism, and he viewed the latter as Jewish-inspired.

Jaime Balmes, a conservative Spanish priest, was most widely known as an educator and a philosopher. He became influential in Argentina, however, during the 1920s and 1930s as yet another extreme critic of the French Revolution. Balmes was remembered further as a precursor of modern corporatism by seeking to resurrect the old guilds that the French Revolution had abolished.[95]

Among these five seminal ideologues of counterrevolution listed by Castellani, the later figure Marcelino Menéndez Pelayo (sometimes Menéndez y Pelayo), "the lay saint of the Falange" as the historian Raymond Carr called him, represented perhaps the most important influence in Argentina. Menéndez Pelayo led the quest to restore Spain's "true Catholic self" and its "providential mission." "Only through [religion]," he declared, "did the Spanish people develop its own way of life and an awareness of its collective strength; only through religion did Spain gain legitimate, well-rooted institutions."

In his quest for the "real Spain," Menéndez Pelayo disparaged the eighteenth century, the age of the Enlightenment, and exalted the medieval era and the Golden Age of the sixteenth century. "In the Middle Ages," he contended, "we never ceased to consider ourselves one People." He maintained that Spain's past greatness would revive when the nation rekindled the Senecan discipline and the militant crusading spirit that had prevailed under Ferdinand and Isabella, "*los reyes católicos.*" At its acme in the sixteenth century, Spain was at its "most intolerant," expelling the Jews and launching the Counter Reformation. At this point, religion inspired "Spain the evangelist over half the earth, Spain the hammer of the heretics, Spain the light of the Council of Trent, Spain the cradle of Saint Ignacio [Loyola]." Menéndez Pelayo lauded the Spanish Inquisition. "Never was there more or better written in Spain than in the two centuries of the Inquisition," he declared.

The eighteenth-century Enlightenment, on the other hand, "the most perverse and ungodly age in history . . . dismantled stone by stone the beautiful edifice of old Spain. . . . Spain then forgot its religion, its language, its science, its arts, and everything that had made it wise, powerful, and feared in the world."[96] At this time, Spain fell victim to the pernicious influence of "philosophes," "Jansenists," "Masons," and "Jews." Menéndez Pelayo abhorred the standards of tolerance, skepticism, relativism, and materialism that arose during the Enlightenment; he declared them incompatible with Spain's primevally "spiritual character."[97] His "myth of Castile" exalted the "most Catholic purity" of both Spain and Spanish America and depicted the Spanish conquest of the Americas as a vast evangelical enterprise accomplished by armies of priests and soldiers: the "union of the Cross and the Sword."[98]

In Argentina the right continually manifested traces of the rhetoric, the historical antimonies, and the conceptual schemes advanced by Menéndez Pelayo. The Catholic church, the right claimed, "represents the historic essence of our nationality."[99] Under the spell of the Menéndez Pelayo "myth of Castile," members of the right in Argentina exalted the "ancient apostolic and warrior spirit of the Middle Ages and the Catholic kings," which had accomplished the conquest of the Americas, as they urged the reunification of Latin America: "the unity of the Peoples on the basis of the Catholic, Apostolic, Roman faith."[100] "We belong to the Christian west," claimed Jordán B. Genta, "because Spain sowed this territory with the spirit of the two Romes, the human spirit of Caesar and the divine spirit of St. Peter."[101]

In the same mode, the Hapsburg king became "the source of honor and authority as the incarnation of the State, the first servant of the *república*, the first slave to duty, and the Minister of God." The Bourbon dynasty, by contrast, was "inspired in French despotism" and, therefore, was "centralist and all-absorbing."[102] The Bourbons had made religion "an issue of the State," and from them came the "foreign and liberal" malignancies that had arisen since the late eighteenth century.[103] Under the Bourbons the "reasoning" that characterized the hated Enlightenment superseded "spiritual vocation and an acceptance of the metaphysical"; a world based on reason replaced that which had been founded on aristocracy, and "Single Truth [the Christian revelation interpreted by an infallible pope] had become a matter for each man's judgment." The Bourbons, declared Federico Ibarguren, had transformed Spanish America, "this ancient land of missionaries and soldiers, into an underdeveloped colony, into an immense factory with no soul."[104]

The Argentine right at first imitated Menéndez Pelayo to the point of plagiarism. But in the late 1930s the "historical revisionists" modified Menéndez Pelayo's basic historical scheme into the autochthonous cult of the longtime governor of Buenos Aires, Juan Manuel de Rosas. In the revisionists' version of Argentine history, Rosas occupied the same role as the Catholic monarchs and the Hapsburgs had in Menéndez Pelayo's Spain, and the Rosas regime became the archetype for the nationalist, Catholic, and paternalist autocracy that the Argentine right wished to establish. Rosas's "liberal" successors—the alleged instigators of spiritual decline and conduits of a destructive materialism—occupied the same position as the Bourbons had for Menéndez Pelayo. Thus, the Argentine right denounced both the French Revolution and "the liberal oligarchy that ruled the country after [the fall of Rosas] under the system of enlightened despotism."[105]

In both of these cases, history became the slave of politics and propaganda. The historians of the right sought to define the future by using myths of a heroic past and erecting cults around the symbolic events and historical figures that embodied the values they aspired to restore. Education, thought Ibarguren, should be based upon a national "historical apologia."[106] "A revision of our history," declared José M. Rosa, a leading revisionist, "is a thankless but deeply patriotic task. . . . From this task will emerge the Argentina of tomorrow."[107]

The Argentine right also bore traces, although they were infrequently acknowledged, of Renan and Taine, the two nineteenth-century French conservative writers mentioned earlier. Renan's influence in Argentina initially stemmed from the writings of the Uruguayan poet Rodó, whose *Ariel* drew heavily upon the Frenchman.[108] Renan lamented what he perceived to be the "profoundly materialist" society that followed adoption of universal suffrage. He yearned for the return of the old, pre-1789 France with its "patriotism, enthusiasm for beauty, love of glory." Renan declared democracy to be at odds with "God's design" and liberal utilitarianism "blind to beauty."[109]

Taine's environmental determinism saw each "civilization" or nationality as the creation of a *faculté maîtresse* (directing principle) that sprang from a synthesis of race, milieu, and "moment," or historical situation. Like that of Renan, Taine's influence in Argentina for the most part spread slowly and indirectly, deriving chiefly from Angel Ganivet's *Idearium Español*, written in 1898, which developed Taine's *faculté maîtresse* into what Ganivet called the *"espíritu territorial,"* that is, the national character founded on the synthesis of environment and history. For Ganivet, the history of Spain from the Roman conquest through the barbarian occupations and the *Reconquista* had been "a permanent struggle for independence." Taine's remark that "at root history is a problem of psychology" reappeared in Ganivet's version as "every society possesses a personality," and for Ganivet, as they did for Taine, "all peoples possess a real or imaginary hero who embodies their own [ideal] qualities." Among the examples of such national heroes submitted by Ganivet were Don Quixote and Robinson Crusoe.[110]

The clerical right in Argentina sprang from assumptions that originally were in conflict with the more secular threads associated with Renan, Taine, and others because the origins of the former lay in the Counter Reformation and those of the latter in the Enlightenment and Idealism. In the early nineteenth century the clerical reactionaries led by de Maistre rejected the idealists, particularly the German philosopher Immanuel Kant, as strongly as they repudiated Rousseau. It was Kant who had invented the pernicious "God of the inward conscience," an idea that mortally threatened Catholic metaphysics based on natural law and the fall of humankind. Kant's German successors led by Johann Gottlieb Fichte and Johann Gottfried von Herder extended the notion of the self-directing individual into the concept of the self-determining *Volk*, an idea that had its outcome in modern European nationalism.[111]

Toward 1870 the nationalist movement in Italy, which was led by Giuseppe Mazzini, the conte di Cavour, and Giuseppe Garibaldi, deprived the church of its jurisdiction over Sicily and the papal states, and for a while nationalism too became anathema to Catholics. Around the same time, Catholics also faced the challenges presented by positivism and Darwinism, the first by claiming the status of a new religion that would replace Christianity and the latter by preaching the "pagan cult of the winners."

Efforts to confront, deflect, or overcome these challenges began mainly in France. The French clerical historian Fustel de Coulanges, for example, sought to demonstrate the "spiritual" foundations of the French nation. His version of nationalism portrayed the church as a primary institutional nucleus of the national community and the clergy as a vital force in each community's origins and development.[112] This scheme thus allowed the history of each nation to be viewed in a pseudopositivist, and even pseudo-Darwinian, form as a process of ascent and progress, but it kept religion and the church at the center of the process.

Attempts to update the primitive tenets of the counterrevolution took many different forms. Writing in late nineteenth-century France, Maurice Barrès developed another reactionary version of nationalism that blended distorted echoes of Darwin and the German idealists with Taine's definition of nationalism as *"l'acceptation d'un déterminisme"* rooted in the triad of race, ancestry, and "spirit." For Barrès "all truth is national truth," and he sought to restore France as a "living unity" through the perception of common roots and a common biological inheritance. French history became a teleological quest for national "character," national "genius," and each nation's *"disposition primitive."* Using historical myth in the same way as Menéndez Pelayo had but omitting his strong clerical emphasis, Barrès contended that France had reached the height of its greatness in the seventeenth century under Louis XIV but then had declined as Voltaire and Montesquieu infected the nation with the "Jewish and German spirit" of the Reformation.[113] In Argentina, Barrès became a major influence on the novelist Manuel Gálvez, who imitated Barrès's cult of rural provincialism.[114]

The works of the psychosociologist Gustave Le Bon, a French contemporary of Barrès, were republished decade after decade in Spanish and Argentine editions. Le Bon stressed instinct and intuition as motivating forces in human behavior. He held that "in all our acts the part played by the unconscious is immense and that played by reason so small. Reason is too new in humanity, and too imperfect to reveal to us the laws of the unconscious, and still less to replace them." Le Bon combined irrationalism with Taine's notion of "the mental constitution of a people," arguing that "the life of a people, its institutions, its beliefs and its arts [represent] the visible thread of its invisible soul. [Each people is] an organism created by the past. . . . Infinitely more numerous than the living, the dead are infinitely more powerful than they."[115]

Among all the luminaries of the French right, however, Charles Maurras commanded the greatest attention and popularity in Argentina.[116] To the Nacionalista historian Zuleta Alvarez, Maurras was "the most notable political thinker to have arisen in France during the past two centuries, and one of the great figures in western letters and thought."[117] "Maurras's influence," declared the Argentine nationalist Marcelo Sánchez Sorondo,"was such that he inspired the first nationalist movements outside France, including ours."[118]

Maurras headed *Action Française*, the leading organization of the French right from the early 1900s to the eve of World War II, and he formulated the famous doctrine of integral nationalism. He devoted his long career, which encompassed a span from the 1890s to the fall of the Pétain regime in 1944, to a campaign to restore the French monarchy. In the present age, Maurras asserted, gold had become "the master of iron . . . the judge of all thinking," and the rule of gold, the *"loi d'or,"* was "indifferent, the most absolute, the least responsible."[119] Resurrection of the ancien régime, he claimed, held the key to replacing the *loi d'or* of a society that had been corrupted by materialism with the *"loi de sang,"* which would reunite France and restore it to greatness. Maurras's desire was for a traditional absolutism like Menéndez Pelayo's that would acknowledge local autonomies and customary rights. Like Barrès, Maurras idealized the folk cults of old, provincial France, where, he asserted, behind its institutional forms and legal superstructures, could be found the true France, *"le pays réel."*

Maurras joined the cult of seventeenth-century France led by Barrès and others; for him also the French Revolution represented the great catastrophe of modern history. To Maurras saving civilization meant destroying Rousseau's optimistic metaphysics, Kantian idealism, and the God of the inward conscience espoused by Protestants and Jews, concepts he viewed as the "microbes of romanticism and Revolution." Liberal-positivism as well was, he declared, the "first beast to kill," and popular democracy was the "monstrous Judaeo-Masonic regime" and the "Dictatorship of the Mob." Maurras lamented the destruction of the guilds, or "natural corporations," in the French Revolution and their replacement by an order that "leaves men naked before Capital and the State" and "exalts the egotism of bad passions. . . . In isolating the individual from his peers, in dragging him systematically out of society, individualism has separated man from the basic requirements of existence."[120]

Maurras's power lay in his striking rhetoric rather than in his originality. Although his republican followers in Argentina ignored his support for monarchy, they took from him the biting epigrammatic instruments he provided to attack the liberal democratic state. "Society arises not from an act of wills, but from a fact of nature," Maurras declared, rejecting the liberal contract theory of the state, whereas democracy falsely assumes that people are "small, similar cubes, equal in height, in dimension, and in weight."[121] Maurras called Protestants "Catholics who have abandoned the idolatry of the Trinity for Jewish monotheism."[122] He hailed the Catholic church as "the last obstacle to the imperialism of gold, the last bastion of free thought."[123] He inveighed against *"les métèques,"* France's foreign residents, and he used anti-Semitism as a tool of popular mobilization. "Everything," he once remarked, "seemed impossible or extremely difficult without the providence of anti-Semitism."[124] Maurras's doctrine of *politique d'abord* presented politics as a pure science.

But in this guise *politique d'abord* became the manifesto of right-wing terror-ism, freeing political activists from all moral restraints and moral responsibili-ties and justifying the seizure of power by a self-anointed "enlightened" elite.

Maurras's influence in Argentina reached its zenith in the late 1920s as *Action Française* became the model for the periodical *La Nueva República*, founded in 1927, and the Liga Republicana of 1929. Maurras's reception in Argentina illustrated the potential tensions between the right's clerical and secular currents. Maurras himself was a militant atheist, whose support for the church derived from its potential utility to the state. In 1927 the Vatican condemned *Action Française* and its doctrines, and in Buenos Aires the church hierarchy quickly followed suit. "To say that politics comes first (as in the concept of *politique d'abord*)," clerical dignitaries declared, "is to assert that the body politic is constructed prior to the existence of Christian morality. . . . For *Action Française* the nation before all: *Salus populus suprema lex est* [Let the welfare of the people be the supreme law]."[125] *La Nueva República*, meanwhile, thought the comparison between itself and *Action Française* "flattering but in part unacceptable. . . . *Action Française* is directed by an unbeliever . . . and its doctrines on the relationship between politics and morality unsatisfactory."[126]

Embryos of the Right in pre-1914 Argentina

During the generation before 1914, liberalism and positivism reached their acmes in Argentina; in this climate the right amounted to no more than a few scattered seeds. At this time the church articulated the little that as yet existed of the counterrevolutionary position. But in Argentina the church always had been much weaker than it had been in Spain and in most other parts of Spanish America. In colonial Argentina, where the native Indian population was much smaller than elsewhere in the Spanish empire, the church had been less able to amass power and wealth from its missionary activities. Clerical influence in the River Plate region suffered a sharp blow following the expulsion of the Jesuits in 1767.[127] Any independent political influence that was wielded by the church largely disappeared during the decades of civil war following the revolution of 1810, when it became almost impossible to maintain communi-cations with Rome.[128] During the 1830s and 1840s, Juan Manuel de Rosas sought to foster a conservative church, but under his rule the church remained tightly subordinated to the government, and the state upheld its control over ecclesiastical appointments and patronage.[129] Rosas, like his predecessors as well as his successors, claimed to exercise the *patronato* (power over the appointment of bishops) as an inheritance from the Spanish Crown, "not as a concession, but as a property inherent to sovereignty."[130]

In early nineteenth-century Argentina, conservative clerical leaders failed to command either the influence enjoyed by the ultramontane priesthood of Spain, Italy, or France or the political stature of a Lucas Alemán, "Mexico's de Maistre," a champion of monarchy, aristocracy, and the interventionist state.[131] During this period the Jujuy priest Juan Ignacio Gorrit supported the federalist opponents of the Buenos Aires liberals in language reminiscent of the counterrevolution's attacks on Rousseau and the Enlightenment. But Gorrit and a few others like him remained isolated, peripheral, and powerless.[132]

Militant clericalism first appeared in Argentina during the 1860s and 1870s, when the church became infected with the conflicts that characterized relations between church and liberals in Europe and Latin America following the 1848 revolutions. These conflicts included the struggle for Italian unification, battles over church land, and disputes over ecclesiastical privilege in Mexico and elsewhere. From 1865 to 1867 the church in Argentina reacted sharply to anticlerical measures in the province of Santa Fe, where the governor, Nicasio Oroño, suppressed a convent, instituted civil matrimony, and sought to remove the church's control over cemeteries.[133] In Buenos Aires in the early 1870s the church sponsored *El Católico*, a periodical that took an ultraconservative position consistent with the recent papal *Syllabus*, that "solemn synthesis and condemnation of the most common and dangerous errors." Foremost among the "errors" denounced in the *Syllabus* stood liberalism.

Its own "noble and holy purpose," declared *El Católico*, was "to leave that monstrous and most evil liberalism without a single unbroken bone, wherever it should raise its ugly snout." Liberalism was a "universal evil," whose nefarious consequences had been most recently visible in the "execrable" Paris Commune. "Liberalism insinuates itself into every part of the world. . . . It represents a falsification of liberty; it is the source and essence of Revolution, . . . the suppression of God." *El Católico* followed with a diatribe against materialism, contending that "everywhere we see the cult of purely material interest, an insatiable thirst for gold, pleasure, enjoyments, rewards, power and honors . . . a resurrection and glorification of paganism and idolatry."

The burning of a Jesuit college by a Buenos Aires mob in 1875 helped spark this clerical onslaught. A few years later Catholic militancy revived, when liberals, taking their cue from similar measures in France and Germany, pressed for anticlerical reform such as lay education, civil matrimony, and the abolition of religious cemeteries, of parish registers, and of religious oaths.[134] Among these proposed measures, educational reform passed Congress in 1883, and a civil matrimony law passed in 1887.

The Catholic response to these lay reforms foreshadowed ideas that ultimately became part of the right's vernacular. Speaking in the Chamber of Deputies in July 1883, for example, Pedro Goyena declared, "A school without religion, a school from which the notion of God has been proscribed, and in which God's name is not even mentioned, that school is damned."[135] The church opposed proposals to abolish ecclesiastical courts in language that recalled the denunciations of the Enlightenment by Spanish clerics almost a century earlier. The doctrine of state supremacy that such legislation implied, Catholics argued, originated with the impious Bourbons, but "a republican and free society should erase the state despotism of the absolutist kings of Spain."[136]

In the 1880s, Catholics remained some distance from a full-fledged counterrevolutionary position. Like the counterrevolutionaries, they opposed liberal "despotism," and drew parallels between the late eighteenth-century Bourbons and the incumbent liberal oligarchy in Argentina. But although Catholics hated liberals, their ideal was a "free Republic" rather than the debased patrimonial absolutism that fifty years later produced the cult of military dictatorship. "While the rift prevails between religion and liberty, [our nation] shall be liberal . . . but never free [*seremos liberales . . . pero no libres*]," declared a speaker at the First Catholic Congress in Buenos Aires in 1884. We are "authentic democrats and republicans," but never liberals, said another Catholic.[137]

In the 1880s this permutation in Argentina between antiliberalism and "free" republicanism was most strikingly apparent in the figure of José Manuel Estrada, the leading Catholic intellectual of his generation. For years Estrada attacked liberalism relentlessly from the orthodox Catholic standpoint as the cause of "upheaval and catastrophes, and as no more than illusions and lies."[138] "What else but liberalism," he asked,

dragged along by its egalitarian delirium, its anxieties to destroy the organic societies and to convert them into disarticulated masses, has wrecked the homes of the poor, shattered the guilds [*gremios*], wiped out families, crumbled small fortunes and small properties? What else but liberalism has annihilated the permanent bonds of cooperation [*patronazgo*]? . . . Liberalism has cast the working classes into the tyranny of wage labor, leaving them subject to the daily contract, incapable of defense against the Rich . . . incited to barbarous explosions of anarchy by the Communist, Socialist or Nihilist sects—sects that are no more than variants and derivatives of liberalism, the originating cause of conflict and conflagration.[139]

Estrada's strictures against liberalism and view that liberalism bred leftist anarchy foreshadowed positions adopted by the Argentine right several decades later. But Estrada also was echoing contemporary Catholic orthodoxy, and he took the standard Catholic line on the issue of political sovereignty as well. "There are only two ways to understand the principle of sovereignty," he declared. "Either you profess the revolutionary version: sovereignty reposes in the capricious will of the masses. Or you profess the alternative: that sovereignty belongs to the Supreme Legislator of the Universe, and the source and essence of all power is Divine. . . . All power comes from God."[140] Under these natural law suppositions it became possible to uphold liberty while attacking liberalism. For Estrada liberty stemmed from God rather than from the social contract developed by Locke or Rousseau, and political liberty meant that the state protected each person's pursuit of "moral duty" and a Christian life. In Argentina, Estrada held, the state had failed to uphold either personal or political liberty. The liberal reforms deprived the church of the power to determine moral conduct and endowed the state with it instead. Secular power of this extent implied the same principle as did the godless revolutionary or Napoleonic "Caesaro-papist" state. Catholic natural law urged rulers to serve the "common good." But the Argentine liberal state was oligarchic, and its congress unrepresentative. With merely a part of the people represented in it Congress could not reflect either the true will of the entire people or the common good.[141]

Estrada's conception of a free and republican society sprang from the teachings of Francisco Suárez, the sixteenth-century Spanish jurist. According to Suárez, society existed as a "natural" part of the divinely ordained cosmos. Government was necessary and "natural" to society, but because "society" meant people, the legitimate exercise of government implied popular consent. In Argentina, Estrada observed, there was "no bond of sympathy between the people and the liberal oligarchy." The leaders of this oligarchy, "whose God is their stomach, . . . forget that peoples and individuals live not only on bread, but on truth and justice." On these grounds Estrada again could follow Suárez in urging revolution against the liberals. "Revolutions," he declared, "are those great invocations [*apelaciones*] of Natural Law which the people may legitimately employ . . . against tyrants who rule contrary to justice."[142]

In 1890, Estrada's semipopulist brand of Catholicism led Catholics to support the insurrection that overthrew the liberal regime of Miguel Juárez Celman (1886–1890). But this "free republican" version of Catholicism proved to be of short duration, and a far more conservative, although still not fully counterrevolutionary, position soon followed it.

This shift occurred in Argentina as the church was being drawn into conflicts stemming from mass immigration and the emergence of an unruly foreign-born proletariat. Between 1890 and 1914 immigration into the now rapidly growing cities fostered class divisions that were simultaneously divisions between natives and foreigners. As Argentine citizenship became roughly coterminous with a middle- or upper-class status, noncitizenship often meant membership in the working class.[143] Meanwhile, as anarchist and socialist groups sought to mobilize the immigrants, much of native Argentina, particularly from the upper classes, began to embrace reaction. During these years the liberal anticlericalism of the 1880s receded in the face of "the Socialist advance" and of an anarchist-led trade union movement, and liberals came to perceive the church as no longer "the guardian of privilege, nor as an enemy of science, but as the ally of the Rich."[144]

The drift toward an alliance of church and state also followed the 1891 papal encyclical *Rerum Novarum*. The encyclical urged Catholics throughout the rapidly urbanizing West to resist "class struggle," using repression if necessary, and to fight for "class harmony" through a program of indoctrination and institution building.[145] The encyclical prompted Estrada and other Catholic leaders in Argentina to found Catholic women's centers to keep working-class women "safe" from socialist or anarchist contagion and to sponsor workers' housing projects to attack the problem of high urban rents.[146] Both these initiatives survived for many years after Estrada's death in 1894, as groups of so-called Social Catholics continued his work.[147]

The most important Catholic institutions to appear after *Rerum Novarum* were the Círculos Obreros, or Workers' Circles, which were copies of entities first established in Europe and introduced in Argentina by the priest Fernando Grote. The Workers' Circles typified late nineteenth-century Catholic thinking and the nostalgic mystique that Catholics had woven around the guilds destroyed by the French Revolution. The circles aspired to unite workers and employers, as Catholics believed the old guilds had done, and they attacked class conflict as antisocial, pledging themselves to "resist . . . the activities of all those who threaten the welfare of the Nation, Religion, Family and Property." Socialist ideas, they claimed, "damage the interests of the workers, and are normally the means for the union leaders to set themselves up as the bosses [*caciques*] of the working masses."[148]

A decade later, in 1902, Catholics created the Christian Democratic League. In aiming to set itself "equally apart from both liberal individualism and socialist collectivism, two different forms of the same tyranny," the league embodied another standard feature of late nineteenth-century Catholic thought.[149] Finally, in more extreme language exceptional in Argentina during this early period, a Catholic-dominated Liga Social Argentina, founded in 1908, pledged "to sustain the Christian organization of society, to combat every error and subversive tendency."

Yet none of these associations was very strong. To José E. Níklison, a National Labor Department official writing during World War I, all of the Catholic groups evinced "passivity and a truly lamentable inertia." By 1913 the Workers' Circles possessed barely twenty thousand members throughout the country and the Liga Social only a few hundred, and the Christian Democratic League had collapsed in 1908.[150] The priest Gustavo Franceschi later recalled the failure of the Christian Democratic League. Its feeble corporatist organizations, which he said merely copied the ideas of "the French sociologist, La Tour du Pin," had proven totally unsuited to the dynamic, mobile society of urban Argentina. According to Franceschi:

> In Italy or Belgium where the streets and houses of the ancient corporations still survive, [corporatism] is possibly applicable. There a professional corporate tradition survives. But here where there are men from all over the world, with so many contrasting customs and backgrounds . . . the very base of the corporation is absent. [In Argentina] corporatism can only be a political instrument rather than a social phenomenon. . . . In Europe the corporation is a resurrection, while here it is an invention.[151]

Such were the earliest manifestations of the clerical right in pre-1914 Argentina. At this stage the clerical right as a movement formed a minor part of the liberal-ecclesiastical alliance created in response to what was for many years called the Social Question. The secular right remained equally embryonic. Its foundations lay in antipathy against immigrants and stretched back several decades into the nineteenth century. In his 1887 novel *En la sangre*, for example, Eugenio Cambaceres depicted Italian immigrant workers as a subhuman species of animal.[152] Physician and writer José M. Ramos Mejía at the turn of the century denounced immigrants as biologically and culturally inferior to the native stock of Argentina.[153] In 1891, Julián Martel's novel *La Bolsa*, which he wrote in the depths of the financial crisis, closely imitated the French anti-Semite Edouard Drumont's *La France Juive* in blaming Jewish financiers for the economic collapse. In 1899, Argentine statesman Miguel Cané began a campaign against "immigrant agitators" that concluded three years later in the xenophobic Law of Residence legislation authorizing the government to deport undesirable foreigners within three days and without trial.[154] From these roots emerged the Argentine nativist movement, which before 1914 had been most intense in 1909 and 1910. In these two years a vigilante band, the Juventud Autonomista, as it called itself, attacked striking workers, tried to destroy working-class newspapers, and in May 1910 led a mob attack against the small Jewish ghetto in Buenos Aires.[155]

In this blend of xenophobia (or "patriotism" as the nativists themselves called it) with violent antileftism could be found another major strand of the Argentine right. Still more complex strands emerged from traditionalism, a literary movement of this period, whose followers upheld the native against the foreign by sanctifying rurality and attacking the corruption they perceived in urban society.[156]

These Argentine leitmotifs bore the strong imprint of Spanish and French mentors. The novelist Manuel Gálvez, for example, imitated Maurice Barrès and the Spanish "Generation of 1898," particularly Angel Ganivet and Miguel Unamuno, and adopted much of the vocabulary and many of the notions that they themselves had derived from Taine, including the ideas of the "historic personality" of the nation and of the nation as an "irreducible nucleus" and a "psychological structure."[157] Spain, which Gálvez visited in 1905 and 1910, especially attracted him. He declared himself "fascinated by Spain, the most profound and disturbing country I know, I experienced the deepest emotions in my life, and I took from Castile many precepts."[158] Gálvez's writings sought to rehabilitate Spain, which in liberal Argentina was "forgotten and ridiculed." Making an implicit comparison with the cold and characterless new cities of the Argentine pampas, Galvez stated that the old Spanish cities were "illustrious and full of essence."[159] Writing about Argentina, Gálvez sought to evoke "the ambience of those provincial cities [of the interior], where as distinct from Buenos Aires the old national spirit, the sentiment of patriotism, and a deep and spiritual sense of ethnicity [*raza*] still remain."[160]

Similar extraneous echoes appear in the work of Leopoldo Lugones. French writers led by Charles-Pierre Baudelaire and Paul Verlaine helped propel Lugones into probing the "mystery of subjective life" and the arena of the intuitive and the subconscious.[161] Years later Gálvez recalled Emilio Becher, another literary figure of this period, as "an Argentine Renan. . . . He thought and he wrote like the French, above all Renan and [Anatole] France, in whose works and spirit he was saturated."[162] Ricardo Rojas's concern with language and his objections to what he saw as its debasement by the immigrants betrayed the influence of Unamuno and behind Unamuno again that of Taine. For Unamuno, language represented "that great psychological archive that conserves the common values of peoples."[163]

The traditionalists adopted these foreign borrowings to combat what they perceived as the destructive consequences of the age of liberal-positivism—an all-engulfing tide of immigrants, foreign languages, and "progress," forces that threatened to destroy the country's essential and Hispanic identity. At the same time, the traditionalists echoed the rural federalist movement that the Argentine liberals had destroyed in the midnineteenth century.[164] Fifty years after its political defeat, federalism lingered as a nostalgic longing for the communities and way of life of the old interior. Typical of this writing was a verse by Leopoldo Lugones:

> En la villa Santa María del Río Seco
> Al pie del Cerro del Romero, nací
> Y esto es todo cuanto diré de mí
> Porque no soy más que un eco
> Del canto natal que traigo aquí.[165]

This literary federalism paralleled and again often imitated the nationalist statements of late nineteenth-century European writers such as Barrès. Like the Europeans who exalted the old provinces and the chartered cities, the traditionalists in Argentina aspired for decentralized government based on local communities and free of the oppressive influence of Buenos Aires. Just as the French idealized the ancien régime and Spaniards the Hapsburgs, the Argentine traditionalists yearned for a world they imagined had existed before the liberals had won political dominance in the 1860s, a world of accepted hierarchy and pastoral changelessness. The traditionalists constantly spoke of their patrician lineages. Lugones, for example, came from a "poor but distinguished family." "Among his ancestors was a colonel in the army of independence. . . . His imposing grandmother would solemnly recall that she had been born in Year Two of the Homeland."[166] Lugones's own poetry commemorated still earlier ancestors:

> A don Juan de Lugones el encomendero
> Que, hijo y nieto de ambos, fue quien sacó primero
> A mención las probanzas, datos y cualidades

De tan buenos servicios a los dos majestades
Con que del rey obtuvo, más por carga que en pago
Doble encomienda de indios en Salta y en
Santiago.[167]

The writers of this generation again echoed the European right as they
denounced the materialism of Buenos Aires. Gálvez declared, "We are seeking to attenuate the ugly materialism that today shames and insults us. . . . This
materialism is a recent phenomenon, that has appeared with the fever for
wealth, and that has come from Europe. The immigrant who has made his
fortune has brought with him a new concept of life. His sole intention is to
enrich himself, and in doing so he has contaminated the Argentines." Lamented Lugones, "We have confused national greatness with money. . . . We
have placed our honor in commerce." Ricardo Oliver, one of Gálvez's friends,
also attacked materialism, declaring that "what we need is some ideal for the
Argentine people."[168] Other writers followed Rodó's *Ariel*, and indirectly
echoed Renan, as they compared Latin America with the United States, much
to the detriment of the latter. "We possess the secret of energy," claimed
Gálvez, "but ours will never be a barbarous, automatic energy like that which
boils away unceasingly in the United States. Ours is a harmonious energy, a
force tempered by Latin energy."[169]

Gálvez and others criticized the ruling liberal elites, which in accepting
"French and British [liberal] ideas too uncritically" embodied the "cosmopolitan spirit" of the age.[170] Rojas's *La Restauración Nacionalista*, the best known
and most widely read of the early right-wing texts, inveighed against "economic and human cosmopolitanism" and complained that the "native element
of the country has abdicated into indifference and intellectual vacuity." Rojas
attacked the "destructive individualism" that prevailed in Buenos Aires and
the immigrants who corrupted the Spanish language with "barbarous dia-
lects."[171] In this society of foreigners that had been wrought by the liberals,
Lugones perceived "anarchy, bereft of any human or even patriotic
solidarity."[172]

To counter these foreign contaminants, the traditionalists scoured the
Argentine past in search of native themes and symbols. They unearthed the
payadores (wandering minstrels), the mestizo gauchos, and the federalist
patriarchs of the Rosas era whom they compared with the "liberal parasites"
who had gained supremacy in the 1860s. They began to weave fantasies
around what Julio Irazusta later called "that feudal democracy of the old
estancia, where the owner was accustomed to live as a country dignitary, and
where the peon received from his master far more than merely a day's wages.
. . . This was a truly cooperative labor system, which blended a sense of
empathy towards the poor with the natural possession of lordship."[173]

In this writing, the rural *estancia* became the local facsimile of the guilds
and corporations idealized by the European right. But before 1914 romanti-
cized formulations like these remained extremely rare; the early nativist

writers were unable to relinquish the liberal world in which they lived. Thus, Gálvez's novels contained numerous stereotypes of the characters who appeared in the works of Emile Zola, one of the leading liberal writers of this generation. Before 1914 many remnants of liberal-positivism survived in the work of Lugones, who at that time believed in "infinite progress" and in "perfect equality as an expression of perfect justice."[174] Lugones insisted upon human dignity for the working class, but he offered little more than the standard liberal recipe of handing out free land to newly arrived immigrants.[175]

The traditionalist writers often identified themselves as supporters of the left. Gálvez recalled that in his youth he and most of his friends were "more or less Socialists or Anarchists. We used to read Kropotkin and Bakunin."[176] For many years Lugones considered himself an anarchist. Even so, from his youth he dreamed of "redemptory enterprises under the dual banner of religion and homeland," and his friend Rubén Darío, the Nicaraguan poet, perceptively recognized that behind Lugones's show of "Red perspectives" lurked a real identity that was "completely White."

Despite Lugones's professed sympathies for the oppressed, he attacked attempts by the French and British governments to reach negotiated agreements with strikers when he visited Europe in 1911, proclaiming *"no se pacta con el desorden."*[177] In 1911, both Lugones and Rojas criticized proposals by the government of Roque Sáenz Peña for male suffrage and the secret ballot, Lugones as an opponent of "mob rule" and Rojas because the reform failed to impose a literacy test on voters. In 1913, Gálvez began to support restrictions on immigration and to sponsor conciliation boards to settle labor disputes in the spirit of the Catholic notion of "class harmony." Foreshadowing corporatist schemes that the right later advanced, Carlos Ibarguren called for a suffrage law that would represent "concrete" entities: farmers, merchants, the professional classes, and workers. A congress of the *"fuerzas vivas,"* he claimed, in terminology typical of corporatism, would sustain "social equilibrium."[178]

Throughout this period, however, "cosmopolitanism," a euphemism for immigration and the threat it was believed to represent, remained the central, indeed obsessive, concern of the traditionalists and the nativist associations. Their main solution to these issues was that offered by Rojas in *La Restauración Nacionalista*: a paternalistic and relatively cost-free dose of "patriotic education" to indoctrinate the new generation of Argentine-born children of immigrants with the habits and values of an unquestioning national allegiance.[179]

Conclusion

Before 1914 the Argentine right possessed little institutional identity. Outside of the Catholic church and the short-lived nativist groups it consisted of not much more than a literary movement, the members of which frequently "betrayed a set of successive identities, all of them of foreign origin, and sometimes to the point that the reproduction becomes a faithful copy of the original."[180] The right found its first self-expressions as uncoordinated reactions to progress and immigration. The traditionalists of this period sometimes published personal manifestos—Rojas's *La Restauración Nacionalista* and Gálvez's *El Diario de Gabriel Quiroga* are examples—that attacked materialism or cosmopolitanism explicitly, as they searched for spiritual or nationalist alternatives. But in this generation the right more commonly broached these issues elliptically or symbolically in verse and novels.

As yet the right had not developed its cult of military authoritarianism or managed to articulate its radical critique of liberalism. This generation did resemble those that followed, however, in linking national identity with class interests and in demanding from society deference to lineage. This generation too evinced the right's ingrained habit of treating working-class movements or ideologies as conspiracies of "professional agitators"—invariably foreigners and occasionally Jews. Before 1914 church leaders, supported by some lay Catholics, began to develop prototypes of corporatist institutions to control a potentially subversive working class. The traditionalists led by Gálvez and Lugones were starting to attack the contemporary society they disliked by expressing their nostalgia for the past: the liberal present was corrupt and decadent, but the conservative, or federalist, past was pure and unsullied. Finally, some of the same writers were displaying the concerns for political order that later would lead the right into its assault on popular democracy.

The Argentine right emerged virtually ex nihilo from the social and economic revolution of the late nineteenth century. Its roots, in contrast to its highly imitative stylistic forms, were local, indigenous, and recent. The counterrevolution in Argentina had a few of its roots in federalism, but for the most part the right developed less as a progression from a local conservative tradition than as a deliberate invention. Before 1914 the right had very shallow contact with the European counterrevolution. Although Gálvez drew from the writings of Barrès and Ganivet, his early writings had few other European points of reference except for the liberal Zola. The Argentine right extended its ideological base and fashioned its dogmas as it grew, and thus it was succeeding generations that attempted to construct the more sophisticated intellectual linkages that ranged from Aristotle to de Maistre, Menéndez Pelayo, and Maurras.

World War I and the Russian Revolution effected the great transition in the right's development, transforming the right from a literary fashion into a political movement. It was the war, insisted Lugones, that finally exposed the claim of the liberals to promote peace as a "noble illusion" and in doing so opened the door to the full force of the counterrevolution. The war achieved "a renaissance of patriotism," declared Lugones. Only after 1914 did Argentina begin "to understand that for the nation power was more important than law, and sovereignty more significant than liberty. Life was no longer a legal or moral system, but a state of force. In this way concept of Homeland came to redefine itself as an expression of Victory, as a Dominion."[181]

After 1918, Lugones and others embarked on the campaign that glorified the nation and the military at the same time as it stridently denounced liberalism. Another twenty years later the Argentine right was developing the doctrine of the "counterrevolutionary war" that it would fight in the 1970s and whose purpose, declared Jordán B. Genta, was "unity of doctrine, above all in the armed forces. And that unity can only be achieved by returning to the Catholic, Roman and Hispanic principles on which this Nation was founded, and which are the same as the Christian west."[182]

Notes

1. National Commission on the Disappeared, *Nunca Más* (New York, 1986), xiii.
2. For a background study stressing social and economic conditions see David Rock, *Argentina, 1516–1987: From Spanish Colonization to Alfonsín*, 2d ed. (Berkeley, 1987).
3. Tulio Halperín, "Liberalism in a Country Born Liberal: Argentina in the Nineteenth Century" (Paper read at the University of Illinois, Urbana, April 1987).
4. Quoted in *Gente*, November 22 , 1977.
5. Quoted in Carlos H. Waisman, "The Ideology of Right-wing Nationalism in Argentina: Capitalism, Socialism and the Jews," in *Proceedings of the 9th World Congress of Jewish Studies* (Jerusalem, 1983), 338.
6. Quoted in Jimmy Burns, *The Land that Lost Its Heroes* (London, 1987), 69.
7. Quoted in *El Bimestre Político y Económico* 28 (March 1986): 26. (Meeting of the association Familiares y Amigos de los Muertos por la Subversión [FAMUS].)
8. *Cabildo*, December 10, 1983.
9. Quoted in Amnesty International, *Report of Amnesty International's Mission to Argentina* (London, 1976), 35.
10. "El General Camps confiesa su responsabilidad directa en la desaparición de cinco mil personas," *El Bimestre Político y Económico* 12 (December 1983): 23–24.
11. Hugh Trevor-Roper, "The Phenomenon of Fascism," in *European Fascism*, ed. S. J. Woolf (London, 1968), 28.
12. Quoted by Trevor-Roper, "Phenomenon of Fascism," 22.
13. Carlos H. Waisman, "The Question of Revolution and the Reversal of Development in Argentina" (San Diego, Mimeographed paper, 1984), 275.
14. There has been much debate on this issue. According to Buchrucker, "The philo-fascists represented an important component of Nacionalismo up till 1945, and in many cases far beyond that decisive year. [During World War II] no one assigned much importance to the tense and problematical relationship between Catholicism and National Socialism. . . . The war against the Soviet Union dissipated practically all sense of reserve that many felt towards the neo-pagans of the Third Reich" (Cristián Buchrucker, *Nacionalismo y peronismo: La Argentina en la crisis ideológica mundial, 1927–1955* [Buenos Aires, 1987], 200). Buchrucker goes further than most commentators in asserting the fascist features of the Argentine right. But note that even here the fascists are mere "philo-fascists" and are, furthermore, only a "component." As Buchrucker would agree, even during the early 1940s religion remained at least a potential obstacle to the full assimilation of fascism by the Argentine right.
15. Federico Ibarguren, *Orígenes del nacionalismo argentino, 1927–1937* (Buenos Aires, 1969), 392.
16. Quoted in Buchrucker, *Nacionalismo y peronismo*, 51.

17. Ernesto Palacio, quoted in Ibarguren, *Orígenes*, 405.

18. A "left nationalism" in Argentina first appeared in 1935 with the creation of the FORJA (Fuerza de Orientación Radical de la Juventud Argentina), a splinter movement of the Radical party. See Mark Falcoff, "Argentine Nationalism on the Eve of Perón: Force of Radical Orientation of Young Argentina and Its Rivals" (Ph.D. diss., Princeton University, 1970).

19. See the discussion of Portuguese *integralismo* in H. Martins, "Portugal," in Woolf, *Fascism*, 302–36.

20. Comisión de Estudios de la Sociedad Argentina de la Defensa de la Tradición, Familia y Propiedad, *El nacionalismo: Una incógnita en constante evolución* (Buenos Aires, 1970), 110–11.

21. Comisión de Estudios, *Nacionalismo*, 149, 176.

22. Marysa Navarro Gerassi, *Los nacionalistas*, trans. Alberto Ciria (Buenos Aires, 1968), 94.

23. Navarro, *Los nacionalistas*, 97.

24. Ibarguren, *Orígenes*, 14.

25. Quoted in Mónica Quijada, *Manuel Gálvez: 60 años de pensamiento nacionalista* (Buenos Aires, 1985), 74, 77.

26. Ibarguren, *Orígenes*, 375, 392; Mario Amadeo, quoted in Navarro, *Los nacionalistas*, 127.

27. Angelo Del Bocca and Mario Giovana, *Fascism Today: A World Survey* (New York, 1969), 53.

28. Quoted in *Criterio*, July 13, 1933.

29. Zeev Sternhell, *La droite révolutionnaire, 1885–1914: Les origines françaises du fascisme* (Paris, 1978), 27.

30. Martins, "Portugal," 302–6.

31. Ibarguren, *Orígenes*, 365; Glen Dealy, "The Tradition of Monistic Democracy in Latin America," in *Politics and Social Change in Latin America: The Distinct Tradition*, ed. Howard J. Wiarda (Amherst, MA, 1974, 1979).

32. Jordán B. Genta, *Acerca de la libertad de enseñar y de la enseñanza de la libertad* (Buenos Aires, 1976), 12.

33. Genta, *Libertad*, 26.

34. Salvador Ferla, *Doctrina del nacionalismo* (Buenos Aires, 1947), 49.

35. Bernice Hamilton, *Political Thought in Sixteenth Century Spain: A Study of the Political Ideas of Vitoria, De Soto, Suárez, and Molina* (Oxford, England, 1963), 33 (quoting Francisco Suárez).

36. *La Nueva República*, April 14, 1929; Ibarguren, *Orígenes*, 54; *Criterio*, October 16, 1930.

37. Quoted in Frederick B. Pike, *Hispanism, 1898–1936: Spanish Conservatives and Liberals and Their Relations with Latin America* (Notre Dame, IN, 1971), 265.

38. Hugo Wast, "El Kahal," in *Obras completas de Hugo Wast*, ed. Hugo Wast (Madrid, 1956), 1726.

39. J. L. Talmon, *The Myth of the Nation and the Vision of Revolution* (Berkeley, 1981), 540.

40. Michael Sutton, *Nationalism, Positivism and Catholicism: The Politics of Charles Maurras and French Catholics, 1890–1914* (Cambridge, England, 1982), 18–37.

41. *Criterio*, March 10, 1932.

42. Ibarguren, *Orígenes*, 80.

43. Enrique P. Osés, *Medios y fines del nacionalismo* (Buenos Aires, 1941), 28.

44. Osés, *Medios*, 64.

45. Ibarguren, *Orígenes*, 231.

46. *Criterio*, October 7, 1930.

47. Ibarguren, *Orígenes*, 189.

48. Carlos Ibarguren, Jr., *Roberto de Laferrère: Periodismo-política-historia* (Buenos Aires, 1970), 36.

49. Ferla, *Doctrina del nacionalismo*, 49.

50. *La Nueva República*, April 23, 1929.

51. Sternhell, *La droite*, 379.

52. *La Nueva República*, December 1, 1927.

53. Talmon, *Myth*, 499.

54. Ibarguren, *Orígenes*, 393, 363, 181–87.

55. José María de Estrada, *El legado de nacionalismo* (Buenos Aires, 1956), 32.

56. Pike, *Hispanism*, 294.

57. Genta, *Libertad*, 179.

58. *Criterio*, April 24, 1930.

59. Genta, *Libertad*, 315.

60. Comisión de Estudios, *Nacionalismo*, 32.

61. Ibarguren, *Orígenes*, 244.

62. Quoted in Talmon, *Myth*, 402.

63. Eugen Weber, *Action Française: Royalism and Reaction in France* (Stanford, 1962), 522.

64. Norman Cohn, *Warrant for Genocide* (New York, 1981), 54.

65. Talmon, *Myth*, 367, 222–23.

66. *Criterio*, April 9, January 29, 1931.

67. Cohn, *Genocide*, 61.

68. Wast, "Kahal," 1766.

69. Jacob Katz, *Freemasons and Jews in Europe* (Cambridge, MA, 1970), 13.

70. Quoted in Katz, *Freemasons*, 150.

71. Cohn, *Genocide*, 25.

72. Marcelino Menéndez Pelayo, *Historia de los ortodoxos* (Madrid, 1956), 446.

73. *Criterio*, May 21, 1931.

74. Genta, *Libertad*, 182.

75. Ibarguren, *Orígenes*, 394.

76. Leopoldo Lugones, *La grande Argentina* (Buenos Aires, 1930), 157.

77. Ibarguren, *Orígenes*, 398, 389.

78. Sternhell, *La droite*, 183. On Spain see Pike, *Hispanism*, 20.

79. *Crisol*, February 14, November 25, 1935.

80. *La Maroma*, January 1940.

81. Osés, *Medios*, 45.

82. Ibarguren, *Orígenes*, 398.

83. Raúl Scalabrini Ortiz, "Bases para la reconstrucción nacional," in *La década infame*, ed. Alberto Ciria (Buenos Aires, 1969), 198.

84. This judgment on Maurras appears in Arturo Jauretche, *FORJA y la década infame* (Buenos Aires, 1984), 21.

85. See, for example, comments in *La Nueva República*, January 1, 1928.

86. Ibarguren, *Orígenes*, 213–14.

87. Enrique Zuleta Alvarez, *El nacionalismo argentino*, 2 vols. (Buenos Aires, 1975), 2:722.

88. On de Maistre see *La Nueva República*, April and May 1929, and Ibarguren, *Orígenes*, 384. On Bonald see Comisión de Estudios, *Nacionalismo*, 19; on Donoso Cortés, see Ibarguren, *Orígenes*, 362; on Balmes see Pike, *Hispanism*, 24. Menéndez Pelayo's influence is less easily documented but may have been transmitted principally by Ramiro de Maeztu, the Spanish ambassador to Argentina (1927-1929); see

Ramiro de Maeztu, *Defensa de la hispanidad* (Buenos Aires, 1945). De Maeztu's writings were derived heavily from nineteenth-century Spanish mentors, but de Maeztu (who was shot and killed by the Republicans on the eve of the Spanish civil war) is regarded by Zuleta Alvarez as "the greatest Spanish thinker of the twentieth century" (Zuleta Alvarez, *Nacionalismo argentino* 1:40).

89. Joseph de Maistre, *Une politique expérimentale* (Paris, 1940), 32, 36, 218, 155; *Criterio*, January 7, 1930; Ibarguren, *Orígenes*, 384.

90. Bonald, *Considérations sur la Révolution Française* (Paris, n.d), vi, vii.

91. Bonald, *Considérations*, 52–53.

92. Gustavo Franceschi in *Criterio*, April 30, 1931.

93. Ibarguren, *Orígenes*, 362.

94. Quoted in *La Nueva República*, May 26, 1928.

95. Pike, *Hispanism*, 21, 24.

96. Menéndez Pelayo, *Historia*, 1192, 1193, 1194, 367, 368.

97. Pike, *Hispanism*, 75.

98. John A. Armstrong, *Nations before Nationalism* (Chapel Hill, NC, 1982), 72–74.

99. Pike, *Hispanism*, 78, 97.

100. Comisión de Estudios, *Nacionalismo*, 55.

101. Genta, *Libertad*, 459.

102. Ibarguren, *Orígenes*, 371.

103. Comisión de Estudios, *Nacionalismo*, 55.

104. Ibarguren, *Orígenes*, 232, 13.

105. Comisión de Estudios, *Nacionalismo*, 55.

106. Ibarguren, *Orígenes*, 189.

107. José M. Rosa, "Defensa y pérdida de nuestra independencia económica," *Revista de Economía Argentina* 41, no. 187 (May 1942): 131.

108. José Enrique Rodó, *Ariel*, ed. Gordon Brotherston (Cambridge, England, 1967), 2–7.

109. Rodó, *Ariel*, 84.

110. H. Ramsden, *Angel Ganivet's "Idearium Español": A Critical Study* (Manchester, England, 1967), 156, 35, 75, 99, 115.

111. Elie Kedourie, *Nationalism* (New York, 1960), 23, 39.

112. For comments on Fustel de Coulanges's *Histoire des institutions politiques de la France* see *Criterio*, December 4, 1930.

113. Sternhell, *La droite*, 170; for Taine's influence on Barrès see William Curt Buthman, *The Rise of Integral Nationalism in France* (New York, 1970), 55–70, 109.

114. Manuel Gálvez, *El solar de la raza*, 5th ed. (Madrid, n.d).

115. Sternhell, *La droite*, 15, 148.

116. For acknowledgments of Maurras's influence see Comisión de Estudios, *Nacionalismo*, 25; Ibarguren, *Orígenes*, 12; Rodolfo Irazusta, *Testimonios* (Buenos Aires, 1980), 20.

117. Zuleta Alvarez, *Nacionalismo argentino*, 1:27.

118. Marcelo Sánchez Sorondo, *La revolución que anunciamos* (Buenos Aires, 1945, 1946).

119. Charles Maurras, *L'Avenir de l'Intelligence* (Paris, 1927), vi, 15.

120. Sternhell, *La droite*, 384–95, 379.

121. Buthman, *Integral Nationalism*, 277,

122. Sutton, *Nationalism*, 41.

123. Maurras, *L'Avenir*, 16.

124. Sternhell, *La droite*, 214.

125. *Criterio*, January 30, 1930, which discusses the 1927 papal ban.

126. *La Nueva República*, December 15, 1929.

127. Rock, *Argentina*, chaps. 1, 2.

128. John J. Kennedy, *Catholicism, Nationalism and Democracy in Argentina* (Notre Dame, IN, 1958), 20–28.

129. John Lynch, *Argentine Dictator: Juan Manuel de Rosas, 1829–1852* (Oxford, England, 1981).

130. Néstor Tomás Auza, *Católicos y liberales en la generación del ochenta*, 2d ed. (Buenos Aires, 1981), 320 (quoting Eduardo Wilde, 1884).

131. David Brading, *Los orígenes del nacionalismo mexicano* (México, 1972), 173.

132. Kennedy, *Catholicism*, 50.

133. Auza, *Católicos*, 14.

134. Héctor Recalde, *La iglesia y la cuestión social, 1871–1910* (Buenos Aires, 1985), 33, 35, 44, 228.

135. Republica Argentina, Cámara de Diputados, *Diario de Sesiones, 1883*, vol. 1 (July 11, 1883), 529.

136. Auza, *Católicos*, 230.

137. Ibid., 430, 274.

138. Ibid., 14.

139. José Manuel Estrada, *Discursos*, 2 vols. (Buenos Aires, 1943), 1:84.

140. Ibid., 99.

141. Ibid., 235; Kennedy, *Catholicism*, 98–105.

142. Kennedy, *Catholicism*, 133; Auza, *Católicos*, 42; Estrada, *Discursos*, 1:333; *Criterio*, September 18, 1930.

143. For an extensive discussion of these social and political changes after 1890 see Rock, *Politics*, chaps. 1–4.

144. Recalde, *Iglesia*, 24.

145. On *Rerum Novarum* see David Rock, "Intellectual Precursors of Conservative Nationalism in Argentina, 1900–1927," *Hispanic American Historical Review* 67, no. 2 (May 1987): 286–87.

146. José Elías Níklison, "Acción social católica," *Boletín del Departamento Nacional del Trabajo* 46 (March 1920): 19.

147. For a lengthy description of these projects see Alejandro E. Bunge, "La acción social obrera," *Revista de economía argentina* 274 (April 1941): 124–31 (first published in 1913).

148. Níklison, "Acción," 197, 120.

149. Rock, "Intellectual Precursors," 287.

150. Níklison, "Acción," 255, 200.

151. *Criterio*, July 6, 1933.

152. Tulio Halperín Donghi, "Para que la inmigración? Ideología y política inmigratoria y aceleración del proceso modernizador: El caso argentino (1810–1914)," *Jahrbuch für Geschichte von Staat, Wirtschaft und Gesellschaft Lateinamerikas* 13 (1976): 468.

153. Waisman, "Question of Revolution," 64.

154. Iaacov Oveid, "El trasfondo histórico de la ley 4144, de residencia," *Desarrollo Económico* 61 (April–June 1976): 123–50.

155. For an account of these events and their background see Sandra McGee Deutsch, *Counterrevolution in Argentina, 1900–1932: The Argentine Patriotic League* (Lincoln, NE, 1986), 35–36. This work contains summary material on the period before 1914. The events of 1909 and 1910 are also described in Carl Solberg, *Immigration and Nationalism in Argentina and Chile, 1890–1914* (Austin, 1970), 112–14.

156. The following passages develop material in Rock, "Intellectual Precursors."

157. Eduardo José Cárdenas and Carlos Manuel Payá, *El primer nacionalismo argentino en Manuel Gálvez y Ricardo Rojas* (Buenos Aires, 1978), 123.

158. Quoted in Quijada, *Gálvez*, 27.

159. Manuel Gálvez, *Amigos y maestros de mi juventud* (Buenos Aires, 1961), 43.

160. Manuel Gálvez, *El espiritualismo español* (Buenos Aires, 1921), 5.

161. Cárdenas and Payá, *Primer nacionalismo*, 25.

162. Gálvez, *Amigos*, 84.

163. Pike, *Hispanism*, 134.

164. Rock, *Argentina*, 120–31.

165. In the village Santa María del Río Seco/At the foot of the Cerro del Romero, I was born/And this is all I will say of myself/Because I am no more than an echo/Of the natal song that I bring here. Leopoldo Lugones in Irazusta, *Lugones*, 23.

166. Irazusta, *Lugones*, 23–24. "Year Two" was 1812.

167. To don Juan de Lugones the *encomendero*/Who, son and grandson of both, was the one who first took/At the mention of proof, times and places and qualities/Of such good services to the two majesties/That from the king he obtained, more as a burden than in payment/Double *encomienda* of Indians in Salta and in/Santiago. Lugones in Irazusta, *Lugones*, 23.

168. Gálvez, *Solar de la raza*, 14; Leopoldo Lugones, "Prometeo," in *Obras en prosa*, ed. Leopoldo Lugones, Jr. (México, 1962), 778; Quijada, *Gálvez*, 18.

169. Quijada, *Gálvez*, 31.

170. Quoted in Waisman, "Question of Revolution," 17.

171. Quoted in María Inés Barbero and Fernando Devoto, *Los nacionalistas* (Buenos Aires, 1983), 19.

172. Lugones, "Prometeo," 1005.

173. Irazusta, *Lugones*, 24.

174. Ibid., 28.

175. Lugones, "Prometeo," 1074.

176. Gálvez, *Amigos*, 127.

177. Irazusta, *Lugones*, 24, 32.

178. Deutsch, *Counterrevolution in Argentina*, 61.

179. Cf. Barbero and Devoto, *Nacionalistas*, 20–28.

180. Roberto Giusti in *Crítica*, July 19, 1923.

181. Quoted in Irazusta, *Lugones*, 111.

182. Genta, *Libertad*, 464.

The Right under Radicalism, 1916–1930

Sandra McGee Deutsch

The years between 1916 and 1930 witnessed the birth of the ultraright in Argentine politics in the shape of two distinct movements: the Liga Patriótica Argentina, founded in 1919, and the self-styled Nacionalistas, who established their first journals and organizations in the second half of the 1920s. The Liga represented a largely homegrown reaction against the immigrant working class, although its members were cognizant of the Russian Revolution and other events abroad. Heavily influenced by European counterrevolutionary thought, the Nacionalistas aimed most of their rhetorical barbs against liberalism.

During these same years, Argentina also experienced democracy under the rule of the Unión Cívica Radical, or Radical party. That this short-lived democratic experiment overlapped the beginnings of the ultraright was no coincidence. Previous administrations had protected the interests of the upper classes, and the elite thus had little need to defend itself under an extremist banner. The Radicals, however, attempted to satisfy a broader constituency than merely the elite. For this reason both the Liga and the Nacionalistas viewed the populist wing of the Radical party and its standard-bearer, Hipólito Yrigoyen, as threats and opposed them. Yet their real enemy was not so much democracy per se as it was the specter of leftist upheaval, for in their opinion the first led inexorably to the second. Antileftism would remain the focus of the Argentine ultraright from its inception to the present. Particularly true for the 1920s, although perhaps less so in later years, a secondary theme would be the superficial character of the right's "nationalism," which was preoccupied more with the need for order *against* the immigrant masses than with the masses' welfare.

Origins

The rise of the ultraright was linked to the political decay of the elite that had governed Argentina from 1880 to 1916. Historians usually have characterized this group as "liberal," because most of its members supported a free market, immigration, public education, a secular society, and rule by a propertied minority. The fact that over time this group entrenched itself in power through fraud and coercion led some scholars to call it the liberal-conservative elite, or *régimen* (regime). The elite's conservatism meant the preservation of the status quo and opposition to progressive change in the form of either democratic or workers' rights, rather than classical conservatism. By the early 1900s the heavily immigrant urban lower and middle classes had become staunch advocates of such rights, the former through unions, anarchist groups, and the Socialist party and the latter through the Radical party, which also attracted some adherents from disaffected sectors of the landowning class. To unify the upper classes and maintain stability in the face of growing labor discontent, the elite reluctantly acceded to Radical party demands for genuine universal male suffrage and in 1912 passed the Sáenz Peña Law. This law opened the way for Radical victories at the polls, including Yrigoyen's election to the presidency in 1916.

Meanwhile, the regime had entered a crisis. Formerly, it had been united under the rubric of the Partido Autonomista Nacional (PAN). When skillful politicians such as President Julio Roca (1880–1886, 1898–1904) left the political scene, the PAN splintered into provincial factions. Even the most powerful of these, the Conservative party of Buenos Aires (1908–), lacked the leadership ability to reforge a national alliance. Most of the provincial conservative parties also failed to offer an alternative to the Radical party's promise of electoral democracy and integrity and, to a lesser extent, to the Socialist party's platform of socioeconomic reform. Their record of electoral fraud and the continued presence of corrupt political hacks in their ranks belied their supposed new devotion to mass rule. Some individuals—most notably, the founders of the Partido Demócrata Progresista (PDP) (1914–)—wanted to create a cohesive, mass-based party combining economic nationalism, democratic principles, a concern for social welfare, and aristocratic leadership. Rivalries between the PDP presidential candidate for 1916, Lisandro de la Torre, and several former PAN figures impeded this attempt to form a modern national conservative party. Faced with a vacuum on the right, those who opposed Radical democracy from a perspective of order moved in increasingly extreme directions.

Labor militancy, however, not the Radical government, supplied the direct impetus for formation of the Argentine ultraright. A history of diverse elite reactions to immigrant working-class activism preceded the birth of the first rightist organization. The regime had used brutal police actions and deportations to repress the labor movement. The Social Catholic movement within the church had encouraged class conciliation through social welfare projects and other methods, including the creation of Workers' Circles—deceptively titled because they included both labor and management. Employers had formed yellow unions and other groups, such as the Asociación del Trabajo (1918), to protect their right to hire and fire workers as they saw fit. In response to widespread labor discontent during the centennial celebration of Argentine independence in May 1910, police and aristocrats had attacked worker organizations and newspaper offices as well as Jewish neighborhoods. Clerics, employers, members of the security forces, and regime figures began to contrast "foreign" working-class protest with the "nationalistic" activities of the privileged sectors.[1] The common feature of these reactions to working-class activism was the desire to subordinate workers and rob them of an ideological platform.

A labor crisis broke out in the post-World War I years that was more serious than previous ones and therefore called for a more permanent solution. The crisis was related to the grave economic problems that Argentina experienced during and after the First World War. Shortages of vital imports during the war hindered industrial and grain production, although meat and wool exports soared. After the war, the demand for both grains and livestock products fell. Unemployment and inflation became the rule.[2] The hardship that these conditions represented for the masses, as well as the inspiration of the European revolutionary movements, led to an unprecedented level of strikes and worker mobilization. Strikes in the transportation and meat-packing sectors between 1916 and 1918, and the first landless rural workers' unions, which directly affected the export economy, particularly threatened the upper class.[3]

Perhaps most troubling to the elite was that it could no longer take government hostility against unions for granted. President Yrigoyen (1916–1922, 1928–1930) appealed to workers for support by portraying himself as an austere man of the people and by meeting with labor representatives. His administration intervened in the major strikes of the war period and helped resolve some of them to the benefit of labor. Unlike previous presidents, Yrigoyen did not deport activists or declare a state of siege, at least before 1919. Although he did not genuinely favor unions, Yrigoyen approached labor with more evenhandedness than previous administrations. The upper class, however, characterized his policy as pro-worker.[4] This perception would strongly influence the formation of the Liga.

The Semana Trágica and the Rise of the Liga

In the midst of economic uncertainty, labor activism, and upper-class discomfort with reformist democracy, the Semana Trágica, a violent struggle between workers, on the one hand, and capitalists and the state, on the other, broke out. It started as a strike in a metallurgical factory in Buenos Aires in

December 1918 and escalated into a general strike the following month. The Semana Trágica, a week of work stoppages, looting, street protest, and violent confrontations between laborers and the police and army, ensued between January 9 and 16. Troops commanded by the Radical general Luis J. Dellepiane arrived in the capital on January 9 and 10 and helped to put an end to the worker-led violence. Soon thereafter, government officials mediated a solution to the strike that had precipitated the disorders.[5]

Throughout the crisis, frightened middle- and upper-class *porteños* (inhabitants of Buenos Aires) wondered if the government had lost control of the situation or, at the very least, if it was coddling the workers. That General Dellepiane had decided on his own to move soldiers into the capital strengthened this perception. This viewpoint was also natural for those who insisted Yrigoyen was pro-worker. Adding to their fears, precisely at this time the leftist revolutionary Spartacists were threatening to take over Germany, an alleged communist plot was "uncovered" in Montevideo, and there were strikes and worker-led demonstrations throughout Chile. The Argentine press devoted considerable attention to these events. As *La Nación* observed, one could not separate occurrences in Buenos Aires from those in the world.[6] Thus it is not surprising that many *porteños* feared that a revolution directed from abroad was imminent. Moreover, because they identified the left with the Soviet Union, they tended to blame local events on Jewish immigrants, most of whom had come from Russia.

Acting on these perceptions, armed groups of civilians took matters into their own hands and patrolled the streets of Buenos Aires from the early hours of January 10 through the 14th. Together with the police, they burst into working-class and Jewish neighborhoods, destroying union and Jewish community institutions, attacking and arresting individuals, and vandalizing Jewish-owned property. Police imprisoned the supposed leaders—Russian-Jewish in origin—of the First Argentine Soviet, which presumably had orchestrated the Semana Trágica. (Later, the authorities quietly released the suspects, having discovered that the "Soviet" was a phantasma.) While the white terror raged, civilians met in police precinct headquarters and created militias to protect their barrios from possible worker incursions. The neighborhood guard movement spread to other cities where labor was active, and guards continued to form after the Semana Trágica had ended.[7]

Various groups were involved in the repression and in the organizations established afterward to maintain order. Leading participants both in the white squads who had attacked the workers and Jews and in the neighborhood guards came from the Comité Nacional de la Juventud, an organization that arose in October 1918 to lobby for the Allied side. When the war ended, the Comité searched for other causes and found them in anti-Yrigoyenism and in the antilabor struggle. Adherents of Yrigoyen's own party were numbered among the vigilantes; indeed, General Dellepiane authorized the distribution of arms to civilians, presumably with the president's approval. Retired military officers, politicians, and upper-class "gentlemen" joined the neighborhood guards. Members of all of these groups, as well as prominent businesspeople and church activists, participated in the Comisión Pro-Defensa del Orden, which collected funds for the families of police, fire fighters, and soldiers killed or wounded by workers. Leading Conservatives and Radicals took part in the Comisión, but, significantly, the latter would join the upper-class Anti-Personalist (anti-Yrigoyenist) wing of the party in succeeding years.[8]

The navy took control of the armed civilians. From the inception of the Semana Trágica, young men had gathered at the Centro Naval, a club for active and retired naval officers, to receive arms and training. On January 12, Rear Admiral Manuel Domecq García created a new citywide civil guard, headquartered in the Centro Naval, which brought together all the disparate vigilante groups. The rear admiral met with representatives from the army and navy on January 15, and they decided to make the citywide militia a permanent one. They invited civic leaders, priests, businesspeople, military officers, and members of prominent organizations, including women's groups, to join the new institution, the Liga Patriótica Argentina, which would uphold "fatherland and order" against "anarchic elements foreign to our nationality."[9]

These guests attended the inaugural meeting of the Liga on January 20 in the Centro Naval, over which Domecq García presided. The participants approved a list of goals, the first of which stated that the Liga would foment the spirit of *argentinidad* among all inhabitants and awareness of a citizen's obligations to the homeland. The Liga would accomplish this task in part by lobbying for greater public and private support for the schools, where children learned to love their country, and for improved wages and benefits for teachers. Motivated by rumors of communist influence in the normal schools, the Liga urged educational authorities to exercise stricter control over teachers' beliefs. The Liga also would encourage the public to celebrate patriotic holidays, to familiarize itself with Argentina's history and habitat, and to revere the military as protector of the nation's homes and freedoms. Another task of the Liga would be to increase the welfare of the poor, thereby reminding the lower classes that all legitimate solutions to current problems fit within the guidelines of the liberal Argentine constitution. Argentina would continue to welcome newcomers who accepted its rules, but it would defend itself against those who advocated alien ideas. The guardians of *argentinidad* would use all legal methods to bring such persons to justice, including cooperating with the authorities to maintain stability in the face of any anarchist threats or violent strikes.[10] The Liga hinted that if legal means did not suffice, it would resort to illegal coercion. Or, as the Liga noted later, when "guests" of the nation abused its hospitality by disturbing the social order, the Liga would protect national interests.[11]

The Liga's statement of purpose reveals its conception of nationalism. It defined *argentinidad* as conformity with the political and social status quo.

Anarchists, union members, socialists, and other dissidents did not fit the Liga's vision of an idyllic Argentine past blessed with social peace; hence, they were "foreign." The immigrant backgrounds of the vast majority of the country's working class reinforced the Liga's distinction between Argentina's "native" upper- and middle-class members, who defended their nation, and their "alien" opponents.[12]

This distinction was more rhetorical than real. Not all protesters came from abroad, nor were Liguistas (league members) necessarily of creole—native-born—lineage. Furthermore, was the maintenance of order in the interest of the upper classes a genuinely nationalist concern? The socialist newspaper *La Vanguardia* regarded the Liga's nationalist claims skeptically. It noted the Liga's following in the military and questioned whether the organization would really protect the constitution against attack from the likeliest quarter—the military. It also pointed out that Argentina hardly treated its foreign-born inhabitants as "guests," for many were forced to live as gypsies, wandering in search of employment, and that a truly nationalistic organization would advocate revising the cumbersome naturalization procedure and make it easier for immigrants to become citizens. The anarchist organ *La Protesta* also asked if those who encouraged divisiveness by sponsoring hatred and violence against a segment of the population—in this case, laborers—were truly nationalistic.[13] The anarchists and Socialists implied that the Liga's nationalism masked antipopular sentiments.

The left raised doubts not only about the Liga's nationalism but also about its commitment to democracy. According to the Socialists, incorporating foreign-born laborers into the political system, rather than singling them out for attack, would strengthen Argentine institutions. Socialists warned of the dangerous overlap between the armed forces and the Liga. Indeed, this collaboration heralded the upper sectors' propensity to rely on the military to protect their interests, which would have tragic consequences for Argentine civilian rule throughout the twentieth century. The implication in the Liga's statement of goals that the Radical administration lacked the strength or desire to perform necessary tasks, and therefore that the Liga would have to fill this vacuum, also alarmed the Socialists. As representatives of the Socialist party insisted on repeated occasions, the Liga was usurping the role of an elected government.[14]

During its first year of existence, the Liga focused on recruiting men and women and organizing itself across the nation. The neighborhood guards formed the core of the ranks. These guards became Liga "brigades," of which there were forty-three in the capital's forty-five police precincts.[15] The guards of the interior also joined the Liga as the brigades of their respective cities. Other urban brigades were organized on the basis of occupation or professional association. Either at the Liga's invitation or through their own initiative, landowners, businesspeople, and civic leaders within the provinces established additional brigades. When landless harvest workers began to strike in the pampas in December 1919, farmers responded by creating rural brigades. The Liga also created "free labor" brigades as counterweights to militant unions. Meanwhile, in the second half of 1919 and early 1920, Liguistas appealed to women to join the organization. Single and married upper-class women created brigades of señoritas and señoras, respectively, in Buenos Aires and other cities, and female teachers of varied backgrounds created teachers' brigades in the city and province of Buenos Aires and the city of Mendoza. By November 1919 the Liga claimed to have 833 brigades throughout the nation.[16] During the following years the Liga's size would fluctuate, but its permanent core would consist of 41 women's brigades and 550 men's brigades, or about 820 female and 11,000 male activists.[17]

Meanwhile, the leadership coalesced. Members of the Círculo Militar (the army counterpart of the Centro Naval), Centro Naval, and Comisión Pro-Defensa del Orden joined the Liga's authorities. Their names appeared on the rosters of the Junta Central, chosen by the brigades, and the Consejo Ejecutivo, elected in turn by the Junta Central. Domecq García served as the provisional head of the organization until April 1919, when the brigades elected Manuel Carlés as president.

Carlés was a complex figure. A lawyer, a professor at the War College and elsewhere, and a former national deputy (1898–1912), Carlés was tied to the regime, yet his closest friends within it had been reformers, such as President Roque Sáenz Peña (1910–1914), who gave his name to the suffrage law. Although his days in the Chamber of Deputies ended with electoral reform, Carlés maintained his interest in politics and his contacts with the Radicals, especially with his good friend President Marcelo T. de Alvear (1922–1928), and with those who would become Anti-Personalists. Yrigoyen named Carlés to preside over the 1918 intervention in the province of Salta, and in February 1919, while the Liga was consolidating itself, the president considered appointing him minister of the navy. Later that year the Conservatives of Buenos Aires province considered Carlés for their slate of candidates.[18] Thus, Carlés's political loyalties were ambiguous.

Ambiguous too was the Liga's relationship with the government. On the one hand, Radicals had participated in the Liga from its beginnings and, at least initially, the Radical administration praised the Liga's defense of order and permitted the military, the police, and the post office to work with the organization. Nevertheless, the Liga's ability to attract thousands of members around the country, including Yrigoyen's upper-class rivals in the opposition and in his own party alike, worried the government, which saw the Liga as a potential political challenger. The growing military involvement in the Liga reinforced official fears. Beginning in mid-1919 (and in response to Socialist warnings), the government issued statements forbidding active military personnel and police from belonging to the Liga, but it was unable to cut the links between the organization and the security forces. The Yrigoyen regime eventually reached an implicit modus vivendi with the Liga. Whereas the regime continued to court native-born, unaffiliated urban workers, it repressed union activities more harshly than it had before the Semana Trágica, and it tacitly accepted the Liga's existence. In turn, the Liga refrained from formally constituting itself as an opposition party or from plotting to overthrow democracy—at least, until Yrigoyen's reelection in 1928.[19] The Radicals could accept the Liga's opposition to labor but not its opposition to their party's rule.

The broad social composition of the Liga indicated the popularity of Liga-style nationalism and explained why the Radicals compromised with it. Liga authorities were aristocratic in background. About 69 percent of the members of the Junta Central and Consejo Ejecutivo between 1920 and 1928 belonged to the upper class, as did virtually all of the female leaders, who were linked by kinship ties. About half of the male leaders owned land themselves or were members of landowning families, and at least 31 percent had been elected or appointed to office before 1916, demonstrating their regime affiliations. Radical fears of military participation in the Liga were justified: 19 percent of those in the Liga's central authorities for whom occupational information was available were officers.[20]

Members of the male brigades were more plebeian in background. Only 18 percent of brigade delegates to the Liga's annual meetings, who tended to be brigade officers, were from the upper class, and 19 percent owned land or belonged to landed families. The Liga's "free laborers" were nonunionized workers already employed by Liguistas or hired by them to break unions and strikes. Because it is unlikely that such workers joined the Liga out of free will or genuine conviction, the middle sectors formed the popular base of the Liga—amounting to perhaps 31 percent of the male national leaders, 82 percent of the delegates, and an even larger percentage of the teachers' brigades and the male rank and file. The urban ranks included professionals, business owners, government and business employees, military officers, and a few priests associated with the Social Catholic movement. In rural areas ranchers and tenant and small farmers and their overseers led the brigades. The brigade members had a stake in society and thus had reason to fear union and leftist agitation.

On behalf of its members' interests, the Liga disrupted union activities, broke strikes, and suppressed the left throughout the nation. Its partner was the Asociación del Trabajo, which took charge of repressing laborers in the capital. The Liga's most significant confrontations with labor occurred outside the city of Buenos Aires, where unions were forming in the agro-export sector so vital to the national economy. One of the first such clashes took place in 1920 in Las Palmas del Chaco Austral, a giant agricultural company in the northeastern corner of El Chaco province. Both Argentines and English citizens were numbered among the firm's directors and owners. Of creole, Paraguayan, Brazilian, and Indian origins, the landless workers on the estate suffered from oppressive conditions, including low wages paid in scrip redeemable only at company stores. To change this situation, laborers formed a union in 1918 and struck the following year, winning higher wages to be paid in national currency, among other concessions. The company, however, insisted on charging a fee for paying wages in cash.[21]

Unwilling to accept an assertive union, the company fought back. Aided by the Liga and the Asociación del Trabajo, Las Palmas recruited mercenaries and criminals and sent them to company lands, starting in January 1920. These armed thugs terrorized the inhabitants and provoked confrontations with union members. By May the firm had organized its agents provocateurs into a Liga brigade headed by one of its administrators, Alberto Danzey. When Las Palmas dismissed union complaints against the Liga in July, the union called a strike, demanding that the company fire Liguistas and stop requiring fees for cash wages.

The strike was protracted, bloody, and indecisive. Several armed battles broke out between workers, on the one side, and Liguistas, company gendarmes, and police on the other. Captain Gregorio Pomar, Radical leader of the Ninth Infantry Regiment, imposed a cease-fire and a settlement favorable to the workers in August. Once the troops left, however, the firm disavowed the agreement and the strike resumed. Liguistas continued to patrol Las Palmas, yet the strike limped on until June 1921. Two years later the union finally won the right to be paid in pesos without fees. Its goal achieved, the union movement in the area declined, and labor conditions remained poor; the brigade of Las Palmas, however, survived at least until the late 1920s.[22] "Nationalism" and the workers essentially had reached a draw.

The Liga's claims of nationalism to the contrary, foreigners and Creoles were found on both sides of the conflict in Las Palmas. The same would be true of worker-Liga clashes in Villaguay, Entre Ríos. Responding to labor mobilization, Liga brigades began to form in that department, located in the zone containing Jewish agricultural settlements, in 1920. In January 1921 a union of peons and manual workers called a strike against farmers and threshing machine owners.[23] Liguistas, including the police, jailed several union activists. The local union, the Socialist party of Villaguay, and the provincial Federación Obrera Comarcal planned a rally to protest these detentions on February 11. Meanwhile, the Villaguay brigade readied itself to meet what it viewed as the Jewish and maximalist "horde." On the scheduled day in the departmental seat of Villaguay, shooting broke out between protestors, on the one hand, and Liguistas and police, on the other. It is not clear who started the gunfire, but most of the approximately thirty-five casualties were laborers. The imprisonment of seventy-six workers and Socialists—and no Liguistas— after the battle also demonstrated that the latter had controlled the events. As eighteen of the prisoners were Jewish, some Liguistas, politicians, and newspapers, including *La Nación* of Buenos Aires, characterized the conflict as one of "Jewish revolutionaries" versus "orderly Creoles." The majority of the prisoners, however, were Creoles.[24]

A few days after it issued its statement on the conflict, *La Nación* changed its mind. The newspaper and other observers realized that Jewish farmers outnumbered Jewish landless workers. Some Jews already belonged to the Liga at the time of the Villaguay incident; whether they belonged or not, however, the interests of most Jewish colonists were the same as those of the organization. After Villaguay, Jews joined the Liga in increasing numbers. By May 1921, twelve of the thirty brigades in the Jewish settlement area had Jewish officers, and others probably had Jewish members.[25] The Liga had used Jews as convenient scapegoats during the Villaguay episode; afterward, just as advantageously, the Liga recruited these "foreigners" as members.

The Liga continued its "nationalistic" mission in Patagonia. Whereas workers throughout the territories of Chubut, Santa Cruz, and Tierra del Fuego formed unions from 1918 on, businesspeople, ranchers, and ranch managers organized an estimated seventy-five brigades in the region between 1920 and 1921.[26] Liga members clashed with unionists in the ports and petroleum installations along the coast. In addition, between November 1921 and January 1922, when the Tenth Cavalry killed as many as fifteen hundred striking ranch workers, Liga brigades furnished the army with fuel, vehicles, housing, and provisions and accompanied it on patrol. After the army decimated union ranks, Liguistas forced workers into joining "free labor" brigades.[27]

That the army and the Liga had destroyed the labor movement in Patagonia was evident; whether in doing so they had countered a "foreign" threat was not as clear. Well aware of the powerful labor movement in southern Chile, Carlés identified the Patagonian unions with an ideology imported from Argentina's neighbor. Indeed, many of the rural workers were Chilean. Foreigners, however, were also found on the employers' side of the struggle. The most prominent entrepreneurs in southern Argentina were European-born landowners and representatives of foreign agro-export firms, and they were leading members of the Patagonian brigades.[28] The Liga made an exception for these and other foreign-born members: They were "beneficial foreigners" who contributed to the nation. This, according to the Liga, set them apart from the working class.

Whereas male Liguistas suppressed those who were in their view harmful foreigners, their female counterparts used peaceful means to "Argentinize" the immigrants. The brigades of señoritas set up free schools for immigrant women in factories in the Buenos Aires area. By 1927 they had established at least nineteen schools, and the Liga claimed that over fifty were operating as late as 1950.[29] The students learned reading, writing, arithmetic, homemaking arts, vocational skills, Argentine history, the catechism, and such "creole" values as patriotism, love of work, punctuality, and obedience. Liga members hoped that the Argentinized pupils would teach their families what they had learned. In this manner, the factory schools, as well as others founded by the Liga in neighborhoods and towns, would help mold rebellious foreigners into a pliable, submissive labor force. To the Liga, this goal signified nationalism. Confirming the nationalistic character of the curriculum, as the Liga defined it, Carlés proudly announced that the señoritas' schools were "exclusively Argentine" in nature.[30]

Liga men and women held some nationalist sentiments that transcended the taming of the proletariat. From 1920 through at least the 1930s, the señoras held annual expositions and sales of textiles made by Indian and creole women of the interior. Their intention was to help an economically deprived group whose origins were genuinely local. Moreover, the textile fairs manifested the Liga's belief that the nation should stimulate and protect its own industries, particularly ones of long standing that used raw materials found within Argentina.[31]

A major theme discussed in the Liga's annual congresses was the problem of Argentine economic dependency. Although some Liguistas were foreign-born businesspeople or worked for foreign companies, speakers warned of the dangers of foreign capital. Liguista speakers noted that the local economy operated for the benefit of other countries rather than for Argentina. The nation, they thought, should reassert control over its own resources and economic life. Luis Zuberbühler, a prominent businessman and Liga official, and president of the business lobby Confederación Argentina del Comercio, de la Industria, y de la Producción (CACIP), implored Argentines to invest funds and ability in industry, so that nationals would control more enterprises. Other Liga members proposed higher tariffs, a national merchant marine, restrictions on foreign investment, public investment funds, and government efforts to reduce the external debt.[32]

The Liga linked the issue of economic nationalism to the labor question. For example, it viewed industrialization as a means of pacifying workers. Liguistas believed that prosperous industries would raise the level of employment and thus reduce labor discontent. A social security system, profit sharing, land reform, and other programs suggested by Liguistas also would quell workers' dissatisfaction. Moreover, some Liga members used the class struggle as an explanation for underdevelopment. They tended to blame the deficiencies of Argentine industry on the workers, thus diverting attention from the issue of foreign control. Several speakers at Liga congresses suggested that in reality laborers in underdeveloped countries shared a common interest with their employers: that of strengthening the economy and thereby increasing the welfare of all. Workers' demands and strikes impeded the functioning of national firms and thus were antinationalistic.[33] Carlés drew a connection between foreign capitalism, which subjected Argentina to orders from abroad, and leftists, who also exploited the country in the service of an alien ideology.[34] In his view, even capitalism was linked to the leftist threat against Argentine autonomy.

Carlés admitted that, in the past, Argentina had adopted some foreign ideas when it had been advantageous to do so, as in science and economics. He also acknowledged his own debt, and the Liga's, to European positivism and Catholic doctrine. Nevertheless, Carlés believed that the left was foreign and the Liga was Argentine. The Liga respected the homeland and its social fabric, based on family, property, and authority, which the left sought to destroy. In place of the Argentine tradition of progress through order, radicals wanted to substitute an ideology of class conflict. Carlés characterized this belief as foreign because it had grown out of circumstances in industrial Europe. He thought it did not express the social reality of an underdeveloped country like Argentina, where, in his opinion, there was neither a proletariat nor a strong capitalist class.[35] (The left, of course, strongly disagreed with these views.) In contrast, the Liga saw its views as indigenous, although it had incorporated some currents of nineteenth-century European thought into native ones.

Had the contemporary European right influenced the Liga? The same postwar crisis had stimulated the formation of both the Liga and European groups. The Liga arose in early 1919, before Fascism in Italy or the Primo de Rivera regime in Spain, and at about the same time as the German Workers' party, the nucleus of National Socialism. The timing of events meant that these movements had no impact on the formative period of the Liga. Nor did the Liga claim any inspiration from Charles Maurras, the foremost French counterrevolutionary of the early twentieth century. The Liga's congressional proceedings and pamphlets contained few references to European movements. During a discussion of land reform, Carlés cited approvingly the Italian Fascist land distribution program, pointing out that landed peasants were unlikely to turn to bolshevism.[36] In another speech Carlés compared the Liga to traditionalist forces in Europe that had united under the banner of the nation to combat and defeat the "red danger."[37] Thus, although European ideas did not determine specific Liga programs or doctrines, Carlés knew of similar antileftist groups abroad.

The Liga contacted foreign dignitaries partly to initiate relations with these groups. The Portuguese and Swiss ministers to Argentina visited Liga headquarters, as did a French government delegation.[38] Before the centennial of Brazilian independence, Carlés congratulated Brazil and sent a pamphlet describing the Liga in Portuguese to the Brazilian legation. (The Liga also had pamphlets prepared in English and German, as well as in Spanish.) Pedro de Toledo of the legation thanked Carlés and invited him to the independence celebration in Rio de Janeiro. He added that by attending, the Liga would strengthen the friendship between the two countries and its ties with similar groups in Brazil.[39] In October 1920, Carlés sent a letter, a pamphlet, and other publications to U.S. Ambassador Frederic J. Stimson. The Liga president asked Stimson to put the Liga in touch with similar institutions in the United States for possible joint action against anarchism. This was a high priority, for "if all men of order were to unite," they could defeat the efforts of those who did not "respect patriotism" and who sought to destroy the social order. Carlés's letter and publications found their way to Attorney General A.

Mitchell Palmer, known for his role in the Red Scare, who compiled a list of antileftist organizations for the Liga. These examples reveal the Liga's desire to strengthen relations with other antileftist groups, as well as the fact that governments were sympathetic to the Liga and its counterparts.[40]

The Liga eventually established contact with antiradical groups in the United States, Uruguay, Chile, Bolivia, Brazil, Peru, Germany, Belgium, France, Great Britain, Denmark, and possibly Switzerland and Portugal. For example, Liga delegates visited the Ligue Civique in France and National Propaganda in Great Britain, and the Liga Patriótica Militar (LPM) of Chile sent representatives to the Liga.[41] The Liga even incorporated an LPM representative into the Junta Central. Carlés cited the Liga's ideals of "international fraternity" to justify this step, and he emphasized the need for the two organizations to work together to strengthen the "nationality" and respect for institutions. The only clear evidence of such collaboration was an LPM ceremony in Santiago in July 1922 honoring the Liga.[42] Nevertheless, for the Liga as well as for the LPM, nationality evidently transcended borders.

Despite its relations with the LPM and other foreign groups, the Liga did not create a "nationalist international." The postwar labor mobilization that had stimulated the formation of the Liga and similar organizations elsewhere in Latin America was short-lived. By 1922 employer interests in the region had quelled the worker threat, rendering far-reaching measures such as an international network of antileftist militias unnecessary. Nevertheless, the Liga's efforts in this direction and its protection of foreign companies demonstrated the tenuous character of its nationalism. True, it showed some concern for Argentine economic independence and for native traditions. Yet the Liga's "visión de patria," as it entitled a film on its campaign against subversion,[43] represented the viewpoint of the upper classes, creole and foreign-born, not that of the nation as a whole. To defeat what it saw as an international threat, the Liga was willing to leap over Argentine boundaries. In its lexicon, nationality did not mean the Argentine people per se, but rather an idealized conception of worker-employer relations, which, according to the Liga, had existed in Argentina and other countries in the past. This definition of nationalism would influence rightist groups throughout the decade and those to come.

Transition to Nacionalismo

According to Liguistas and other figures, the threat to the Argentine nationality reemerged in the late 1920s. In response to this situation, a new rightist movement, the Nacionalistas, coalesced. Unlike the Liga, a united group founded in January 1919, Nacionalistas gathered in various circles and organizations, and no specific date marked their beginning. Also in contrast to their predecessor, Nacionalistas devoted more attention to thought than to action.

Thus, to explain their origins one must emphasize the conditions that sparked their mobilization, and the evolution of their thinking.

Yrigoyen seemed to the right to threaten its position. He and his wing of the Radical party had increased the power of the immigrant middle class. Through his recognition of the university reform movement, Yrigoyen helped open university faculties and administrations, as well as the liberal professions and, hence, government service, to greater middle-class participation. The new government oil monopoly, Yacimientos Petrolíferos Fiscales, and the enlarged bureaucracy provided more employment for members of this sector, who also joined the party organization and were elected to office. Such policies, along with the Radicals' image of integrity and democracy, won popular favor and translated into success at the polls. Yrigoyen had removed local conservatives from provincial governments through interventions in his first term. His colleague Marcelo T. de Alvear became president when he left office, and he was reelected when Alvear's presidency concluded. Yrigoyen's victory in 1928 and his previous interventions also enabled his party to win a majority in the Chamber of Deputies that year. Only the Senate remained in opposition hands. To Yrigoyen's opponents—the Anti-Personalist Radicals, the various conservative factions, the Liga, and young scions of the elite— democracy seemed to mean a permanent loss of political control to the "New Argentines" that they despised. They identified Yrigoyen's seemingly per- petual rule with dictatorship. However, because the people had consented to Yrigoyen's augmentation of power, his was what his opponents called a dictatorship of the masses and, therefore, in their view resembled or could lead to communism.

In contrast to the Liga's broad definition of dictatorship, its conception of civil rights in a democracy had always been a narrow one. For Carlés, "to live, to work, and to acquire goods" with the earnings of one's labor constituted the "essential rights" of the individual. The only other liberty he approved of was that of workers to remain "free" of unions, a liberty promoted by the Liga's union-busting tactics. He opposed freedom of thought, for having the permis- sion to think freely did not guarantee that people would exercise this right responsibly.[44] The Liga's repression of the Socialist party and peaceful worker demonstrations further manifested its disdain for liberty of expression. More- over, its emphasis on authority and lower-class deference contradicted the democratic ideal of equality. Indeed, Carlés's view of democracy did not include equality or self-assertion. In 1920 he defined this type of political system as a "state of justice for all." As the decade wore on, however, he increasingly preferred the term "republic" to "democracy," noting that the founders of the Argentine nation had established the first, not the second. A republic assured the well-being of all on the basis of mutual respect, he proclaimed. In 1928 he praised a republic as a "social state where discipline, the principle of authority, the security of the individual and in one's work, and civil peace reign."[45] Implicitly, Carlés was contrasting the supposed stability of elite rule with what he saw as the turbulence and leftist bent of democracy. The numerous conflicts of the years between 1880 and 1916, however, belied his view.

Carlés and other members of the elite feared that behind Yrigoyenist democracy lurked the danger of social dissolution. This opinion had been the main factor behind the creation of the Liga. The pacification of the labor movement by 1922 and the presidency of the aristocratic Alvear, however, had calmed upper-class apprehensions of democracy. Yet these apprehensions had not disappeared. In 1923, Carlés denounced "the evil political breeds that stimulate all the sensuality of the low social depths in exchange for the electoral vote."[46] In that same year, the Liga cosponsored Leopoldo Lugones's series of talks in which the poet definitively repudiated the revolutionary sympathies of his youth. Lugones linked his newfound dislike for foreign leftism with his revulsion for "the clientele of the ballot box and the committee." He placed his hopes for social peace and nationalism in the military, rather than in democracy, and restated these views in stronger fashion in his famous "Hour of the Sword" speech in Lima in 1924 published, significantly, by the Círculo Militar.[47]

Yrigoyen's reelection and memories of his supposed pro-worker sentiments exacerbated these fears of the ties between democracy and leftism. In April 1928, just after the Radical caudillo's electoral victory, Carlés called together the presidents of the brigades of the federal capital in a secret session to make sure they were prepared to maintain order if authorities did not take firm action against labor provocations. A few days after Yrigoyen's inauguration in October, the metropolitan brigades approved Carlés's proposal to reestablish the militia formation that the Liga had used against workers in its early days. The following year, when Yrigoyen took his time in responding to strikes in Rosario, members of the upper classes complained that the government lacked the strength to combat bolshevism. In actuality, there was little evidence of labor militancy. Nevertheless, Carlés insisted that the university reform movement had lowered discipline and authority in education and had helped spread Bolshevik ideas. The Liga also announced that Radicals were cooperating with anarchists to secure the labor vote (the fact that anarchists do not vote notwithstanding) and conceal labor abuses. Indeed, in May 1930, Carlés claimed that the Yrigoyen administration had made a pact with "the leaders of anarchism."[48]

By this time the Great Depression had reached Argentina, and the septuagenarian Yrigoyen appeared unable to combat either the economic crisis, the chaos within his administration, or his resolute opposition in the Senate. Violence between Radicals and their opponents furnished evidence of political decay, which the elderly president was powerless to halt or to which he may have contributed. Bitterly divided by partisan disputes, Congress was equally impotent. It is not surprising that, within this atmosphere, popular support for political change grew. Other groups joined the Liga, conservative factions, and Anti-Personalists in opposition to Yrigoyen. The most important of these was the military. Angered by the president's meddling in their concerns, officers began to plot against the government. Some of these conspirators found antidemocratic ideas attractive.[49]

Antidemocratic ideas had been taking shape slowly since the early part of the decade. Indeed, the same situation that inspired the formation of the Liga—postwar labor militancy—catalyzed this new rightist current, that of the Nacionalistas. The worker-led disorders in the Semana Trágica had repelled such future Nacionalistas as Lugones, the former PDP figure Carlos Ibarguren, and Juan Carulla, a medical doctor, and awakened in them a concern for order. Already, during a visit to wartime Europe, Carulla had "learned" that socialists had not supported their respective countries' war efforts—an inaccurate lesson—and that true nationalists would have to oppose them out of patriotism.[50]

Repugnance for the left turned many upper-class intellectual youths toward Catholicism. This was another by-product of January 1919. The Social Catholic movement had responded to the Semana Trágica by organizing the Gran Colecta Nacional, a fund-raising drive "for reestablishing and consolidating Argentine social peace." Its opposition to unions and class conflict resembled that of the Liga; in fact, seven of the Colecta's eleven-member financial committee were Liguistas, as were other organizers and contributors. The Colecta spent most of the proceeds on projects designed to alleviate working-class discontent, such as housing. However, believing that social peace required carrying the antirevolutionary message not only to workers but also to future leaders, it also directed some funds toward Catholic education. Thus the Colecta sent aid to the Ateneo Social de la Juventud, which had been founded in 1917 by Atilio Dell'Oro Maini, a Liga and Asociación del Trabajo member, Tomás Casares, a judge and professor, and others as a means of inculcating youths with Catholic values.[51]

More importantly, Dell'Oro Maini, Casares, and the Catholic scholar César Pico helped establish with Colecta funding the Cursos de Cultura Católica in 1922. The students read and discussed Thomist doctrine and the works of European orthodox Catholic and rightist authors. One participant later recalled the Cursos as "dissident toward tradition and toward the right, but dissident." Their growing appreciation of hierarchy, spiritualism, heroism, discipline, and corporativism—the values of the Catholic Middle Ages—put the participants in the Cursos and its spin-off groups, Convivio and Baluarte, at odds with the contemporary order. This hostility toward the status quo also characterized the Catholic journals *Criterio* (1928–) and *Número* (1930–31), whose contributors attended the Cursos.[52]

The Catholics frequently discussed the works of Charles Maurras, who would exert the most important foreign influence on Nacionalismo during this period. In 1925, Julio Irazusta, soon to become one of the most prominent Nacionalista intellectuals, characterized the French counterrevolutionary's thought as "a most magnificent model for conservative action."[53] Maurras lauded the Old Regime and detested the revolution that had overthrown it. In his view, before 1789 a hereditary system of mediating institutions, including estates, families, guilds, the monarchy, and, in particular, the church, promoted hierarchy, obedience, and harmony. Maurras attributed the fall of the admirable Old Regime to the forces of Judaism and "Jewish" (non-Romanized) Christianity and to German tribalism and Protestantism, which, with their pernicious emphasis on individualistic freedom and humanism, created the doctrine of the French Revolution. Liberal republicans founded a new system under which abstract concepts such as freedom and democracy assumed precedence over national well-being. Rule by the rich, the greedy, the ignorant masses, and those pandering to these groups replaced the old elite of the monarchist period, which had been trained to govern well. Moreover, the anarchic and materialistic tendencies of liberal democracy led inevitably, in Maurras's view, to the threat of proletarian revolution. Because liberalism had initiated the entire process of French decay, however, Maurras directed most of his ire toward it rather than toward leftism.

Maurras considered it axiomatic that the monarchy, which was responsible for French glory, should return to power. Only a conspiracy of foreign enemies and their internal allies could explain the failure to reinstitute this "natural" system of government. The revolutionary currents of liberalism and leftism and the other forces that threatened French unity and stability, such as international capitalism, anticlericalism, and pacifism, were also foreign, primarily of Jewish and German origin, in his view.

Maurras posed some difficulties for Argentine Nacionalistas. For example, his idealized conception of the Old Regime was as much an abstraction as the liberal principles he despised. Nevertheless, despite his utopian view of the past, he considered himself a keen observer of concrete reality. Irazusta recognized the flaw in Maurras's thought, that is, that Maurras believed that politics was the science of the particular and could not be reduced to a system, but he had gone ahead and created his own system.[54] With a few exceptions, most Nacionalistas rejected Maurrasian-style monarchism, for it had little relevance in a country with firm republican traditions. Most importantly, in 1926 the pope condemned Maurras for converting religion into the handmaiden of politics, forcing the latter's Nacionalista admirers to temper their enthusiasm.

Although the Nacionalistas, then, did not blindly adopt all of Maurras's teachings, they found much in them that was attractive. They shared his opposition to liberalism, parliamentarianism, and Marxism and his linkage of these doctrines under the heading of "dissolvent." They, too, advocated a powerful state under elitist rule; responsible for Argentine progress in the past, the regime should be returned to power. According to the Nacionalistas, "functional democracy" representing genuine social forces—those that had ruled in Maurras's idealized monarchy—should replace the Argentine version of democracy, which they believed represented only demagogic professional politicians and promoted anarchy. Opponents of immigration, Nacionalistas shared Maurras's hatred of foreigners. And, increasingly after 1930, the Nacionalistas assumed the existence of a conspiracy against Argentine interests directed from abroad, one that united liberals, democrats, leftists, foreign capitalists, and Jews.[55]

To a lesser extent than Maurras, Benito Mussolini also elicited praise from Nacionalistas. Some were suspicious of his one-man dictatorial tendencies, but they nonetheless approved of his strong interventionist government, defeat of the left, and good relations with the church. A frequent contributor to *Criterio* and Nacionalista publications, the novelist Manuel Gálvez was one of *Il Duce*'s admirers. Starting with the Italian Fascist regime, the modern dictatorship, in his view, represented the first stage of a return to the classical political principles of order and equilibrium, reason, Roman law, and the primacy of the spiritual over the material. He admitted that Mussolini had used extreme means to restore classical politics and quash the revolutionary spirit, but such methods were subordinate to a worthy goal: "a new revolution, founded in principles opposite to those which animated the French revolution and its derivates socialism and bolshevism."[56]

Budding Nacionalismo also claimed Spanish sources of inspiration. Cultural nationalists such as Gálvez, an unabashed Hispanist, were breaking down upper-class distaste for its Spanish heritage. The visits to Argentina in 1928 of the Spanish writer and philosopher José Ortega y Gasset, whose articulate elitism found a mouthpiece in César Pico, and of Ramiro de Maeztu, Spain's ambassador to Argentina, helped arouse interest in the nineteenth-century Spanish conservative thinkers Juan Donoso Cortés and Juan Vásquez de Mella. Nacionalistas greeted Maeztu with praise for the Spain of Primo de Rivera, the prime minister. They saw Maeztu as someone who could help reunite Spain and Spanish America into a Hispanic community devoted to common counterrevolutionary aspirations.[57] Reminiscent of the Liga's interest in creating an antileftist world network, this manifestation of internationalism similarly contradicted the Nacionalistas' supposed devotion to Argentine political and cultural autonomy. At any rate, Maeztu met frequently with Julio Irazusta and his brother Rodolfo as well as with participants in the Cursos. According to Julio Irazusta, much of Maeztu's book *Defensa de la Hispanidad* (1934) drew upon these discussions; the influence, therefore, went both ways.[58]

Nacionalismo was indebted not only to Catholicism, Maurras, and Hispanism, but to Lugones as well. The poet followed his antileftist, antiliberal speeches of 1923 and 1924 with the publication of *La organización de la paz* (1925), a diatribe against democracy, Christianity, Marxism, and all other notions of universal fraternity. In opposition to these abstractions, Lugones emphasized what he considered to be concrete realities: biology, race, nation, force, and hierarchy. A sympathetic biographer, Julio Irazusta later admitted that Lugones carried his social Darwinist and Nietzschean views to "incredible" extremes.[59] Another leading Nacionalista, Ernesto Palacio, described Lugones as a fascist.[60] The Catholic influence on Nacionalistas led them to repudiate Lugones's paganism and radicalism, although they admired him as a teacher and shared with him some of the same enemies. After the revolution of 1930, the Nacionalistas' economic, social, and political ideas converged with those of Lugones, who would join their organizations; before that year, however, the poet did not belong to their camp.

Drawn eclectically from foreign and local sources, Nacionalista ideology was discussed in two newspapers during these years: *La Voz Nacional* and *La Nueva República* (LNR). *La Voz Nacional* appeared between March and November 1925. Its sponsors included Juan Carulla and several foreigners— an inauspicious beginning for a nationalist organ. The paper, however, brought General José F. Uriburu, the future leader of the 1930 revolution, into the Nacionalista fold. One of the few subscribers, Uriburu had participated in the revolution of 1890 against the regime and in the PDP, and he was disillusioned with democracy.[61]

Launched two years after *La Voz Nacional* ran out of money, *LNR* was the principal voice of Nacionalismo from 1927 to 1931. The political origins of its editorial circle were diverse; the Irazusta brothers came from an Anti-Personalist provincial family, Palacio and Carulla from the left, and several from the ranks of Personalism and the PDP. Maurras held great appeal for Carulla, the Irazustas, and others, and less for the Catholic conservative Pico and recently converted Palacio. One Maurrasian monarchist left the fledgling paper over the issue of its republicanism, reflected in the title, and there were other ideological defections. Nevertheless, opposition to Yrigoyenist demagogy, liberalism, socialism, immigration, university reform, and electoralism—what they viewed as foreign dissolvent elements—united those who remained, as did their preference for a strong corporativist state headed by a nonpartisan elite. They interpreted their task to be the reversal of a forty-year trend, one that began after Roca's presidency, of "spiritual disorientation" and ideological "chaos" in the ruling sectors. Changing the elite's notions of government was the *LNR*'s chief preoccupation before September 1930.[62]

Part of the *LNR*'s educational duty was to convince its readers of its view that democracy contradicted the nation's republican traditions and best interests. As Rodolfo Irazusta wrote in a series of articles, "Democracy is not in the Constitution." The founding fathers, he believed, had omitted this word because it meant disorder. The Argentine constitution reflected its authors' republican sentiments. Republicanism elevated the national interest over individual interests and thus represented the opposite of democracy, according to the *LNR* circle. The constitution and republicanism contrasted with democracy in that they stood for the rule of law rather than the rule of the masses, federalism rather than centralist dictatorship, and representation of the so-called *fuerzas vivas* rather than of political parties. The *LNR* claimed that true Argentine nationalists were firmly republican.[63]

LNR writers derived their republican views partly from classical sources. Much of their inspiration, however, came from Carlés, who by the late 1920s emerged as a leading antiadministration spokesperson. The similarities between Carlés's thought and that of the *LNR* were not surprising, noted Rodolfo Irazusta, for the Liga president was a "precursor of the real republicanism" disseminated in the newspaper. Years before, Carlés had begun to distinguish republics from democracies and praise the former.[64] *LNR* often covered Carlés's speaking engagements and lauded his ideas. He agreed with the Nacionalistas on the need for religious values, hierarchy, and subordination of individual liberties to the national interest. He, too, equated nationalism with order and characterized Argentina's internal enemies as foreign. Both the Nacionalistas and Carlés criticized liberalism, socialism, and partisan political struggle, and both favored elitist rule. By the late 1920s, Carlés even grouped liberal democrats with leftist workers as agents of dissolution.

Moreover, Carlés and many Nacionalistas admired the original spirit of Radicalism and considered themselves its successors. Carlés had initiated his political career by attending the first meeting of the Unión Cívica, the predecessor of the Unión Cívica Radical, which rebelled against the liberal, corrupt Miguel Juárez Celman regime (1886–1890) in 1890. Two Nacionalistas, Uriburu and his cousin Carlos Ibarguren, were also active in the Unión Cívica. Carlés participated in the abortive Radical revolution of 1893, and his continuing sympathies for the Radical party have been noted already. Early Radicalism had defended the constitution with weapons, and it leaned toward clericalism, according to the Nacionalistas. Moreover, it had been creole, unlike what they saw as the immigrant, parvenu UCR under Yrigoyen. Now the party represented "the revolution in all its crudeness," and as such, Nacionalistas opposed it.[65] As they described it, this revolution included the lower as well as the middle class.

Some Nacionalistas also admired the PDP. Ibarguren helped write its platform of 1916 and ran for the presidency on the PDP ticket in 1922. Other former Progressive Democrats included Uriburu and his cousin Francisco Uriburu, editor of *La Fronda*, a Conservative party organ and strong supporter of the Liga and the *LNR*. Nacionalistas pointed out that the PDP leader Lisandro de la Torre had opposed not only the corrupt, partisan regime but also Yrigoyen's "demagogy without ideas." His resolute anticlericalism, however, diminished his attractiveness to the Catholic Nacionalistas, who also began to judge the PDP to be excessively democratic.[66]

These sympathies indicated Nacionalista ambivalence toward the regime and its successors. Initially, Julio Irazusta and Carulla favored returning to a Roca-style government. They thought that under this president the spirit of the ruling class, whose interest was associated with that of the nation, had reigned above the competing parties. Yet a few months later, Rodolfo Irazusta wrote that installing a republican elite did not mean returning to the "*gobiernos de familia*" that had governed Argentina for half a century. Others questioned whether Roca was indeed a nationalist, deriding the sterile, partisan, anti-clerical, and bourgeois tone of his administration and the regime he had helped create. They criticized the regime for engendering demagogy through the universal suffrage law and the Conservative party for competing with Radicalism for mass support. The Conservatives' opportunism and lack of firm doctrine were leading the party to the left of Radicalism, in their opinion. Thus, in Nacionalista eyes the Conservative party had forfeited the right to rule, for the first task of a truly national party was to resist revolution, that is, to resist the left.[67] Yet despite these statements, Nacionalistas would seek recruits in the Conservative party. Evidently, opportunism went both ways.

Conservatives and *LNR* writers joined the various Nacionalista forces seeking to overthrow the president.[68] Founded in 1929, the Liga Republicana carried Carlés's and the *LNR*'s ideological battle against Yrigoyen into the streets. Its members loudly demonstrated against the government, spread anti-Yrigoyenist propaganda, and fought Radicals, university students, and, increasingly in the months before September 1930, the police. By 1930 the Liga Republicana had amassed a few hundred core members and powerful allies— *La Fronda* and General Uriburu and his military associates, who were planning a coup. In the course of their conspiratorial activity, the *LNR* and the Republicanos shifted their political thinking. They declared their support to be merely for the constitution's preamble, and not for the entire constitution as before. Evidently, the constitution was more democratic than they had thought. From here it was a short step to their postrevolution statements that the constitution should be revised to permit a corporativist system and that only the military could accomplish this task, for the military was above all parties. As with the Liga in the early 1920s, order took precedence over Argentine tradition.

A new group, the Legión de Mayo, became part of the revolutionary struggle in August 1930. Unlike their Republicano comrades-in-arms, who opposed not only the ruling party but also the electoral system, Legionarios criticized Yrigoyenist abuses yet praised the supposed democracy that had existed from 1810 to 1912. They voiced the ideas of Conservatives, who simply wished to reinstall themselves in office, and in so doing drew fire from the *LNR*. The thousand-odd revolutionaries papered over their differences, united under the Conservative deputy and Legionario Alberto Viñas, and helped the military bring Uriburu to power on September 6, 1930 (as discussed in the chapter by Ronald H. Dolkart). However, the disagreement between the extremist Liga Republicana and the *LNR*, on the one hand, and the moderate Legión de Mayo, on the other, presaged future tensions between Nacionalistas and Conservatives in Uriburu's government (1930–31) and throughout the 1930s.

Many Argentines saw the Uriburu regime as the restoration of elitist rule. Indeed, the composition of the Nacionalista groups that helped bring him to power also reflected aristocratic roots.[69] About 60 percent of the members of the *LNR* circle, Liga Republicana, and Legión de Mayo were from the upper class, rising to 84 percent among the most ardent Nacionalistas, the militants who belonged to more than one group. Moreover, many Nacionalistas tended to come from interconnected families; 36 percent of the entire group that was studied, and 47 percent of the militants, were closely related to other Nacionalistas. Three percent had participated in the Liga Patriótica Argentina, and 14 percent were closely related to members of that group, indicating relatively little linkage with it. Because the Nacionalistas tended to be young— their average age in 1930 was thirty-one—few were in government before the Radicals assumed power. Yet 35 percent either had been elected or appointed to office before 1916 or, more commonly, had close relatives in such positions; the same was true of 47 percent of the militant Nacionalistas. Over one half, or 54 percent, either owned land or belonged to landholding families, as did 69 percent of the militants but only 33 percent of the *LNR* group. The heavy concentration of the latter in the liberal professions as well as their relative absence from the land suggests that the *LNR* writers were aristocrats with little left to them but their names. However, although some observers characterized all Nacionalistas as in general downwardly mobile,[70] there is scant evidence for this assertion as of 1930.

Surprisingly, only one member of a Nacionalista group was a military officer compared to the much higher figure for the Liga Patriótica Argentina. Yet many officers were sympathetic to Nacionalismo, particularly because it assigned to them the leading role in the creation of a new political system. They manifested their sympathies by supporting Uriburu in 1930 and afterward and by opposing his rival, the more moderate General Agustín P. Justo (president, 1932–1938). Moreover, officers would join Nacionalista organizations in the 1930s.

The degree of military participation was only one of the differences between the Liga and the Nacionalistas. Another was age: the average Nacionalista was sixteen years younger than his Liga counterpart of 1920, who averaged forty-seven years of age. Even though more of the Liga's leaders and the women who were Liguistas came from the aristocracy, the Nacionalistas' popular base was smaller than that of their predecessors. Close family links reinforced class allegiances among Nacionalistas (and among female Liguistas), but not among the Liga's male members. Of course, Nacionalista organizations were far smaller than the postwar Liga, and unlike the Liguistas, the Nacionalistas denigrated the middle class and made little effort to recruit members from its rank before September 1930. Nor did Nacionalistas seek to attract women to their cause at this time. With their traditional roles in the home and in charity work, women were suited for the Liga's social welfare projects but not evidently for the Nacionalistas' ideological endeavors and street fighting.

The one important resemblance between Liguistas and their successors was a similar degree of participation in the regime, either through their own political offices or those of their families. Yet even this similarity hints at a difference: A group shut out of power for fourteen years—indeed, one that had never known political power—was bound to be more dissatisfied with the status quo than was a group that had exercised but had lost power only a few years before, which was the situation of those Liguistas tied to the regime in 1920.

The foregoing comparison reveals that Nacionalistas were younger, more homogeneous, and more dispossessed than their precursors. They were also far more radical. Nacionalista and Liguista reactions to the Uriburu government demonstrated this difference. Both Carlés and the Nacionalistas applauded the regime's persecution of labor and the left. Uriburu's repression of Alvear and other Radicals, however, angered Carlés, who turned against the revolutionary government. The Nacionalistas approved of this repression but were disappointed and disillusioned by Uriburu's failure to implant a corporativist dictatorship. Nacionalistas in the 1930s continued to favor a corporativist system, whereas Carlés and the Liga now favored liberal democracy.[71]

Nacionalistas were more extreme than Liguistas in other respects as well. One measure of their extremism was their anti-Semitism. The pragmatic Liga could welcome "foreign" Jews as members; Nacionalistas could never see the Jews as anything but foreign interlopers. In contrast to Liga members, who rarely made anti-Semitic comments after Villaguay, *LNR* writers frequently indulged in the expression of such sentiments. They demanded an end to Jewish immigration, which they judged harmed the country, and identified Jews with their enemies: leftism, liberalism, internationalism, the grain exporters who exploited Argentine farmers. After the revolution they "discovered" a capitalist-communist-Jewish "conspiracy" against the nation. Maurras and other French counterrevolutionaries helped inspire these anti-Semitic views but so too did the Nacionalistas' own frustration over their political impotence and Argentina's economic decline in the Great Depression.

There were also other differences between Nacionalistas and Liguistas. In contrast to the latter, Nacionalistas had little interest in questions of social justice or economics, although this would change after the revolution of 1930. This attitude reflected another variance: The Liga directed its efforts toward co-opting and repressing workers, whereas Nacionalistas attempted to convert the military and the upper class to their view of the need to change the form of government.

Despite these differences between Liguistas and Nacionalistas, there was an underlying continuity between the two ultra-rightist currents of the Radical period. Foreign ideas and events influenced both movements, especially the Nacionalistas, but so, too, did local preoccupations influence them. Both groups were connected to the upper class and the former elite, although in each case tensions and ambiguities marked the relationship. Both Liguistas and, particularly, Nacionalistas were suspicious of democracy, yet they also

sympathized with those who had rebelled against the regime. Most importantly, the concern for order of the Liguistas and their successors outweighed
their national sentiments, and the strongest threat to order, in the view of these
groups, was the immigrant left. Inheritor of the *LNR*'s mantle, the Nacionalista
organ *Crisol* in 1932 acknowledged this link between the Liga and
Nacionalismo. It praised the Liga as the first organization in Argentina to
oppose "extremism," adding that it had opened the path "on which all nationalist institutions since have marched."[72] Both before and after 1930 the right
was, above all else, antileftist.

Notes

1. I discuss these and other precedents to the Liga in *Counterrevolution in
Argentina, 1900–1932: The Argentine Patriotic League* (Lincoln, NE, 1986), chap. 2.
On the Asociación del Trabajo, see María Silvia Ospital, "Acción empresaria y
conflictos laborales: La Asociación del Trabajo, 1918–1930," ms., 1987. Note that
"Conservative" refers to the Conservative party of Buenos Aires, and "local conserva-
tive" refers to the provincial parties tied to the regime; "nationalism" signifies that
philosophy in general, whereas "Nacionalismo" means a specific rightist movement.
Anti-immigrant sentiments are described in detail in this essay.

2. On economic conditions in Argentina see Guido Di Tella and Manuel
Zymelman, *Los ciclos económicos argentinos* (Buenos Aires, 1973), 129–86; Joseph
S. Tulchin, "The Argentine Economy during the First World War," *Review of the
River Plate* (June 19, 30, July 10, 1970); Darío Cantón, José L. Moreno, and Alberto
Ciria, *Argentina, la democracia constitucional y su crisis* (Buenos Aires, 1972), 21–
50; and Vicente Vázquez-Presedo, *Estadísticas históricas argentinas* (comparadas), 3
vols. (Buenos Aires, 1971–1988), 2:46.

3. Vázquez-Presedo, *Estadísticas* 2:47. On labor see David Rock, *Politics in
Argentina, 1890–1930: The Rise and Fall of Radicalism* (London, 1975), 125–56;
Robert Edward Shipley, "On the Outside Looking In: A Social History of the 'Porteño'
Worker during the 'Golden Age' of Argentine Development, 1914–1930" (Ph.D.
diss., Rutgers University, 1977); Edgardo J. Bilsky, *La semana trágica* (Buenos
Aires, 1984); and Richard J. Walter, *The Socialist Party of Argentina, 1890–1930*
(Austin, 1977), 150–57.

4. *La Nación*, January 8, 1919; Alain Rouquié, *Poder militar y sociedad política
en la Argentina*, 2 vols., trans. Arturo Iglesias Echegaray (Buenos Aires, 1981),
1:140–41, 143–44, 150; Chargé d'Affaires ad interim Donald White to Secretary of
State Charles Evans Hughes, June 1, 1921, Dispatch no. 1567, U.S., Department of
State Records Related to the Internal Affairs of Argentina, 1910–1929, National
Archives Microfilm Copy M514, 835.00/237.

5. On the Semana Trágica see the daily press of Buenos Aires for those days;
David Rock, "Lucha civil en la Argentina: La semana trágica de enero de 1919,"
Desarrollo Económico 11 (March 1972): 165–215; Nicolás Babini, "La semana
trágica: Pesadilla de una siesta de verano," *Todo Es Historia* (September 1967): 8–20;
and Julio Godio, *La semana trágica de enero de 1919* (Buenos Aires, 1972).

6. *La Nación*, January 8, 1919. On events in Chile see Peter DeShazo, *Urban
Workers and Labor Unions in Chile, 1902–1927* (Madison, WI, 1983), 161–62.

7. On the civilian-led repression and the formation of militias see Nahum
Solominsky, *La semana trágica en la Argentina* (Buenos Aires, 1971), 17–21; José R.

Romariz, *La semana trágica: Relato de los hechos sangrientos del año 1919* (Buenos Aires, 1952); and *La Prensa, La Nación*, and *La Epoca*, January 10–15, 1919.

8. Romariz, *La semana trágica*, 170; *La Epoca*, January 16–17, 1919.

9. *Revista Militar* 19 (January 1919): 198–202; *La Razón*, January 17, 1919; *La Prensa*, January 21, 1919.

10. *La Epoca*, January 20, 1919.

11. Liga Patriótica Argentina, *Definición de la Liga Patriótica Argentina* (Guía del buen sentido social) (Buenos Aires, 1921), 3; Liga Patriótica Argentina, *Discursos pronunciados en el acto inaugural y veredicto del Jurado de la Tercera Exposición Nacional de Tejidos y Bordados, 1–15 julio 1922* (Buenos Aires, 1922), 7.

12. Liga Patriótica Argentina, *Primer Congreso de Trabajadores de la Liga Patriótica Argentina* (Buenos Aires, 1920), 39–40.

13. *La Vanguardia*, April 1, May 13, 1919; *La Protesta*, November 9, 1919.

14. See, for example, Nicolás Repetto's remarks in the Cámara de Diputados, cited in *La Vanguardia*, June 11, 1919.

15. Liga Patriótica Argentina, *Solemne homenaje de la Liga Patriótica Militar de Chile a la Liga Patriótica Argentina* (Santiago, 1922), 16; República Argentina, Policía de la Capital Federal, *Orden del día* 34 (1920): 832–34. The press reported daily on the creation of brigades.

16. *El Pueblo*, June 30–July 1, July 21–22, 1919; *La Fronda*, October 8, November 1, 1919; *La Nación*, November 4, 1919, August 13, 1920; *La Capital* (Rosario), January 26, 1921. The figure for brigades appeared in *La Fronda*, November 2, 1919.

17. See Deutsch, *Counterrevolution in Argentina*, 93–94.

18. *La Prensa*, April 6, 1919, October 26, 1946; Pedro P. Maglione Jaimes, "Una figura señera—Manuel Carlés," *La Nación*, January 12, 1969; Rock, *Politics in Argentina*, 183; *La Voz del Interior* (Córdoba), December 12, 1919; *La Protesta*, January 13, 1920.

19. Deutsch, *Counterrevolution in Argentina*, 97–102; *El Pueblo*, July 24, 1919.

20. These and the following comments on the Liga's social composition are based on a sample of 146 brigade delegates to the annual congresses from 1920 to 1928 and of 71 members of the Junta Central and Consejo Executivo for those years. Sources included the *Guía de sociedades anónimas* (Buenos Aires, 1923, 1932, 1950); Jockey Club, *Nómina de los socios* (Buenos Aires, 1926, 1943), *Libro de oro* (Buenos Aires, 1911, 1923, 1932, 1936, 1941); "Nómina de socios," *Anales de la Sociedad Rural Argentina* 52 (February 1918): 116–34; Sociedad Rural Argentina, *Nómina de socios* (Buenos Aires, 1938, 1948, 1956, 1962); Carlos Calvo, *Nobiliario del Antiguo Virreynato del Río de la Plata*, 6 vols. (Buenos Aires, 1936–1943); and others listed in Deutsch, *Counterrevolution in Argentina*, 284–86. Those who belonged to the Jockey Club, the Sociedad Rural or other rural associations, prestigious social registers, and/or the Círculos de Armas were considered upper class. I thank Néstor Tomás Auza and José Luis de Imaz for checking the lists of persons studied (both Liguistas and Nacionalistas, see note 69) and confirming their class background.

21. On the conflict in Las Palmas see Crisanto Domínguez, *Rebelión en la selva* (Buenos Aires, 1948); *La Vanguardia*, August 12, 14, 17, 19, 24, 26, 30, 1920; Ramón Tissera, "Revolución social en la selva," *Todo Es Historia* (April 1968): 64–75. Company directors and owners are named in W. H. Morton Cameron, ed., *Enciclopedia comercial (Encyclopedia Commercial): Unico órgano oficial, anual o bienal, de la British and Latin American Chamber of Commerce. Argentina, Brasil, Chile, Perú, Uruguay, Suplemento Británico* (London, 1922), 305. *La Protesta*, April 29, 1922, and *La Organización Obrera*, December 4, 1920, discussed the ties between the Liga and the Asociación del Trabajo.

22. The Las Palmas brigade was represented at all the congresses of the 1920s. On the union movement see José García Pulido, *El Gran Chaco y su imperio Las Palmas* (Buenos Aires, 1951), 134–44.

23. On the events in Villaguay see *La Vanguardia*, February 15–21, 24–28, 1919; República Argentina, Congreso Nacional, *Diario de sesiones de la Cámara de Diputados* 6 (February 18, 23, 1921, in 1920 series): 311–16, 355–92.

24. *La Nación*, February 17, 1921; *La Fronda*, February 27, 1921.

25. *La Nación*, February 19, 1921. Members of brigade juntas were mentioned in the press and in Liga Patriótica Argentina, *Primero de Mayo Argentino: Conmemoración del pronunciamiento de Urquiza en Entre Ríos* (Buenos Aires, 1921).

26. The number of brigades was taken from Liga congresses and press reports. Carlés claimed, however, that there were over two hundred. See Liga Patriótica Argentina, *El culto de la Patagonia: Sucesos de Santa Cruz* (Buenos Aires, 1922), 9.

27. Osvaldo Bayer, *Los vengadores de la Patagonia trágica*, 4 vols. (Buenos Aires, 1972–1984); Susana Fiorito, "Un drama olvidado: Las huelgas patagónicas de 1920–1921," *Polémica* 54 (1971): 92–96; Liga, *El culto*.

28. Bayer, *Los vengadores* 1:38, 55–56; José María Borrero, *La Patagonia trágica*, 2d ed. (Buenos Aires, 1957), 63–65, 84; Carlés in Liga, *El culto*, 27.

29. Liga publications and the press mentioned nineteen schools; Liga Patriótica Argentina, *La verdad de la Liga Patriótica Argentina* (Buenos Aires, 1950), 11, gave the figure of fifty schools.

30. Carlés in Comisión de Señoritas de la Liga Patriótica Argentina, *Sus escuelas de obreras en las fábricas* (Buenos Aires, 1922), 1. Also see Comisión, *Sus escuelas* (in its entirety); Comisión Central de Señoritas, *Memoria de diez escuelas obreras, 1924-mayo-1925* (Buenos Aires, 1925); idem, *Memoria, 1927-mayo-1928* (Buenos Aires, 1928); and Liga Patriótica Argentina, *Brevario de historia nacional* (Buenos Aires, 1922). I discuss women's activities at greater length in "The Visible and Invisible Liga Patriótica Argentina, 1919–1928: Gender Roles and the Right Wing," *Hispanic American Historical Review* 64, no. 2 (May 1984): 233–58.

31. Liga, *Tercera Exposición*, 1–5; Liga Patriótica Argentina, *Discursos pronunciados en el acto inaugural y veredicto del Jurado de la Cuarta Exposición Nacional de Tejidos y Bordados, 4–20 agosto 1923* (Buenos Aires, 1923), 2.

32. Zuberbühler in Liga Patriótica Argentina, *El abaratamiento de la vida. Influencia del costo de producción industrial. Reajuste de salarios* (Buenos Aires, 1921), 1, 4. Also see, for example, Liga Patriótica Argentina, *Tercer Congreso de Trabajadores de la Liga Patriótica Argentina* (Buenos Aires, 1922), 109–13, 116; Liga Patriótica Argentina, *Congreso General de Territorios Nacionales* (Buenos Aires, 1927), 95, 115; Liga Patriótica Argentina, *Cuarto Congreso Nacionalista de la Liga Patriótica Argentina* (Buenos Aires, 1923), 131, 330–34.

33. Liga, *Primer Congreso*, 173–74; Liga, *Cuarto Congreso*, 268–71.

34. Carlés in Liga Patriótica Argentina, *Organización de la soberanía o escuela de bienestar* (Buenos Aires, 1928), 11.

35. Carlés in Liga, *Primer Congreso*, 37–39; Liga, *Tercera Exposición*, 6; Liga, *Primero de Mayo*, 37; Liga Patriótica Argentina, *Declaración de principios, organización y propósitos de los Soviets Argentinos: Con introducción y notas marginales del sentido común por la Liga Patriótica Argentina* (Buenos Aires, 1920), 4–5, 9, 12; Liga Patriótica Argentina, *Humanitarismo práctico: La Liga Patriótica Argentina en Gualeguaychú* (Buenos Aires, 1921), 18.

36. Carlés in Liga Patriótica Argentina, *Quinto Congreso Nacionalista de Trabajadores, organizado por la Liga Patriótica Argentina* (Buenos Aires, 1924), 39–40.

37. Carlés in Liga, *Tercera Exposición*, 7. Also see Carlés to Ambassador Frederic J. Stimson, December 21, 1920, Dispatch no. 1422, 835.43L62. Rouquié, in *Poder militar*, 1:146 n. 65, found another example of a Liguista expressing sympathy for Italian Fascism.

38. May 2, 1921, Dispatch no. 1547, 835.00/226; *La Fronda*, April 16, June 30, 1920; *La Prensa*, April 16, 29, 1920. On antileftist militias abroad see Arno J. Mayer, "Postwar Nationalisms, 1918-1919," *Past and Present* (July 1966): 114–18; James M. Diehl, *Paramilitary Politics in Weimar Germany* (Bloomington, IN, 1977); David Large, "The Politics of Law and Order: Counterrevolutionary Self-Defense Organizations in Central Europe, 1918-1923" (Ph.D. diss., University of California—Berkeley, 1974).

39. This correspondence is cited in Liga Patriótica Argentina, *Definição de Liga Patriótica Argentina (Guía do bom senso social)* (Buenos Aires, 1922), in Liga Patriótica Argentina, *Historia documental de la Liga Patriótica Argentina* (Buenos Aires, 1922). This collection of pamphlets also includes copies of this publication in English, Spanish, and German.

40. December 21, 1920, February 16, 1921, March 3, 1921, Dispatch no. 1422, 835.43L62-/1. On ties with the American Legion see *La Prensa*, March 17, 1920; on Palmer see Robert K. Murray, *Red Scare: A Study in National Hysteria, 1919–1920*, 2d ed. (New York, 1964).

41. Names of such groups were mentioned in the press between 1919 and 1921. Also see *La Fronda*, July 9, 1920; *La Nación*, August 7, 1920; and *El Mercurio* (Santiago), August 26, 1920.

42. Liga, *Solemne homenaje*; *El Mercurio*, January 30, June 11, 1919, August 26, October 24, 1920, July 27–28, 1922.

43. *El Mercurio*, July 27, 1922. On such "internationals" in Europe see Large, "The Politics of Law and Order," 1–45. Also see Michael Arthur Ledeen, *Universal Fascism: The Theory and Practice of the Fascist International, 1928–1936* (New York, 1971).

44. Liga Patriótica Argentina, *Catecismo de la doctrina patria* (Buenos Aires, 1921), 8; Liga, *Primer Congreso*, 38–39.

45. Liga, *Primer Congreso*, 41; Liga Patriótica Argentina, *Discurso pronunciado por el presidente de la Liga Patriótica Argentina, Dr. Manuel Carlés en la reunión celebrada por la honorable Junta de Gobierno en honor de los delegados de la Asociación de Empleados de Comercio de Rio de Janeiro* (Buenos Aires, 1924); *El Pueblo*, February 19, 1921; Liga Patriótica Argentina, *Misión y doctrina de la Liga Patriótica Argentina* (Buenos Aires, 1956), 1; Liga Patriótica Argentina, *Sexto Congreso Nacionalista de Trabajadores organizado por la Liga Patrióica Argentina* (Buenos Aires, 1925), 39; *La Nueva República* (hereafter LNR) 29 (August 25, 1928): 2.

46. Liga, *Cuarto Congreso*, 32.

47. Cited in Julio Irazusta, *Genio y figura de Leopoldo Lugones* (Buenos Aires, 1968), 98–101, 105–6. Also see Gladys S. Onega, *La inmigración en la literatura argentina* (Buenos Aires, 1969), 216–19.

48. Liga Patriótica Argentina, *Noveno Congreso Nacionalista organizado por la Liga Patriótica Argentina* (Buenos Aires, 1928), 555; July 31, 1929, Dispatch no. 617, 835.00/436; Liga Patriótica Argentina, *Restauración de la moral argentina* (Buenos Aires, 1930), 6. Also see "A," August 2, 1928, Report no. 184, and October 19, 1928, Report no. 249, C-10-K; August 7, 1929, Report no. 209, C-10-L; U.S. Chief of Naval Operations, Intelligence Division, Naval Attaché Reports, 1886–1939, Record Group 38, National Archives, Washington, DC.

49. Rouquié, *Poder militar*, 1:171–210. On the preparations for the revolution of 1930 see Robert A. Potash, *The Army and Politics in Argentina, 1928–1945: Yrigoyen*

to Perón (Stanford, 1969), 29–54; Marvin Goldwert, *Democracy, Militarism, and Nationalism in Argentina, 1930–1966: An Interpretation* (Austin, 1972), 12–29; Roberto Etchepareborda, "Aspectos políticos de la crisis de 1930," *Revista de Historia* 3 (1958): 7–40; José María Sarobe, *Memorias sobre la revolución del 6 de septiembre de 1930* (Buenos Aires, 1957); and Juan Perón, *Tres revoluciones militares* (Buenos Aires, 1963), 13–82. On the Nacionalistas and the revolution see Marysa Navarro Gerassi, *Los nacionalistas*, trans. Alberto Ciria (Buenos Aires, 1968), 55–67; Enrique Zuleta Alvarez, *El nacionalismo argentino*, 2 vols. (Buenos Aires, 1975), 1: 237–41; and Ronald H. Dolkart, "The Right in the Década Infame, 1930–1943," in this volume.

50. Carlos Ibarguren, *La historia que he vivido*, 2d ed. (Buenos Aires, 1969), 323–25; Juan E. Carulla, *Al filo del medio siglo* (Buenos Aires, 1951), 97–98, 138, 145–49, 158–60; Carlos Ibarguren, Jr., *Roberto de Laferrère: Periodismo-política-historia* (Buenos Aires, 1970), 25–26; Rodolfo Irazusta, "La política," *LNR*, no. 57 (August 9, 1930): 1.

51. Comité Ejecutivo de la Gran Colecta Nacional, *La paz social* (Buenos Aires, 1919); Miguel de Andrea, *La perturbación social contemporánea* (Buenos Aires, 1944), 81, 128–29.

52. See the following articles in *Universitas* 9, no. 38 (July–September 1975): Mario Amadeo, "El grupo 'Baluarte' y los Cursos de Cultura Católica," 23–26; Alberto Ezpezel Berro, "Un fragmento," 46–48; and Bernadino Montejano, Jr., "Un hogar espiritual," 51–52. The quotation comes from Ezpezel Berro, 46.

53. Julio Irazusta to Enrique Pérez Mariluz, December 3, 1925, in Julio Irazusta Papers, Notebook 1, Las Casuarinas, Entre Ríos, Argentina.

54. Ibid.; Julio Irazusta, Diary, August 15, 1925, Irazusta Papers, Notebook 2. On Maurras see J. S. McClelland, ed., *The French Right: From De Maistre to Maurras*, trans. John Frears (London, 1970), 213–304; Enrique Zuleta Alvarez, *Introducción a Maurras* (Buenos Aires, 1965); Ernst Nolte, *Three Faces of Fascism: Action Française, Italian Fascism, National Socialism*, trans. Leila Vennewitz (New York, 1964), 139–89; and this essay.

55. Ibarguren, *La historia*, 369; Julio Irazusta, "Los libros," *LNR*, no. 1 (December 1, 1927): 3.

56. Manuel Gálvez, "Interpretación de las dictaduras," *Criterio* 32 (October 11, 1928): 43–44. Also see " 'Action Française' y el fascismo ante la Santa Sede," *Criterio* 58 (April 11, 1929): 457–59. Julio Irazusta, in *Memorias: Historia de un historiador a la fuerza* (Buenos Aires, 1975), 153–54, was not very impressed with Mussolini.

57. *LNR* 7 (March 1, 1928): 1.

58. Julio Irazusta, interview, July 1977, Las Casuarinas, Entre Ríos.

59. Irazusta, *Lugones*, 111.

60. Ernesto Palacio, "El nacionalismo," *LNR* 24 (July 21, 1928): 1.

61. Carulla, *Al filo*, 228–31; Ibarguren, *Laferrére*, 28–29.

62. Julio Irazusta, "Historia de La Nueva República," ms., n.d., in Irazusta Papers, Notebook 2; Carulla, *Al filo*, 241–42; Irazusta, *Memorias*, 176–78, 181; quotation from *LNR*, no. 1 (December 1, 1927): 1. On *LNR* and early Nacionalista doctrine also see Cristián Buchrucker, *Nacionalismo y peronismo: La Argentina en la crisis ideológica mundial, 1927–1955* (Buenos Aires, 1987), 45–77.

63. Palacio, "La doctrina de la Nueva Republica," *LNR*, no. 43 (December 1, 1928): 4; Rodolfo Irazusta, "La política," *LNR*, no. 12 (April 28, 1928): 1.

64. Rodolfo Irazusta, "La política," *LNR*, no. 29 (August 25, 1928): 1.

65. Ibid. Ibarguren, *La historia*, 68–69; Ibarguren, *Laferrère*, 21–22; Irazusta, "La política" 12: 1.

66. Mario Garay, "Ecos," *LNR* 51 (June 28, 1930): 2; Ibarguren, *La historia,* 285–86, 326; Ibarguren, *Laferrère,* 23; E. J. M. (h.), "En Babia," *LNR* 60 (August 30, 1930): 2.

67. Irazusta, "La política" 12: 1; Abel Galíndez, "Nuestros conservadores," *LNR* 38 (October 27, 1928): 1; *LNR* 49 (June 14, 1930): 4; Irazusta, "Los libros," 2; Ibarguren, *Laferrère,* 12–13; Ibarguren, *Orígenes,* 17.

68. On the Legión de Mayo, Liga Republicana, and the revolution of 1930 see Carlos Ibarguren (h.), *Respuestas a un cuestionario acerca del nacionalismo, 1930–1945* (Buenos Aires, 1971), 5–11; *La Fronda,* July 11, 1929; *LNR* 52–60 (July–August 1930); Julio Quesada, *Orígenes de la revolución del 6 de septiembre de 1930 (Rosas e Yrigoyen)* (Buenos Aires, 1930), 74–77, 80; and V. Gutiérrez de Miguel, *La revolución argentina: Relato de un testigo presencial* (Madrid, 1930), 112, 173. On the Liga's role see Liga Patriótica Argentina, *La Liga Patriótica y la revolución del 6 de septiembre de 1930* (Buenos Aires, 1930). The Legión de Mayo turned against electoralism after September 1930. The Liga Republicana and *LNR* did not always agree. See Zuleta Alvarez, *Nacionalismo argentino,* 1:238.

69. This biographical information comes from a study of 154 members of the Legión de Mayo, 134 members of the Liga Republicana, 18 *LNR* contributors, and 32 members of two or more of these groups, for a total of 338. The biographical sources are the same as those for the Liga (see note 20). Differences between the groups were insignificant unless noted. "Close relationships" are defined as those of siblings, first and second cousins, fathers and sons, grandfathers and grandsons, uncles and nephews, and brothers-in-law. On the restoration of the regime see Manuel Gálvez, *Hombres en soledad* (Buenos Aires, 1935).

70. See, for example, Arturo Jauretche, interview, April 1, 1971, Oral History Project, Instituto Torcuato Di Tella, Buenos Aires.

71. On Carlés's participation in the coup and his falling-out with Uriburu, as well as the Nacionalistas' reaction to the Uriburu regime, see Deutsch, *Counterrevolution in Argentina,* 203–4, 206–8, 214–15, 223–34.

72. *Crisol,* September 1, 1932. Also see the statement of Guillermo Patricio Kelly, former member of the Alianza Libertadora Nacionalista, a group of the 1940s and 1950s, on how the Liga's murders of workers represented the beginnings of Nacionalismo, in *Mayoría,* April 21, 1958.

The Right in the Década Infame, 1930–1943

Ronald H. Dolkart

The revolution of September 6, 1930, brought to power a right that was united in proclaiming victory for its vision of Argentina's future. Both the old right conservatives and the new right Nacionalistas joined together to depose the hated Radicals and to install a military regime. Rightists saw this break with the constitutional succession as an opportunity for a "revolution"—or counterrevolution—that would legitimize them as the only viable political force in Argentina. In the ensuing thirteen years known as the Década Infame, a high point of right-wing thought and influence, major tensions between the two persuasions of the right developed and persisted well beyond the next period of Argentine history, starting in 1943.

The old right was reconstituted as the dominant "conservative" alliance, although it called itself the Partido Demócrata Nacional (PDN). The conditions of the worldwide depression reinforced the authority of the PDN's main supporters, the great landowning families, major exporters, big bankers, and their many retainers, because these elites appeared to provide the only opportunity for Argentina to improve its economic position by selling its beef and wheat abroad. Conservatives remained especially powerful in the provinces, where *estancieros* (landowners) controlled votes. The upper class favored the constitutional and institutional structure that it had created as the "liberal" oligarchy of the nineteenth century, using the mechanisms of fraudulent elections and corrupt payoffs to maintain control behind a facade of representative government. Conservatives furnished most of the federal and provincial officials of the 1930s and set policies that steered a cautious course in domestic and international matters.

The new right emerged as the militant Nacionalistas, energized by the defeat of Radicalism and the triumph of the army. The times seemed made for their cause: the successes of European fascism coincided with the Nacionalistas' own struggle against Argentina's "democratic" tradition. At the head of the Nacionalistas were often capable leaders, individuals who spoke and wrote prolifically, members of the old elite and the more affluent middle class. These spokespersons attracted a growing following to large paramilitary bands through appeals to patriotism and to hopes for a new corporativist direction for the nation. The rank and file could read a variety of newspapers and magazines, often filled with vituperation against their opponents. Out of these expanding organizations, although they represented only a minority of the politically active in Argentina, came an increased Nacionalista influence in institutions such as the army, university, church, and business. They had their greatest impact in Buenos Aires and other urban areas, despite attempts to proselytize throughout the republic. The Nacionalistas' weakness remained a tendency to divide into myriad personalist groups, the multitude of "Ligas" and "Legiones," a dozen major ones and many minor ones, and this fragmentation made them easy prey for manipulation by the conservatives.

The right in the period from 1930 to 1943 thus was made up of two dispensations, old and new, with certain principles and goals in common and periods of cooperation but equally important differences in programs and activities. Consequently, the persistent force in shaping the actions of the right was the tension between conservatives and Nacionalistas. Conflict developed as a result of the political events of the Década Infame and the disputes over specific issues. The right in this period, therefore, is discussed in three major sections that focus on national politics and doctrinal differences.

The first part deals with the revolution of 1930 and its aftermath. At this time, the bonds linking the conservatives and Nacionalistas remained strong and optimism about their ability to determine the destiny of Argentina pervaded their relationship. Yet circumstances soon created a rift when Radicalism revived. To counter the Radical threat, the conservatives insisted on a return to rigged elections rather than make the extreme institutional changes the Nacionalistas wanted. The second part examines the controversies that arose through the middle years of the depression decade. There were a wide range of interrelated issues; most involved the long-standing concerns of the right that had developed in the early part of the century out of the fear of bolshevism but were given new urgency by the conditions of the 1930s. As the splits became more sharply defined between the Nacionalistas and conservatives, and thus threatened the right's control of the country, prominent leaders tried to construct bridges to reconnect them once again. Finally, the third section explores the crisis for the right that began in the early 1940s when what unity remained started to disintegrate, torn apart by government instability and by the circumstances of the Second World War. The rupture was completed as the conservatives joined in attacking Nacionalistas for their fascist sympathies and consequent subservience to foreign ideologies and the Nacionalistas denounced conservatives as corrupt exploiters serving British interests. The Década Infame ended with a disunited right whose disarray opened the way for a new political alignment after the army took over in 1943.

The Revolution of 1930

The alliance between the old right conservatives and the new right Nacionalistas was strongest in opposition to Hipólito Yrigoyen, the leader of the Unión Cívica Radical (UCR), after his reelection in 1928. Rightist organizations fomented a climate of extreme instability and distrust. With the blessing of the right, the army undertook the task of overthrowing the Yrigoyen government. The Radical leader had displayed attitudes at odds with the military mentality of rigidity and hierarchy; he interfered with internal military decisions and promotion schedules. And so the rightist campaign against Yrigoyen had a strong impact on active and retired officers, notably on General José F. Uriburu, who had given up regular duty in order to denounce the government. Uriburu's activities quickly turned into a plot to take over power. In this goal he was joined by another retired general, Agustín P. Justo. But the two officers had different views on what to achieve. Uriburu desired a long-term military rule that would bring about a fundamental restructuring of the political system; Justo foresaw only a brief transition government and a return to civilian control as it had operated under the constitution of 1853, thus preserving the army's reputation as a protector of the fundamental charter.[1]

By early summer 1930 the conspiracy was under way; military officers and civilian politicians joined together, some favoring the Uriburu position, others that of Justo. In the end, all agreed that Uriburu would be the provisional president only, to be replaced when new elections were held under either the old constitution or a new system of government. Thus, on September 6, 1930, using relatively little violence, a small force deposed Yrigoyen and took him prisoner. The military quickly rationalized the entire operation as a popular uprising supported by the vast majority.[2] The backing and participation of the right was downplayed. But clearly Uriburu and many of his supporters in the army subscribed to its political views.

The right was ecstatic at the fall of Yrigoyen. This achievement of its goal, however, immediately created tension among the two major rightist views, conservative and Nacionalista. Although most members of his cabinet represented old-line conservative politicians, General Uriburu communicated his desire to make significant political changes in the system, notably to end use of the secret ballot (which had opened the way for Radical victories when it was put in force some years earlier) and to initiate indirect, authoritarian, corporativist rule.[3] He was opposed by his rival Justo, representing the opinion of powerful leaders who insisted on retaining the electoral system they were certain could be manipulated. And so Uriburu opted for a tactic that would permit a series of provincial elections in those areas where overwhelming support for his government seemed assured. With this backing he believed that he might then change the constitution.[4] No province seemed more suitable than Buenos Aires, where major sentiment for the revolution made the Uriburu forces confident of electoral victory. A bitter lesson was learned in Buenos Aires province on April 5, 1931, when the Radicals won a stunning upset over the local Conservative party. Although the elections were annulled, the provisional government was obviously in serious trouble.

As Uriburu saw his power slipping away, he turned initially to the Nacionalistas, who formed the Legión Cívica Argentina (LCA), dedicated specifically to supporting the principles of the September Revolution. The general issued a decree on May 20, 1931, giving the LCA official status and a formal association with Argentina's armed forces. Subsequently, the LCA was organized into paramilitary units and trained regularly with the army. It operated out of a government-owned building, and its so-called Consejo Superior included members of the various military services. The LCA became a large and visible organization engaged in intimidating those who might try to pressure Uriburu toward a more moderate policy. An early estimate put membership at around fifteen thousand,[5] but opponents charged that many enrollees were impressed from the ranks of government employees.[6] On the national holiday, May 25, 1931,

> thirty thousand members of this organization [the LCR] passed in review before the President of the Nation. They wore civilian clothes and only carried company flags, but they were formed in platoon formation, marched well, and the majority showed evidence of having completed their military service. They were a very inspiring sight and, as the head of each platoon arrived within six paces of the President, he would give "eyes right" and then call loudly "Legioneros," the whole platoon giving the Fascisti salute at the same time and replying "Viva la Patria."[7]

The LCA continued to grow until reports showed fifty thousand had signed up in Buenos Aires alone, with uncounted additional members as it spread throughout the rest of Argentina.[8] Active recruiting required that each member attempt to find ten others. This method of organization made the LCA a model for many of the later Nacionalista organizations, and it remained important during most of the decade of the 1930s. Yet not even its threat to put one hundred thousand legionnaires in the street in order to support Uriburu as a candidate to succeed himself could save the provisional president. General Justo demanded his retirement as the price for not splitting the military, and Uriburu had to agree.

The revolution of September 6, 1930, and its leader General José F. Uriburu became the central images in the mythologies that both factions of the right created. In the conservatives' view, the revolution was Argentina's opportunity to reject "the empire of immorality as the norm, of bribery as an administrative system, of fraud and corruption in all acts of political life."[9] The old right, then, saw in the revolution a symbol of a return to the golden age of national harmony before the rise of the Radicals. September 6 would serve to remind Argentines that preserving the past was their only hope.

In the Nacionalistas' interpretation, the revolution was Argentina's call to forge ahead because "it gives the opportunity to reconstruct our country morally, politically and economically . . . [for] the high enterprise of national salvation."[10] The Nacionalistas insisted that this event acted as a beginning for radical change, as the leap forward toward an as-yet-undefined new Argentine state. Most of all, they attempted to create and preserve a "Myth of September." The revolution marked the Nacionalistas' start as a political—and, they believed, moral—force in Argentina. To guard its ideals was their sacred trust. The Nacionalistas insistently made it a benchmark for discussion of issues they found important. For them the annual celebration of September 6 reflected their own impact on the nation. On the first anniversary there was "popular delirium" as Uriburu spoke and the LCA marched by.[11] But then in April of the following year, after he had left office, the general died, so 1932 became a memorial. By the third year's celebration, Nacionalistas were complaining that the government was shifting emphasis from an exaltation of political principles to a sentimental homage to the few people killed in the uprising. And in 1939 the loud complaint surfaced that "the ninth anniversary of the September Revolution has passed without any action on the part of public powers to remember it on the national level."[12] Although the conservative right tried quietly to bury this symbol of Nacionalista fervor, it would rise once again with another military revolution in 1943.

The revolution of 1930, which had inspired right-wing unity and raised high the hopes of the Nacionalistas, gradually turned into a conservative-dominated return to fraudulent elections. The process began in September 1931 when General Uriburu found himself forced by his rival, General Justo, to call presidential elections. All of the right feared continued voter allegiance to the UCR. When the Uriburu government refused to sanction a UCR candidacy by charging a plot against the government, the Radicals opted to use their favorite tactic of denouncing the election and calling upon supporters to cast blank ballots. The opposition then fell to the Alianza Civil. A combination of moderate, left-of-center parties, the Alianza put forth its two great leaders, Lisandro de la Torre for president and Nicolás Repetto for vice president.

Even with the ban on the UCR and the lack of widespread popularity for the Alianza, the conservatives and Nacionalistas still needed a political platform upon which to run. Justo had forced Uriburu to deny any ambition to continue as president, and Justo then hoped that the mantle of the revolution would fall upon him. But he lacked Uriburu's charisma and had to find wider political support. Thus to underwrite Justo's candidacy the Concordancia, an alliance of strange bedfellows, came together. Its nucleus was the PDN, itself a conglomerate of provincial groups under the control of regional oligarchies and political bosses, the most important of which was the Partido Conservador of Buenos Aires province. The PDN eschewed any ideological program, only declaring itself against Radicalism and for the revolution of 1930, thereby seeking to embrace conservatives and Nacionalistas alike. The Concordancia included two other factions: the Socialistas Independientes, who were anything but socialist (they were more nineteenth-century liberal), and the Anti-

Personalistas, a breakaway group of the UCR, opposed to Yrigoyen's dominance of the party.[13]

The Concordancia proclaimed the ticket of Agustín P. Justo, whose official connection was with the Anti-Personalistas, for president, and Julio A. Roca, Jr., whose father had been the oligarchy's favorite head of state under the regime, for vice president. The election indeed brought back the former tactics of fraud and corruption at the ballot box, and so the Concordancia won easily with some 600,000 votes to only 488,000 for the Alianza. Justo, an ambitious and clever politician, was determined to give Argentina a pragmatic, some would say an opportunistic, emphasis on administrative efficiency. At his inauguration he embraced principles of the revolution of 1930, as he turned to General Uriburu and proclaimed: "I recognize myself as the repository of the hopes of our people and charged by them to continue directing the work which, hard and bitter, has been realized by the provisional government."[14] Thus, in hopes of pleasing the forces on the right, Justo fostered the idea that his policies were the direct outgrowth of the Uriburu ideology of corporativism and authoritarianism. At the same time, he realized that Argentina was passing through a period of economic and social transition toward a more urban industrial nation, and he had no intention of precipitating a crisis by instituting sweeping political changes. The government faced far too many pressing economic problems growing out of the world depression. The new president's technique was to gain support from as wide a spectrum of public opinion as possible by telling various groups what they wanted to hear as he forged ahead with programs of central government planning, a key process in rebuilding financial stability. The conservatives generally remained loyal; the Nacionalistas gradually became alienated.

Historical treatments of the Justo period often have concentrated on the president's political skill in governing Argentina without opposition while he worked on economic problems. But beneath this seemingly benign surface the thirties remained a period of constant political turmoil, much of it manifested in street violence. The newspapers were filled with reports of shootings, beatings, and clashes directly related to partisan issues. The source for much of this disorder came from rightist provocations and Radical and leftist responses. The right-wing newspapers spent much ink lamenting that "Yrigoyenism . . . conferred citizenship on noxious social agitators, white slavers and members of nationalities that always will be undesirable among us"[15] and denouncing the "innate cowardice of socialism . . . sons of an unmanly doctrine so that they are emasculated and ignoble."[16] No wonder the Radicals often attacked the publication *La Fronda* as they did in the early hours of February 28, 1932, when a number of shots were fired at its offices.

More serious were the events of mid-1932, when Marcelo T. de Alvear had returned to Buenos Aires to promote his Radical candidacy. Articles denounced the threats, attacks, clubbings, and brawling.[17] Such acts were recognized as the preconceived plans of right-wing groups that the authorities seemed unwilling to control. A march by the LCA in 1933 provoked a counterdemonstration of opponents shouting "Death to the Nacionalistas" in front of the *La Fronda* office; shots were fired, and two people were killed.[18] Undoubtedly, the most infamous crime of the decade was the assassination in 1934 of the senator-elect, Enzo Bordabehere, in the Senate chamber during a fiery debate about the government's beef regulation policy. Lisandro de la Torre, his fellow senator from Santa Fe, was vigorously denouncing Minister of Agriculture Luis F. Dahau and Minister of Treasury Federico Pinedo; personal insults were exchanged, shots rang out, and Bordabehere fell, mortally wounded. The perpetrator, Ramón Valdez Cora, claimed that he had only been trying to protect the government ministers from violence, but he was known as a fanatical member of the PDN and, rumor had it, a deeply committed Nacionalista as well.[19]

A center of conflict was the provincial capital of Córdoba, where the Nacionalistas were particularly strong and often were opposed by local leftist university students. Constant turmoil throughout 1933 peaked when it was reported that a provincial Socialist deputy had insulted members of the LCA, "even against their mothers."[20] In the ensuing fight dozens of shots were fired, and a local deputy was killed and ten persons wounded. Such violence in Córdoba continued throughout the decade. In 1936 the university was closed down after groups of students clashed, causing the police to intervene when one of the participants was gravely wounded; the rightist press blamed the persecution of right-wing students on Amadeo Sabbatini, governor of the province, one of the first Radicals to stand and win election after 1930.[21] And two years later three students were killed in a disputed election in the law school, an election that the right claimed to have won.

Furthermore, the decade was one of rampant rumors and scandals. The press ridiculed the climate of rumor mongering: "The president of the republic has been kidnapped! . . . Armed groups are advancing down the Avenida de Mayo! . . . Two generals have committed suicide in the passageway of Government House . . . et cetera."[22] Argentina seemed constantly beset by such tales of political violence, many involving supposed rightist plots. A favorite report found the right in league with foreign governments to take over or set up espionage centers in such remote areas as Patagonia.

The violence of the 1930s contributed to an ever-expanding number of right-wing organizations. These ranged across a spectrum from moderate conservative to openly fascist. There were a variety of types: the broad-based Milicia Cívica Nacionalista, the age-linked Alianza de la Juventud Nacionalista (AJN), the gender-defined Asociación de Damas Argentinas, the institutionally organized Unión Nacionalista Universitaria, the professional Corporación Nacionalista de Maestros, the workers' Federación Obrera Nacionalista Argentina. Some gained a wider membership and audience, such as Acción Nacionalista Argentina (ANA), estimated around fifteen thousand at its height in 1934. This group published a popular manifesto directed against the electoral system and liberal individualism and in favor of corporativist representation and authoritarian government.[23] The majority of these organizations remained small and ineffectual. Finally, total membership of Nacionalistas cannot be estimated accurately. Most of the groups refused to discuss numbers: even if such statistics were available, the sum of all groups would not provide a total because most adherents went from one Nacionalista association to another and the growth of one usually meant loss of membership for another.

Division meant weakness and thus a determined effort was made to promote unity. The initial attempt came from Acción Nacionalista when it issued its "Afirmación de Una Nueva Argentina," referred to as ADUNA. The major goal remained that of the September Revolution's corporativist representation "by legislators who embody the fundamental interest of each trade union or profession,"[24] but this emphasis alienated the moderate conservatives. A more serious effort grew out of the establishment of the Frente Nacional (National Front). On May 1, 1936, a combination of socialists and Radicals announced the formation of the Popular Front, in clear imitation of similar centrist-left alliances in Europe. Only in such a manner, it was argued, could the Concordancia be effectively challenged in presidential elections the following year. Three days later, rightist reaction produced the Frente Nacional, which included the PDN and the other conservative parties, and looked for the adherence of the Nacionalistas. But these groups were deeply suspicious of what they saw as an attempt once again to get their support for a perpetuation of the old landowning interests, and they denounced the Frente.[25] It played an active role in the 1937 presidential elections but then faded away.

A clear enunciation of aims and objectives of the right was necessary to increase its appeal. The proclamation of such principles came from the Nacionalistas during the Década Infame, and the principles have remained remarkably consistent since that time, but their diffusion was often limited and the profusion of such statements from various groups made them seem confusing and contradictory. One significant source was Enzo Valenti Ferro's *Que quieren los Nacionalistas?* He was a member of the Legion Cívica Argentina, and he used his manifesto in an attempt to convince all rightist factions to agree on these beliefs. The most interesting proposals included the establishment of a homestead law that would provide every Argentine family with ownership of an urban or rural property, as a means of making each citizen a "small capitalist" and of "implanting social justice which benefits Nacionalismo"; the protection of workers through a national workers' relief program, including medical care and injury compensation; and the regulation of capital and labor through a department of labor that would bring together unions and industry in order to negotiate contracts. Clearly, the Nacionalistas envisioned a system that did more than repress the working class. Valenti Ferro hoped that this program would reach out to a majority of Argentines, but in the end he put his faith in *El Jefe*: "There will arrive the man who will attract in his person all the Nacionalista energy."[26]

Despite Valenti Ferro's optimism, the lack of a charismatic and popular leader prevented the right wing from coalescing into a united, powerful organization. The early hope that General Uriburu would be such a figure vanished. Although army officers largely supported the right, none of them ever rose to a position of enthusiastic rightist acclaim. The many civilian politicians clamoring for this role came and went; the strongest claimant to the mantle of a rightist leader was the governor of the province of Buenos Aires, Manuel Fresco, but he, like many others, was caught in the crossfire between conservatives and Nacionalistas. This tension left leadership principally in the hands of intellectuals and journalists who wrote a great deal and sometimes founded their own organizations. These men were often young, in their thirties and forties, well educated in the liberal professions, members of the upper and middle class, and deeply disillusioned by the perceived decline of Argentina and the failures of Radicalism.[27]

Perhaps the most revered intellectual figure remained Leopoldo Lugones, one of Argentina's and Latin America's greatest poets of the early twentieth century. His literary odyssey was accompanied by a political one, from socialist to Nacionalista. The literature of Nacionalismo credited Lugones with much of the inspiration for the movement. And he remained active until his death in 1938, attempting to form a Guardia Argentina to promote his ideas, but he was too aged to become an effective leader.[28]

There was never a lack, however, of journals and newspapers to discuss the issues of concern to the right. Most of them were ephemeral and irregular. A few became more prominent and visible. Established early in the century (1919), *La Fronda* endured longer than any other right-wing daily and, thus, stands as the newspaper of record for information about the right in the Década Infame. It was founded as the voice of opposition to Yrigoyen and became a center for the conspiracy leading to the revolution of 1930. *La Fronda* attracted many young journalists and possessed a lively style, but its circulation probably never exceeded fifteen hundred.[29] *Bandera Argentina* was edited by Juan E. Carulla, a founder of the LCA, and it followed a middle-of-the-road line within the rightist camp. This position meant the worship of the figure of General Uriburu with the view that "the Revolution of September constituted the apex of the desire of a patriotic and inspired group."[30] Carulla refused to bow to the pressure of more strident voices. That lot fell to *Crisol*, directed by Enrique P. Osés, who was a virulent opponent of the oligarchy and therefore of the Justo government. He called himself not only a Nacionalista but also a national-socialist, and he was infamous for his attacks on the regime and the newspapers that supported it.

The major subject in most of these newspapers remained the public activities of the right, their marches and *actos* (functions). Buenos Aires or a provincial capital would be filled with posters announcing events at some auditorium or city square to commemorate an anniversary or theme. The rightist press invariably would announce that the meeting had "reached magnificent proportions." There might be, as in La Plata, the capital of the province of Buenos Aires, the parade of a Nacionalista group, in this case Avancismo: "A thousand uniformed young men, with the blue and white flag waving in the breeze, demonstrated to the astonished crowd that patriotic feeling has not disappeared among the new generations."[31] In metropolitan Buenos Aires a favorite gathering place was the large Coliseo Theater, where, for example, in 1936 on the anniversary of the death of General José de San Martín, hero of Argentine independence, speakers invited by the Comité de la Juventud Argentina used the occasion to denounce communism before an overflow crowd.[32]

The Justo Years

The political events following the September Revolution had generally favored cooperation between old right conservatives and new right Nacionalistas. But the election of Justo and the Concordancia brought out the tension between the two factions. The old-line conservatives had formed the Concordancia to support Justo, and they hoped that the end of "Yrigoyenismo" meant a return to their former domination of Argentine politics by fraudulent means in order to administer the nation in their own interests. Under Justo they were able to control most of the ministerial posts and thus exercise the greatest influence on him. These conservatives viewed the Nacionalistas with deep suspicion as too extreme and a threat to the long-standing cordial international relationship Argentina maintained with Western European democracies— even if they sympathized with many of the principles espoused by Nacionalismo.

The Nacionalistas were much more precise in their growing denunciation of the conservatives. Their major criticism condemned conservatives for being opposed to "nationalism," defined as the interests of Argentina, and dedicated to the well-being of Argentina's European customers, from whom these landowners derived their wealth. This antipathy can be demonstrated in terms of those issues that divided the old from the new right as the 1930s progressed: British relations, historical interpretation, communist influence, Spanish civil war, European fascism, Jewish Argentines, Catholic church, social concerns. The dynamics of the right shifted as both factions reacted to these questions from varying perspectives.

The Roca-Runciman Pact of 1933 between Argentina and Great Britain provided evidence for the Nacionalista claim that conservatives were nothing more than *vendepatrias* (sellouts to foreign interests). The world depression made Argentina's beef and wheat exports vulnerable to the trade protectionism that characterized this period. Argentina's principal customer, Great

Britain, seemed to be turning against Argentine suppliers when London signed an agreement in Ottawa in 1932 that gave imperial preference to Commonwealth countries. The Justo government's major support, the landowners, became fearful that their markets would disappear. And so an Argentine mission was dispatched to England, led by Vice President Roca, to negotiate with the head of the British Board of Trade, Walter Runciman. In what seemed a humiliating process for the Argentines, they were forced to spend all proceeds earned from the sale of a fixed quota of Argentine beef on English finished goods.[33]

The reaction to the Roca-Runciman Pact was muted when it was announced; most sectors of public opinion were critical, although they admitted that the circumstances of the world economic situation forced Argentina to make such choices. But it proved a seminal event for the Nacionalistas. Soon after the treaty was signed, two brothers, Julio and Rudolfo Irazusta, published a book on British imperialism in Argentina that made a profound impression and elevated the authors to the front ranks of Nacionalismo's leadership. The first part of the Irazustas' indictment analyzed the Roca mission, accusing the Argentine representatives of simply not defending the nation's interests, "failure from the very first declarations."[34] The second section continued with a discussion of the treaty itself, noting that "unconsciously or not, what the Roca mission has brought us to are new bonds destined to maintain and if possible reinforce our dependence on Great Britain, dependency that the natural evolution of economic and political affairs in our country and the world had weakened."[35] Finally, the third part, a "History of the Argentine Oligarchy," brought home the point, the dominance of the ruling class, in which "material progress, the specific effort of the oligarchy, has compromised our independence, has left nothing to the country in terms of the output of intensive exploitation."[36]

The rest of the 1930s and 1940s witnessed a rising tide of Nacionalista denunciation against England for its unofficial dominion over Argentina, as well as for its continued hold over what was proclaimed to be Argentine territory, the Islas Malvinas, and a growing admiration for Britain's European enemies, Germany and Italy. More significant was the Irazustas' influence in laying the ultimate blame on those in Argentina who conspired with the British—the regime, the oligarchy, the landowners and exporters—all in league with foreign interests. The Nacionalistas constrasted these rentiers with the agricultural workers, portraying the former as selling out the national patrimony and the latter as representing an Argentine authenticity beyond materialism. For the right, unfortunately, the offensive in exposing scandals of British dominance in Argentina was seized by the left. In 1935 the issues of British-owned municipal trams and railroads and a Senate debate on foreign-owned packinghouses dominated the news.[37] These vehement exposés by the socialists put the right in a quandary, but the Nacionalista response was to condemn all foreign influence at once, Britain's and the socialists'.

If the Roca-Runciman agreement caused the Argentine right to question its historical relationship with Great Britain, the Nacionalistas were now prepared to go much further. There emerged a complete reevaluation of Argentine history, which came to be known as Revisionism. It had its cast of heroes and villains, and among those beatified none was greater than Juan Manuel de Rosas. Although it was during his ascendency in Argentina in the 1830s and 1840s that the Malvinas were lost, Rosas, as governor of Buenos Aires, had contended with the power of Britain, as in the attempted Anglo-French blockade of Paraná, and successfully held it at bay. But he had not been dealt with kindly by Argentine history. He was dismissed with the rest of his generation of leaders in Latin America as a typical caudillo, and the liberals who had written most of that history left him little glory. Although there had been attempts to resurrect him earlier, the right during the 1930s brought this effort to a new level of intensity and gave to it a character that reflected the movement's own concerns.

Revisionism reached its apogee with the establishment of the Juan Manuel de Rosas Institute in 1938, which published both a bulletin and a journal named for its hero. Interest in Revisionism resulted in a flood of publications, much of it based on a historical concern with documentary support.[38] One of the most ardent Rosistas was the Nacionalista journalist and writer Roberto de Laferrère. In his aptly titled *El nacionalismo de Rosas*, he wrote that "the figure of Rosas is gigantic as the principal defender of our nationality in a struggle to the death which lasted, for him, more than thirty years. He is the representative of 'Argentineness,' of ourselves in conflict with 'foreignness,' whose hostile proposals have nothing to do with civilization nor with culture."[39] Consequently, for the revisionists, Rosas now became a figure of veneration as the prototypical "nationalist." In this historiographical debate, the conservatives continued to scorn him. They dated their rise to power from the liberal overthrow of Rosas and, therefore, had other champions. The comparable hero for the conservatives was General Julio A. Roca, the epitome of the liberal regime, president from 1880 to 1886 and again from 1898 to 1904. Not coincidentally, his son, Julio A. Roca, Jr., was selected as vice president to Justo, providing a direct link to the conservative legacy.

Through Rosas the Nacionalistas sought to glorify a lost tradition of opposition to foreign dominance in Argentina and to castigate the liberal oligarchy and its governments that followed Rosas. This antipathy toward nineteenth-century liberalism and its conservative heirs joined with the right's hatred of Marxism, communism, and bolshevism. Indeed, Ramón Doll, an important essayist among the Nacionalistas, titled one of his articles "Como el liberalismo vehiculiza al comunismo," in which he stated that "under the pretext of assuring liberty of thought, liberalism permits the diffusion of communism . . . and because of the demagogic nature of the electoral democracies, liberalism makes significant gestures to communism."[40] The obsession with communism grew ever more intense in the 1930s. But who precisely were the "communists" in Argentina? The U.S. embassy, preoccupied with this question, received its information immediately after the September Revolution from Manuel Carlés of the Liga Patriótica Argentina. One of his documents, labeled "Official Communist Party," stated that the Communists undertook agitation and propaganda in their publication, *La Internacional*, and had ward committees and factory cells. But the U.S. ambassador commented that "Bolshevism and communism are so closely allied in Argentina that it is difficult, if not wellnigh impossible to draw a line of demarcation between the two sects. Their members are almost entirely foreigners, some of whom are unable to speak Spanish."[41] Even the Nacionalistas would admit, at one of their typical meetings where "an enormous crowd proved its repudiation of communism," that "here there are few communists. . . . There are few communists in plain sight but many in the shadows, and these are the cowardly anti-Argentine socialists."[42] "Communist," then, was always a broad term in the view of the right, one that covered all of the right's opponents on the left and often in the center as well.

One of the right's favorite legal changes was a proposed law for the "repression of communism," making punishable by up to five years in prison "that which teaches or propagandizes the doctrine of . . . 'dictatorship of the proletariat' or any other based on the system of collective property and the abolition of private property." This bill was introduced in the Argentine Senate in 1932 and again in 1936 by Matías G. Sánchez Sorondo.[43] He spoke at length, a dissertation on the history of communism and its means of subverting Argentine society. To illustrate his points, Sánchez Sorondo inserted into the record a list of 127 "Communist and other extremist publications," including *The Gastronomic Sentinel* and the *Bulletin of the Red Cross*.[44] He talked almost continually through thirteen sessions of the Senate and then had the entire 184-page transcript published.[45] The measure was finally approved at the end of 1936.

What aroused both the conservatives and Nacionalistas so vehemently about communism in 1936 was the outbreak of the Spanish civil war in the summer of that year. Argentines, a large number of whom were Spanish immigrants and their immediate descendants, had followed closely the abdication of King Alfonso XIII and the establishment of the Second Republic in 1931. Very soon the Nacionalistas were declaring: "Either communists or fascists. All parties in between, including socialists, are destined to disappear. We see it in Spain where the government is practically communist."[46] When the Spanish conflict erupted the Argentine right declared its strong sympathy for the nationalist forces of General Francisco Franco. The conservative members of the Senate sent a dispatch to the revolutionary junta of Burgos: "Our message of love and solidarity to Spain, which, obeying the mandate of its history, struggles against communism as the essential requirement of our civilization."[47] Clearly, both persuasions of the right were outraged; however, the Nacionalistas insisted that fascism was now the only alternative, whereas conservatives were more restrained, seeking only the defeat of the republican left.

Equal fervor was found among the centrist Radicals and the left socialists in favor of the Spanish republic. Although their expressions of support in the socialist press and telegrams to the government in Madrid made their position clear, of greater importance was the material aid they collected and sent to Spain. There were a number of organizations in Argentina that raised money under the banner of the Federación de Organismos de Ayuda a la República Española, and the total collected was estimated to be the considerable sum of over three million Argentine pesos. In addition, an undetermined number of Argentine volunteers went to Spain to fight for the Loyalist cause.[48]

The right, infuriated at such activities, responded by establishing a Centro de Acción Española, which was the headquarters of such organizations as the Agrupación Tradicionalista Española, the Agrupación Monárquica, and, most important, the Falange Española de Buenos Aires. This Falange, fully uniformed, marched in and out of the Centro giving the fascist salute; it provided a point of contact when the Franco forces sent a representative to Argentina, Juan Pablo de Lojendio. It also showed a series of documentary films about the war in Spain, which, the rightist press noted, attracted large crowds, and it was responsible for attempts to organize similar groups in the Argentine interior. Fund-raising involved the work of the Legionarios Civiles de Franco, presided over by Soledad Alonso de Drysdale, a society matron, which reported 7,964 members and 211,754 pesos in donations by early 1938.[49] Soon Franco's agents had established a press service, "News and Commentary from Nationalist Spain," to which the rightist dailies subscribed.[50] By early 1939, Franco's victory seemed certain, and such events as the fall of Barcelona occasioned activities at theaters throughout the capital, staged by a variety of Nacionalista groups.

Their support for General Franco in the Spanish civil war united the right in its sympathy for all European anticommunist political movements. But the other European parties with which the Spanish Falange was linked, those generic fascists, would stir deep divisions in the ranks of the Argentine right. In the early years of the Década Infame, it seemed as if the September Revolution had put Argentina on the side of history. "The world is marching politically toward the right."[51] Admiration for Benito Mussolini's Italy, a nation from which many Argentines originally came and continued to derive cultural support, poured from rightist pens; much acclaim soon appeared for Adolf Hitler's National Socialism as well. These two movements were becoming, in the view of the right, a universal imperative, with imitators spreading throughout Europe, to France, Austria, Belgium. But their vociferous approval placed the right in a difficult position. After all the right's denunciations of international communism controlling leftist groups from Moscow, that same left now could berate the right as a puppet speaking in the voice of Rome or Berlin. In its defense, a rightist daily responded:

For several months, some of the red newspapers, and now individuals—in good or bad faith—have spread the rumor that La Fronda is a fascist daily. Our powerful reserves of good humor let us smile before such a picturesque and capricious definition. However, it might be well to say that La Fronda is not fascist, but nationalist, that is to say, before all and above all an Argentine newspaper, for the defense of Argentine interests . . . we fight all extremes and repudiate all demagogues, and if they appear in the Partido Demócrata Nacional we will also fight them with equal decisiveness.[52]

Indeed, the term "fascist" came to be used with almost the same ease by the left as the word "communist" by the right. Of course, literal fascists did exist. As early as 1923 the Partido Nacional Fascista had been formed, principally for the purpose of propagandizing on behalf of Mussolini's Italy.[53] It sponsored ceremonies on Fascist holidays when the Italian ambassador spoke, and in general it became the link between the immigrant Italian population and the politics of the mother country. By the 1930s the Italian government was showing a serious attempt to promote its interests in Argentina. The Italian press attaché made liberal use of influence and money in order to see that the Italian-language dailies in Argentina, such as *Il Mattino d'Italia*, gave ample coverage to Il Duce's accomplishments.[54] The formation of the Partido Fascista Argentina (PFA) in 1932 marked another concerted effort to influence Argentine politics. To avoid accusations of foreign control, the manifestos of the PFA spoke of a *fascismo criollo* and attempted to indicate the differences between the PFA and other Nacionalista groups. The other groups were challenged as tools of the conservative ruling class, whereas the fascists portrayed themselves as a mass, revolutionary movement of social justice, but of course in opposition to Marxism. In the interior, the Unión Nacional Fascista became an important organization, and its leader, Nimio de Anquín, enjoyed a solid reputation in Nacionalista circles.[55] The U.S. embassy estimated that in total there were in Argentina ten thousand "Italian Fascists who pay fees regularly to various organizations throughout the country."[56]

Despite the threat of potential disorder growing out of Italian Fascism's mass movements, support for Mussolini persisted among adherents of the Argentine right. This backing was transferred to Hitler as his party grew in strength in Germany and then came to power in 1933. In the years immediately thereafter, the main thrust of Germany's policy was to get the support of the local German community, but Nazism had one significant dark influence in Argentina, the intensification of anti-Semitism.[57] Antipathy toward Jews, of course, had appeared in Argentina before the formation of the Nazi party and was a tenet of the right from its earliest days when the supposed Red terror of the Semana Trágica (1919) was blamed on Jewish agitators. From that time on, in the view of rightists, "Judaism and communism are a single problem."[58] The right-wing press focused on those Jews who were members of the Socialist party, such as Enrique Dickmann, associating them with a class of despised immigrants who could never shed their "internationalism" for an Argentine identity. In the course of the 1930s, Jews fleeing European persecution arrived in ever larger numbers in Argentina, despite restrictive immigration laws that gave preference to rural, agricultural settlers. Anti-Semitic cartoons caricatured Jews as those who came into Argentina under false pretenses in order to set up exploitive businesses.

The European policies of open persecution of Jews met with unrestrained approval by the right. All Nazi propaganda was accepted wholesale—that "90 percent" of commerce, law, medicine, public, and university positions were in the hands of Jews and that Hitler wanted only to lift this burden from the backs of the German people.[59] When the Radical and socialist leaders of Buenos Aires fought anti-Semitism by forming a Comité Antiracista that identified widespread discrimination as a result of rightist propaganda against Argentine Jews, the Nacionalista press called a for violent response. Street fights broke out at meetings threatening the committee. The Liga Republicana declared a "campaign of opposition to the Semitic invasion of the country." And when the committee protested formally to the Ministry of the Interior about anti-Semitism, editorials sought to obscure the issue by protesting a Jewish conspiracy to silence the right, directed by a "Grupo Idiomático Judío," which labeled attacks on communism as "racial persecution or persecution of the working class or fascist penetration organized by foreign governments."[60]

One of the fountains out of which anti-Semitism flowed and out of which the right drew its inspiration was the Catholic church. The relationship between church and state in Argentina was a contradictory one: on the one hand, the constitution declared that the nation supported the Roman Catholic faith (Article 2), giving it an established position; on the other, during the 1880s a series of laws laicized such institutions as education and set up a state-run school system without religious teaching. The result was a current of criticism among the hierarchy and the devout that condemned government based on nineteenth-century liberal anticlericalism. This critique joined with the virulently anti-Communist position of the church in order to inspire a right-wing Catholic political position even before the revolution of 1930.

The Década Infame produced a convergence between these militant Catholics and the political right, especially the Nacionalistas. Many believers supported a strongly authoritarian state in order to stop a feared spread of socialism during the darkest days of the world economic depression. Although most conservatives wanted to reinforce the position of the church in society, they stopped short of demanding an end to the legal limits placed upon it; the Nacionalistas had no such doubts and demanded above all a generous amount of religious education in the public schools.

The church's close relationship to the right appeared in its journals, its outspoken priests, and its action groups and their activities. Much of the inspiration and continuity of right-wing Catholic thought came from its regular publications, including *Criterio*, a widely read journal after 1928. Originally a literary magazine for young, avant-garde authors, such as Eduardo Mallea and Jorge Luis Borges, in 1930 it fell into the hands of a group of more militant Catholics, including Ernesto Palacio. The editor was Enrique P. Osés, who was to become a violent critic of the regime and spokesperson for a fascist type of government in Argentina. Under his direction the tone of Catholic involvement in national affairs was set: the principles of the 1930 revolution meant a return to an enhanced role for the church in Argentine institutions.[61]

The next editor of *Criterio*, Gustavo Franceschi, represented the activist clerics who became important allies of the right. Franceschi declared himself an admirer of the Nacionalista crusade to purify Argentina. Julio Meinvielle was the most prolific popularizer of the Catholic position. He wrote a series of books beginning with an early important essay, *Concepción católica de la política*, a rather tentative effort to criticize mass democracy as outside the Thomistic conceptions of official doctrine that "the state ought primarily to protect and support the educational efforts of family and Church."[62] As the decade wore on, Meinvielle grew more rabid and anti-Semitic. Another cleric, Virgilio Filippo, a priest from the parish of Belgrano, took to the airwaves, denouncing "the socialist manifesto of the Jew, Karl Marx, elevated to delirium in the USSR."[63]

The gathering of the International Eucharistic Congress in Buenos Aires (October 1934) received much attention from the right, which attempted to tie the Congress closely to its influence in Argentina. The public enthusiasm for the meeting, the rightist press indicated, provided evidence of a continuation of support for the 1930 revolution, a signal of the rejection of the secular state.[64] In addition, the church's organizational activities and teaching functions were much praised and seen as essential in any future government where the right's authoritarianism would reflect that of Catholicism. Catholic Action was a movement set up in many European and Western Hemisphere nations; its goal was to work for governments friendly to the church without becoming a "political organization." The establishment of Acción Católica Argentina (ACA) caused the Nacionalistas to claim it as one of their own. The ACA continued a series of "Courses in Catholic Culture," taught by some of the most notable figures of the right, such as César Pico; a major theme was that only a rightist-dominated state could save Catholic values and the church in a time of secular, materialist onslaughts.[65]

For their part, however, the church and its spokespeople remained cautious about embracing the Argentine right. Its traditional role was to steer clear of politics and press only for those few policies it considered vital. During the 1930s the hierarchy most desired the introduction of religious education into the public schools. Beyond this specific objective, those who spoke for the church advanced only vague generalities such as: "the reestablishment of the State in Christ must be the basic point of a Nacionalista program."[66] It was the right that took for granted the firm adherence and even active support of the church and its followers, a supposition that the Argentine hierarchy did little to counteract.

The right and the church indeed were united in one major concern: the so-called social question of workers, increasingly industrial, who provided fertile ground for the growth of all the doctrines that the right and the church despised, from Radicalism to Marxism. By 1930, Argentina was entering upon a new stage of economic development as import-substitution industrialization made manufacturing an important source of employment in urban centers. Strike activity increased during the late 1920s, so that after September 1930 a state of siege forbade such work actions. Because the conservative government remained fearful of workers' revolutionary potential, it promoted the Nacionalistas' emerging tactic for dealing with labor: turn any organized movement into a government-controlled group.

The largest labor organization of the period was the recently formed Confederación General del Trabajo (CGT). Its declared policy was to avoid political involvement, even in the face of the repression of the Uriburu and Justo administrations. But factions within the CGT demanded denunciations of fascism, and on May Day 1936 it joined with other elements of the Popular Front and, thereafter, followed a policy of greater labor militancy.[67]

Many rightist organizations said little about the concrete aspects of the Argentine economy and its effects on the working class, but Acción Nacionalista Argentina made a clear declaration about the government's failure to deal with the misery of unemployment, pointing out that "such conduct compromises the situation of the government, the security and stability of the state . . . opening the way for demagogic and extremist action."[68] Thus the ANA issued a list, "Economic Bases," which included statements about using national production for the benefit of the working class, making the state responsible for giving work to citizens, and subdividing land so that every family might have a home or farm—all to be accomplished within a Nacionalista framework.[69] And the Milicia Cívica Nacionalista announced its opposition to "capital which produces nothing" and "organizations which call themselves working class but spread class hatred" and its support of "corporativist union representation" and "legislation which guarantees a rational balance between capital and labor."[70]

Indeed, some unions showed the influence of Nacionalista ideas. A dock workers' group (Sindicato Obrero de Diques y Darsenas Puerto de la Capital) issued its own manifesto, declaring that socialist, communist, and anarchist influence among workers had led them only to jail cells, that Argentina's economic life was controlled by "giant Jewish trusts," and that all workers ought to assemble on May Day in order to reaffirm the principles of Nacionalismo.[71] Then there was an attempt, never successful, to form an umbrella group, the Federación Obrera Nacionalista Argentina (FONA). The rightist press complained that FONA was denied permission by the police to hold meetings at the Church of Our Lady of Mercy or to affix posters welcoming wounded German war veterans,[72] which indicated the Justo administration's fear of union activism.

It was precisely this question of how to deal with an Argentina that was changing economically and socially that proved so divisive in the split between conservatives and Nacionalistas. On the one hand, the conservatives tended to see Argentine industrialization and diversification as an economic strength. Many of the elite invested in the manufacturing sector and believed industrial workers could be controlled by mere repression; their only interest was to keep labor costs as low as possible. Thus, the formation of unions and the conditions of workers interested them little. On the other, the Nacionalistas insisted that workers be taught a gospel of deference, obedience, and patriotism, which would ensure their rejection of the left. Exploitive employers forced labor toward discontent, they insisted, and social harmony, therefore, was supported by decent wages and working conditions. Despite these differences, both sides realized the dangers of uncontrolled unionism and followed a policy critical of organized labor. In this effort they sought leaders who might bring them together and bridge their differences. Two individuals were prominent in this effort: Matías G. Sánchez Sorondo and Manuel A. Fresco.

First elected as a national deputy in 1918, Sánchez Sorondo was a significant activist in the old Conservative party of the province of Buenos Aires. A member of one of Argentina's aristocratic families with a fortune made through the export trade, he gained an early reputation defending meat producers from the fluctuations of the world market. He had a distinguished career as lawyer, academic, author, and diplomat,[73] then became active in the struggle to oust Yrigoyen and the Radicals from power. His role in the conspiracy made him one of General Uriburu's closest political advisers, and he emerged as the communication link with civilian elements, urging them to support the coup and trying to reassure them that there would be no major change in the constitutional system (despite Uriburu's real intentions). As a reward he was named minister of the interior in the provisional government, and at one point, while Uriburu was traveling outside Buenos Aires, he became acting president. Throughout this period he was closely associated with the Nacionalista elements that supported Uriburu.

Sánchez Sorondo never joined in the formal Nacionalista network, and the Nacionalistas always harbored deep suspicion of and even animosity toward him. Someone so close to the regime of electoral fraud, whom the British had honored with the award of CBE (Commander of the British Empire), could scarcely be looked upon sympathetically. In fact, when he was named minister of the interior during the Uriburu administration, the Irazusta brothers declared that the Nacionalistas now had lost the opportunity to establish a government that fit their ideology.[74] Nevertheless, the rest of the 1930s witnessed Sánchez Sorondo's attempts to reach out to the Nacionalistas as he moved further toward the extreme right, hoping to lead other conservatives with him in that direction.

With the election of Agustín Justo as president on the Concordancia ticket, Sánchez Sorondo became a member of the Argentine Senate, where he maintained a high visibility. His principal cause was the campaign against communism, and his bill to ban it, as has been noted, inspired him to speak for days on end, emphasizing a defense of right-wing regimes in Europe as the bulwark against Marxism: "It is absurd to speak of the extremism of the right. . . . Extremism . . . because the forces attacked defend themselves and employ more or less rigor, more or less violence in their repression!"[75] The crisis for Sánchez Sorondo came with Justo's intervention to depose the governor of the province of Buenos Aires, Federico Martínez de Hoz. A large landowner but a favorite of the Nacionalistas, Martínez de Hoz feuded with the regular elements of his Conservative party. When the federal authorities arrived to oust him, hundreds of members of the LCA showed up to save the governor but finally refused any direct confrontation with troops. Sánchez Sorondo was deeply involved in getting the LCA's participation and then was either driven out of the PDN (to which the Conservatives belonged) or, as he preferred to announce, had resigned.[76] He kept his seat in the Senate and there denounced the electoral system as "bastardized democracy."

In late March 1937, Sánchez Sorondo left on a trip to Italy, in response to "an exceptional invitation for a member of the Argentine parliament . . . only made to emperors, kings and heads of state,"[77] to meet with Mussolini and then to Spain to meet with Franco. This journey led the U.S. embassy to label Sánchez Sorondo "as the outstanding Fascist figure in Argentina."[78] Upon his return he sounded increasingly like a committed Nacionalista in the Senate, expressing endless admiration for the fascist regimes of Europe yet insisting that Argentine Nacionalismo demanded a system responsive to its own "reality," not a slavish imitation,[79] which was the essence of the right-wing's propaganda. He was involved ever more deeply in political circles attempting to push Argentina further to the right in the late 1930s and early 1940s. However, the Nacionalistas remained unconvinced of his sincerity.

The other politician who aspired to form a bridge between conservatism and Nacionalismo, Manuel Fresco, aimed at a much greater role than did Sánchez Sorondo. The right understood its weakness in terms of the lack of a charismatic leader, an Argentine Mussolini or Franco, capable of bringing all the various rightist elements together; this leadership principle formed the essence of right-wing victories in Europe. After the demise of Uriburu, only Fresco arose to attempt such a grab at power.

Fresco's origins, unlike those of Sánchez Sorondo, were distinctly middle class, and his rightist views can be seen as typical of many professionals. He had been born in the province of Buenos Aires of a family that "had the smell of the countertop," small shopkeepers in a rural community.[80] He moved up the social ladder by graduating from the faculty of medicine at the University of Buenos Aires in 1915 and then practicing before entering politics. He became a staunch advocate of the Buenos Aires Conservative party, which was controlled by an old-line political boss, Alberto Barceló, but he demonstrated early on his affinity for a more extreme right-wing ideology by joining the Liga Patriótica.[81] For his obvious abilities at organization and oratory, he was rewarded with a number of important provincial positions. He played an active role in the conspiracy and successful outcome of the 1930 revolution and remained closely associated with its ideals. During the early 1930s he kept his feet firmly planted in the conservative camp as the head of Buenos Aires province's section of the PDN and also as a provincial representative in the national Chamber of Deputies, where he served as presiding officer. Whereas Sánchez Sorondo broke with the PDN over the intervention in the province of Buenos Aires that deposed the Nacionalista favorite Governor Martínez de Hoz, Fresco succeeded him as governor. The conservatives hoped that Fresco would attract Nacionalistas to his cause, and Fresco hoped that he could use the governorship to launch a broad-based rightist crusade that might propel him to the presidency of Argentina.

Once in the governor's office, Fresco began to promote himself to the Nacionalistas, and his popularity among their various factions grew, although some of them complained that he was only a tool of the oligarchy sent to co-opt them. At one of the typical banquets offered by the Nacionalistas soon after Fresco became governor, seven thousand devotees met him with a "wild confusion of cheers."[82] And Fresco replied by announcing a philosophy that embraced both old right conservatives and new right Nacionalistas:

> My government is conservative, in respect to conserving, defending and rendering homage to the traditional values of Argentine social groups, in respect to asserting its force and prestige over the basic institutions of the Western Christian World, the family, property, nationality, hierarchy; it aspires to be modern and directive in respect to applying technological systems and procedures to public functions. . . . It is a government of the right in respect to recognizing and protecting the expansion of capital and private enterprise as necessary elements to promote the economic greatness of the province and in respect to affirming the domain of authority and discipline, for without its vigilance the state falls into anarchy and society ends in chaos; and it is at the same time a government of defined social orientation because its actions are founded on the eternal notions of distributive justice consecrated by Christian morals.[83]

Fresco then undertook the propaganda campaign that would spread his name across Argentina under the slogan so closely associated with him and Nacionalismo, "Dios, Patria, Hogar" (God, Fatherland, Home). To demonstrate his commitment to these tenets, he compelled provincial teachers to join the Corporación Nacionalista de Maestros, which required taking an oath filled with Nacionalista principles.[84] This initiative in education was a starting point for Fresco's wide range of activities in the province of Buenos Aires, where he was determined to base his appeal on concrete rightist accomplishments. Indeed, he was one of the most visible and dynamic politicians of the decade.

At the end of his administration, Fresco boasted about the passage of some four hundred laws for the improvement of the province and the establishment of vast programs of public works, agricultural colonization, police reform, and health benefits. However, his efforts to solidify ties with all rightist factions rested on three major achievements that demonstrated the activist nature of the government.

The suppression of communism was a cause Fresco championed, expanding on the effort by Sánchez Sorondo in the national legislature. Fresco never tired of denouncing "the liberal marxist dogma" and the penetration of communism in "all the intellectual and pseudo-intellectual centers, the universities and the schools."[85] Early in his governorship, on May 20, 1936, he issued a decree that banned all communist propaganda. The definition of "communist" remained so broad that police power censored whatever it chose.

The introduction of compulsory religious education contravened a long-established policy of secular schools, but Fresco tried nonetheless to require Catholic teaching. The resulting pressure from conservatives forced his retreat. However, in his last year in office he pushed through a law that mandated the hierarchy to certify public schoolteachers to give a period of religious instruction, with the provision that parents could stipulate that their children need not attend.[86] This action won Fresco the open admiration of the Nacionalistas, who saw it as a direct frontal attack on the liberal state.

Finally, the control over labor became Fresco's major effort to build a system of social control along corporativist lines. The province of Buenos Aires was the most industrialized in Argentina, and this manufacturing sector continued to grow during the 1930s. The right's major fear remained the revolutionary potential of industrial workers. Fresco's solution was the Labor Code, passed by his legislature on May 12, 1937. A lengthy document, its core was the stipulation for compulsory arbitration of all labor disputes.[87] Whereas the socialists decried this law as a means for suppressing workers' rights and union activity, Fresco heralded it as a "fascist" model that protected the working class from the blatant exploitation of irresponsible capitalists. The record, often emphasized in the governor's propaganda, showed that hundreds of worker-management controversies were settled under the law with a resultant improvement in wages and working conditions. Fresco's ultimate aim remained the formation of rightist workers' organizations under state control, although this goal eluded him as he became embroiled in the political divisions of the late 1930s.

The Fascist Threat

The Justo administration had tried to attract the support of, or at least neutralize any threat from, the right by portraying itself as the anointed successor of General Uriburu's government. Justo insisted upon a dominant voice in the choice of the Concordancia's next candidate as the presidential elections of 1937 approached. He selected Roberto M. Ortiz, his minister of finance. Ortiz made the right, especially the Nacionalistas, very apprehensive because he was a civilian and an Anti-Personalist Radical of unknown views beyond his economic expertise. But most of the rightists rallied around his candidacy as representative of the line of succession from the 1930 revolution. Ramón S. Castillo received the nomination for vice president precisely because he was closer to the right, although not a known Nacionalista. Thus, the right wing dutifully noted that "the triumph of the Concordancia will assure the continuity of the official work and progress which has been realized since the 6th of September 1930, the movement of salvation."[88] Once again the election was a foregone conclusion through the use of fraudulent vote counts. However, Ortiz had a hidden agenda that soon came to light: the return of uncorrupted elections and thus the probability that the Radicals would regain national power. The fear of a revived Radicalism did more than anything to push the Nacionalistas toward the more extremist European voices of the late 1930s.

The Ortiz presidency lasted for almost two and one-half years, a stable period of improving economic conditions. But the deteriorating situation in Europe deeply affected Argentina and polarized public opinion. The triumph of Franco in Spain and the threatening demands of Hitler and Mussolini inspired the right to proclaim these governments as models for a future Argentina. Only one important group of Nacionalistas resisted the European fascist prototype. These intellectuals expounded the doctrine termed "Nacionalismo republicano."[89] Their journal, *Nuevo Orden*, insisted on rigid independence from all foreign influence, British or German, denunciation of the old landowning regime, and the formation of a popular party espousing majoritarian interests. Obviously, such precepts were not so distant from those of Radicalism, a party these writers validated in its general views but criticized as having turned to Yrigoyenism. Nevertheless, most Nacionalistas became closely aligned with the images of European fascism. For example, as German expansionism became evident the organization calling itself "Restauración" went on the offensive against those who had burned a German flag in protest of the German-Austrian *Anschluss*. They issued a statement to the German ambassador in Argentina scorning the "Jewish-Communist" perpetrators of this act and congratulating him on the "union" of the two states.[90]

In fact, "La Cuestión Nazi," the issue of Germany's influence in Argentina, became a center of attention. Soon after Hitler took power in 1933 a new ambassador, Edmund von Thermann, arrived in Buenos Aires; he played an active role in propagandizing on behalf of his government and was often an invited guest of Nacionalista groups. Particularly after 1938, as fascist power grew in Europe and brought out praise from Argentine rightist admirers, Nazism became an ever more virulent issue in Argentina. Of course, Nacionalista newspapers attemped to dismiss the entire matter: "A great deal has been said, too much, about 'Nazi infiltration' in these moments. The expression is very fashionable. . . . There are journals that dedicate entire pages to this thoroughly partisan campaign, inspired by absolutely bad faith. . . . What there is indeed in this country is hebraic and communistic infiltration."[91]

The left replied by introducing a resolution in the Chamber of Deputies, sponsored by the Socialist member Enrique Dickmann, one of the most hated subjects of rightist denunciation. He asked for an investigation of "illicit activities of foreign organizations," to which was added a like-minded amendment naming the "National Socialist ideology opposed to Argentine institutional systems and threatening to its sovereignty." The investigation was put off until the following year, when the issue of Nazi influence took on more ominous tones.[92]

Early in 1939 the sensationalist press in Argentina began to expose in the most lurid terms the supposed but unproved plans for a German takeover of Argentine territory. Headlines proclaimed, "Patagonia is no one's territory and we can annex it—official documents communicated from Berlin to Buenos Aires." A story followed, based on photocopies, indicating that the German embassy was directing an Argentine Nazi party to subvert national control over the sparsely populated interior of the country.[93] Within one week it was reported that "the Nazis have a military organization in Córdoba," including the accusation that "the relations between National Socialism and Nacionalismo are of various kinds and recognize the subordination of the Argentines to foreigners."[94] Then numerous charges appeared that German-Argentines maintained their German-language schools for the purpose of inculcating students with National Socialist principles. These assertions implicated the Argentine right directly or indirectly in support of activities controlled by foreign governments. In a fury, Nacionalistas denied such connections ever existed or that Nazism had any links to their doctrine, however much they might admire Hitler's Germany! Meanwhile, the rightist press began using the Transoceanic News Service, a propaganda agency of the German government, insisting that it was "totally Argentine."[95]

A slate of books soon followed, the most important by Dickmann, giving detailed evidence of the German attempts to infiltrate Argentina through links forged with the Nacionalistas. Dickmann quoted a confidential memorandum from the LCA to the German embassy of "warmest congratulations on the brilliant triumph obtained by the führer Adolf Hitler upon annexing Austria to the great German state" and a list of the membership of the LCA in the southern territory of Neuquén, in the majority German, Italian, and Spanish nationals— "that is how they recruit legionnaires for the Legión Cívica Argentina."[96]

The right quickly published its own exposé, which attempted to tie all groups, such as the Organización Popular Contra el Facismo y el Antisemitismo, to "Jewish vengeance" and Marxist duplicity: "The function of this committee was to stir up the racial problem which constituted the beginning of the great campaign planned by the Communist party."[97] The popular outcry had its effect in forcing those straddling the fence between conservatives and Nacionalistas to move away from the more extreme groups. Senator Sánchez Sorondo made it clear that "I profess admiration for Mussolini . . . but in its political aspect Fascism is a phenomenon completely Italian. . . . I do not want my country to have disguises or imitations."[98] This statement raises the issue of assessing the extent of European fascist influence. Although German and Italian governments and press organizations furnished information and, undoubtedly, money, the Nacionalistas remained committed to their sui generis image and, therefore, focused primarily on domestic concerns.

The outbreak of the Second World War on September 1, 1939, was preceded by the Hitler-Stalin nonaggression pact, which the right excused as a tactical gesture in no way diminishing the superiority of Nazism because of its "religious sense of existence." But war meant a further deterioration in any solidarity that might have kept the right unified. The socialists and the Radicals clearly sympathized with the Allied cause, particularly after the fall of France in 1940; the Nacionalistas not only praised Italian and German militarism, but they also exulted in the imminent downfall of Great Britain. The conservative right found itself in a quandary between emotional and financial attachment to England and admiration for the authoritarian nature of fascism. Some still tried to find a middle ground to bring the right together. Alejandro Ruiz-Guiñazú, a distinguished and influential conservative, published an essay calling for a "constructive state" based on all of the catchwords: "authority, liberty, order, responsibility, common good, justice, hierarchy, discipline, evolution, continuity, dynamism."[99] But these clichés would no longer satisfy militant Nacionalistas.

War also meant that the Ortiz government was faced with a much clearer issue about Italian and German influence among the elements of the Argentine right. The president, whose feeling for the European democracies was strong, followed the pattern of other Western Hemisphere nations and proclaimed a firm neutrality. Although the Nacionalistas praised this policy, they felt certain that the coming triumph of the Axis only would increase their prestige in Argentina and, consequently, their influence over the government. But Ortiz soon made clear his detestation for the Nacionalistas in a crisis with Governor Fresco. From the time of his election, Fresco was condemned (or sometimes praised) as a fascist; *La Prensa* noted snidely that "the present government of Buenos Aires province has been considered fascist and we limit ourselves to repeating the word with which it has been classified."[100] Fresco became the object of the severest philippic in the national Chamber of Deputies from a member of his own party, Aquiles Guglialmelli. A PDN member who had had a falling out with his party over Fresco's policies, Guglialmelli insisted that "all the action of Fresco is directed at implanting fascism, not only in Buenos Aires, but in the entire republic."[101]

Ortiz found Fresco's brand of government increasingly repugnant, particularly in light of future provincial elections. The newspapers hinted at the tension developing as "a struggle of tendencies which have manifested themselves for some time in the official party linked to the future gubernatorial elections."[102] Apparently, Ortiz put pressure on Fresco to purge the most visible Nacionalista elements in his administration, and he agreed to replace the minister of government, Roberto J. Noble, and the minister of finance, César Ameghino. What further enraged the president was Fresco's choice of the next governor, Alberto Barceló, the corrupt political boss of the industrial city of Avellaneda, who won the election by clearly fraudulent means. This situation provided Ortiz with the opportunity to move against Fresco before Barceló could be inaugurated. On March 7, 1940, President Ortiz intervened in the province of Buenos Aires, denouncing Fresco's undemocratic intent to influence "the political panorama of the country."[103] Ortiz paid a heavy price for his move against Fresco: it provoked a ministerial crisis in his cabinet resulting in two resignations and solidified the Nacionalistas' absolute opposition to his government and, increasingly, to the PDN.

The cause of Ortiz's political troubles, Manuel Fresco, believed that the PDN might have supported him as a popular candidate in the next presidential elections, but when his party remained silent in the face of intervention, he resigned. He then openly took up the Nacionalista cause and founded a new organization, Unión Nacional Argentina (UNA), or as he preferred to call it, Patria. The UNA called for a Nacionalista revolution and made the old landowners' political regime, which in the past had supported Fresco, a subject of particular scorn. Its thirteen-point program included many of the former governor's provincial measures directed toward the working class.[104] To spread his ideas, he founded a newspaper, *Cabildo*, in 1942. A morning tabloid rather more given to newsreporting than most rightist publications, it espoused the continued neutrality of Argentina in the war while at the same time praising the fascist cause. Overtaken by events after 1943, a mass following for Fresco never materialized and he faded away. Yet Juan Perón later would implement many of the governor's ideas on labor relations.[105]

Not only the opposition of the Nacionalistas but also a debilitating illness caused Ortiz to lose his grip on the presidency. On July 3, 1940, he took leave (never to return), handing over the office to Vice President Castillo, a politician who would try once again to bridge the widening gap between conservatives and Nacionalistas. Indeed, the Nacionalistas felt much revived, both by the march of fascism abroad in the early part of the war and the possibilities, with Castillo's benign support, for forming a broad front or political party that could allow them to take power either by ballot or by revolution.

In this rightist alignment, the most important group to emerge by the end of the 1930s was the Alianza de la Juventud Nacionalista. The AJN put great energy into organizing both "militants," who wore uniforms and contracted "special obligations," such as military training, and "supporters"; a special effort was made to recruit among the working class, and indoctrination came in heavy doses at an AJN school.[106] By the early 1940s, AJN members were everywhere in evidence, especially in support of President Castillo, who received the plaudits of "the well-organized, banner-waving mobs of the Alianza de Juventud Nacionalista, shouting: 'Neutralidad' and 'Argentinos, si, Judios, no.'"[107] The Alianza had a much clearer and more radical program than most of the Nacionalista groups, insisting on the nationalization of public service industries and land reform programs in order to assure broad-based Argentine support.[108] Despite the AJN's hope to lead the right, such policies put it at odds with the conservatives and their regime. This anticonservative stance reflected the views of the Alianza's leader, General Juan Bautista Molina. He had been involved in right-wing politics since the 1930 revolution when he had been an adviser to Uriburu, pushing him to change the constitutional system in Argentina. Afterward, Molina participated in various Nacionalista organizations, taking part in plots against both Justo and Ortiz. In an attempt to bring all the Nacionalista groups together, Molina founded the Consejo Superior del Nacionalismo in 1941; its aim was to set up a political party and support candidates in the 1943 election. But this effort failed.

Molina, although retired from active duty, represented the politicization of the military, particularly in support of the right. When Castillo became acting president, Molina and his supporters hoped to have an important influence over him, as his right-wing views were known.[109] The constraints on Castillo remained strong, however, because Ortiz had not officially relinquished his office. Although the general officers still followed the dictates of the former president, Justo, in upholding the constitutional system of Argentina, the lower ranks increasingly became influenced by Nacionalista thought and accepted the view once again that only the army could save Argentina.

Furthermore, the army officers, like other Argentines in the early 1940s, were responding to the circumstances of the European conflict. As German military forces closed in on Great Britain, the right became more vociferous in its admiration for the fascist cause. And the European right reached out to inspire these followers. Mussolini's Italy had been cultivating Argentina for some two decades; Hitler's Germany now made a determined effort to influence public opinion and to take advantage of the unstable political situation.

A major medium for Nazi propaganda was the newspaper *El Pampero*, reputedly subsidized from the German embassy,[110] and edited by the vitriolic Enrique Osés. His aim was to show the "catastrophic magnitude of the British yoke on our republic" by exposing such typical corruption as the "tragic statistics of the victims of the British railways, trying to overcome all the secrets and silences that protect foreign enterprise."[111] At the same time, the "Nazi preoccupation" was satirized editorially as the mania of communists and Jews. The American writer Waldo Frank was particularly scathing about *El Pampero*, which called him the "Yankee-Jew." Frank charged that the German embassy, through Osés and his paper, had him declared persona non grata and hired thugs to attack him physically during a 1942 visit to Buenos Aires, a clear indication to Frank of the influence of Nazism and its methods among the Nacionalistas.[112] Osés himself used the newspaper to make a final repudiation of the conservatives, the Old Regime, who had supposedly betrayed the revolution of 1930: "We rejected before, we reject now, the pretension of those conservative political forces which in spite of all our rejection still try to get themselves into our ranks. We will march alone and against them."[113]

As the Axis forces advanced along the road to world conquest and the Argentine Nacionalistas moved closer to a defiant fascist position, the majority of Argentines continued to express sympathy for the European democracies through organized groups such as Acción Argentina. Public opinion now supported the Chamber of Deputies' proposal to form a Comisión Investigadora de Actividades Antiargentinas. Thus, Dickmann's earlier recommendation resulted in a final version of the resolution adopted in 1940 intended "to designate a special commission of five members to propose emergency laws to prevent or repress activities of organizations foreign to our institutional system and dangerous to the national sovereignty."[114] Much of the work of the commission centered on the German and Italian efforts to spy, to use the German community and businesses, to take over territory, and to propagandize in Argentina. The congressional findings received wide publicity in a separately published series of documents. This material showed convincingly the influence of a German National Socialist party operating in Argentina and included evidence of its infiltration in such institutions as railways, schools, labor unions, and scientific organizations, as well as evidence of efforts by the German embassy to pursue espionage and to finance sympathetic individuals and organizations.[115] The investigation of Axis nations' penetration turned up direct connections of rightist groups with German and Italian agents. But these revelations about foreign influence loosed a storm against the commission from Nacionalistas who continued to defend their independence. For example, when the commission president, Deputy Juan Antonio Solari, called a press conference to show photographs of a Nacionalista gathering in Entre Rios, where the fascist salute was being given (ironically, pictures published in a rightist provincial newspaper), *El Pampero* sardonically replied that "with the arm extended and the palm up—which is the Nacionalista salute—they swore the oath of [Argentine] independence, the delegates of Tucumán. Therefore, disregarding exotic examples, the Argentine Nacionalistas salute that way. We don't find the same origins in the fist held up or the V for victory."[116]

The early 1940s witnessed the growing isolation of President Castillo and the Nacionalistas, with no love lost between them, but forced to depend on one another and on a policy of strict neutrality in the face of increasing centrist and leftist demands to favor Great Britain and France. After the Japanese attack on Pearl Harbor and the entrance of the United States into the Second World War, Castillo declared a state of siege in order to minimize dissent against his administration. But the Nacionalistas never trusted Castillo, with his ties in the Old Regime, and when he selected Robustiano Patrón Costas, a sugar grower and politician from Tucumán, as the official candidate of the PDN to succeed him, Nacionalista elements were incensed that a large landowner would continue political control by the class they had come so to despise.

Nacionalista groups scarcely had the power to take action; however, their mentality had permeated important sectors of the armed forces. Military journals showed the growth of right-wing views when officers like Juan Carlos Sanguinetti, a Nazi sympathizer, and civilians such as Sánchez Sorondo wrote articles praising the military state.[117] And so Nacionalista officers, including Juan Perón, organized into the Grupo de Oficiales Unidos (GOU) and plotted to take over the government. The result was the "revolution" of June 4, 1943, which ended the Castillo presidency and the expected election of Patrón Costas and, with it, the period of the Década Infame.

Conclusion

Argentines continue to look back to the period from 1930 to 1943 as the crucial stage in their twentieth-century history. For the democratic majority, it began a downward spiral toward the crisis that now envelops Argentina. This was indeed a Década Infame: the revolution of 1930 interrupted the long period of constitutional succession and would initiate a regular pattern of military intervention. The right corrupted not only the 1930s but also bequeathed its perverse influence that brought to power Juan Perón and the generals of the Dirty War. For the rightists, the revolution may have been Argentina's last opportunity to prevent the onslaught against order and authenticity. Both conservatives and Nacionalistas, however, see the 1930s as a golden age because of a flourishing of rightist thought and confidence that has never been repeated.

Still, the role of the right remains an unresolved historical problem. Of the many questions surrounding its place in Argentine history during the 1930s, three are especially relevant. Why did rightists fail to find a leader to bring them together and to galvanize a following? The cast of potential rulers was large and varied within the ranks of the right, both military and civilian. And the chiefs of the various Nacionalista groups certainly tried to promote themselves. Yet not until the rise of Perón did an all-powerful leader emerge. The answer, therefore, lies in the next question. Why did the right fail to gain a wide, even majoritarian, constituency? The right recognized the changes in Argentina, the transformation from an agricultural to an industrial economy, and the consequent increase in the urban working class. Even though repression remained the order of the day, there was a dawning realization that the loyalty of laborers could be harnessed to counter the left and build the way to power for the right. But again, Perón proved to be the one who capitalized on this potential. So a final issue arises. Why was the right unable to project a positive image in the propitious circumstances of the 1930s? Instead, its enemies tarred it with the brush of European fascism. The commonality of the right throughout the Western world during the interwar period is clear. The Argentine right's interest in, sympathy for, and adoption of European fascist ideas did not automatically undercut its sui generis characteristics. Yet it certainly gained and retained the image of Argentine Nazis. Nevertheless, the Argentine right responded to concrete concerns reflecting the Argentine reality. Cristián Buchrucker, a recent commentator on Nacionalismo, argues that the right's influence derived from its involvement with the "principal tensions in Argentine society during that time [the 1930s]," such as the antagonisms between old Argentines and immigrants, the maldistribution of wealth, and the political exclusion of the masses.[118]

The answer to these questions lies in the failure of the right to seize the opportunity the 1930s presented it for a broad-based organization that compellingly advanced its program. Instead, the tendency to divide and atomize overtook it. Undoubtedly, the split of conservatives and Nacionalistas grew out of quite distinct worldviews. The old right looked back to its dominance during the late nineteenth century and sought to recreate those circumstances once again, whereas the new right, on the one hand, looked back even further to a mythic criollismo that existed before the oligarchy's rule and, on the other, looked forward to a radically changed Argentina after the bankrupt elitist control was defeated. Fear of the left rather than a comprehensive program held them together for temporary alliances. More difficult to understand was the inclination of the militant Nacionalistas to fragment into so many competing organizations and the failure of attempts to produce an overriding leadership. Divided, they fell easy prey to conservative domination. And in the 1930s their connection with European fascism tarnished their image.

The revolution of June 4, 1943, brought the right together in unanimous praise for the uprising, believing, once again, as they had in 1930, that a military coup from the top would catapult them to power and alter the institutional basis of Argentina. Once again they would be co-opted and deluded, to their great despair, as Juan Domingo Perón seized power.

Notes

1. See detailed examination in Robert A. Potash, *The Army and Politics in Argentina, 1928–1945: Yrigoyen to Perón* (Stanford, 1969), 42–44.

2. This attitude is well expressed in Enrique I. Rottjer, "La revolución del 6 de septiembre desde el punto de vista militar," *Revista Militar* 357 (October 1930): 575–90.

3. General José F. Uriburu, manifesto of October 1, 1930, and speech at the Escuela Superior de Guerra on December 15, 1930, in Alberto E. Uriburu, *La palabra del General Uriburu* (Buenos Aires, 1933), 21–25, 47–53.

4. Potash, *Army and Politics*, 64–65.

5. U.S. naval attaché, report, April 20, 1931, 835.00/543, *Records of the Department of State Relating to the Internal Affairs of Argentina, 1930–1939*, U.S. National Archives Microfilm Publication M1230, Washington, DC, 1982 (hereafter cited as Embassy Dispatch, with date and file number).

6. *La Vanguardia*, May 20, 1931.

7. Embassy Dispatch, June 10, 1931, 835.00/543.

8. Ibid. Cristián Buchrucker, *Nacionalismo y peronismo: La Argentina en la crisis ideológica mundial, 1927–1955* (Buenos Aires, 1987), 234 n. 2, estimates only six thousand to ten thousand LCA members.

9. *La revolución del 6 de septiembre: Su motivo, sus hombres, su gobierno* (Buenos Aires, 1931), 7. This oversized, illustrated, expensively produced encomium is of mysterious origin, having no publication information.

10. Juan E. Carulla, *Valor ético de la revolución del 6 de septiembre 1930* (Buenos Aires, 1931), 124.

11. *La Fronda*, September 7, 1931.

12. Ibid., September 7, 1939.

13. Alberto Ciria, *Partidos y poder en la Argentina moderna* (Buenos Aires, 1964), 147.

14. *La Prensa*, February 21, 1932.

15. *La Fronda*, December 21, 1931.

16. Ibid., February 7, 1932.

17. *La Nación*, July 23, 1932.

18. *La Fronda*, May 27, 1933.

19. In the Argentine film *Asesinato en el Senado de la Nación* (1984) Director Juan José Jusid focuses on this incident but ties Ramón Valdez Cora to the oligarchy that is seen as imbued with fascist ideas—indicative of a popular interpretation of the 1930s in Argentina. The events also are covered in Peter H. Smith, *Politics and Beef in Argentina* (New York, 1969), 182–87.

20. *La Fronda*, September 29, 1933.

21. Ibid., August 26, 1936.

22. Ibid., November 23, 1935.

23. *La Nación*, May 24, 1933. For membership figures see Buchrucker, *Nacionalismo y peronismo*, 234 n. 2. He has compiled the most complete list of Nacionalista groups labeled "Restaurador," 116–17.

24. *La Fronda*, May 24, 1933.

25. See Marilú Bou, "1936: El fraude, el frente, el fascismo," *Todo Es Historia* 237 (February 1987): 8–25.

26. See Enzo Valenti Ferro, *Qué quieren los nacionalistas?* (Buenos Aires, 1934), esp. 59–100, 110–12.

27. A large body of writing exists by these individuals, much of it autobiographical, such as Juan E. Carulla, *Al filo del medio siglo* (Buenos Aires, 1951). Because the aim here is not to write an intellectual history of the right, the best source is Enrique Zuleta Alvarez, *El nacionalismo argentino*, 2 vols. (Buenos Aires, 1975).

28. See Leopoldo Lugones (h.), *Mi padre* (Buenos Aires, 1949), for a sympathetic treatment among the many biographies.

29. Ysabel F. Rennie, *The Argentine Republic* (New York, 1945), 277.

30. Carulla, *Al filo*, 228.

31. *La Fronda*, July 9, 1932.

32. *La Prensa*, August 18, 1936.

33. See discussion of the Roca-Runciman Pact in Javier Villaneuva, "Economic Development," and Joseph S. Tulchin, "Foreign Policy," in *Prologue to Perón: Argentina in Depression and War, 1930–1945*, ed. Mark Falcoff and Ronald H. Dolkart (Berkeley, 1975), 65–67, 95–101.

34. Rodolfo Irazusta and Julio Irazusta, *La Argentina y el imperialismo británico* (Buenos Aires, n.d.), 55.

35. Ibid., 87.

36. Ibid., 136.

37. Rennie, *Argentine Republic*, 238–44, 248–57.

38. See José María Rosa, *El revisionismo responde* (Buenos Aires, 1964), 193–206.

39. Roberto de Laferrère, *El nacionalismo de Rosas* (Buenos Aires, 1953), 16 (first published in the *Revista del Instituto de Investigaciones Historicas, "Juan Manuel de Rosas"* 2–3 [August 1939]).

40. Ramón Doll, *Acerca de una política nacional* (1939; reprint ed., Buenos Aires, 1975), 130.

41. Embassy Dispatch, September 8, October 30, 1930, 835.00B/30.

42. *La Fronda*, August 21, 1932.

43. República Argentina, Cámara de Senadores, *Diario de Sesiones, 1936–1937*, vol. 3 (Buenos Aires, 1937), 24–26 (hereafter cited as Cámara de Senadores or Cámara de Diputados).

44. Ibid., 95–98.

45. Matías G. Sánchez Sorondo, *Represión del comunismo* (Buenos Aires, 1937).

46. *La Fronda*, January 17, 1933.

47. Ibid., September 2, 1936.

48. Mark Falcoff, "Argentina," in *The Spanish Civil War, 1936–39: American Hemisphere Perspectives*, ed. Mark Falcoff and Frederick B. Pike (Lincoln, NE, 1982), 316–20.

49. *La Fronda*, January 21, 1938; Falcoff, "Argentina," 322.

50. *La Fronda*, February 5, 1938.

51. Ibid., October 31, 1931.

52. Ibid., February 17, 1932.

53. Marysa Navarro Gerassi, *Los nacionalistas*, trans. Alberto Ciria (Buenos Aires, 1968), 95–96.

54. Embassy Dispatch, March 3, 1938, 835.00F/3.

55. For the PFA see H. V. Passalacqua Elicabe, *El movimiento fascista argentina* (Buenos Aires, 1935). For the UNF see Buchrucker, *Nacionalismo y peronismo*, 176.

56. Embassy Dispatch, March 3, 1938, 835.00F/3.

57. Ronald C. Newton, "The United States, the German-Argentines, and the Myth of the Fourth Reich, 1943–1947," *Hispanic American Historical Review* 64, no. 1 (February 1984): 86.

58. Carlos M. Silveyra, *La cuestión nazi en la Argentina*, 2d ed. (Buenos Aires, 1939), 7. Silveyra was the director of *Clarinada*, a rabidly anti-Semitic journal.

59. *La Fronda*, May 7, 1937.

60. Ibid., October 20, 1938.

61. See Héctor René Lafleur, Sergio D. Orovenzano, and Fernando Pedro Alonso, *Las revistas literarias argentinas, 1893–1960* (Buenos Aires, 1962), 118–19.

62. Julio Meinvielle, *Concepción católica de la política*, 3d ed. (1932; reprint ed., Buenos Aires, 1961), 128.

63. Virgilio Filippo, *Habla el padre Filippo* (Buenos Aires, 1941), 96–97.

64. *La Fronda*, October 17, 1934.

65. See Navarro, *Los nacionalistas*, 110–12.

66. Alberto Ezcurra Medrano, *Catolicismo y nacionalismo*, 2d ed. (Buenos Aires, 1939), 96.

67. Samuel L. Baily, *Labor, Nationalism, and Politics in Argentina* (New Brunswick, NJ, 1967), 51–61.

68. *La Fronda*, October 13, 1932.

69. Ibid., January 4, 1933.

70. Ibid., May 9, 1933.

71. Ibid., April 6, 1933.

72. Ibid., August 1, 1933.

73. *Quién es quién en la Argentina, año 1939* (Buenos Aires, 1939), 392.

74. Zuleta Alvarez, *Nacionalismo argentino* 1:246.
75. Cámara de Senadores, *1936–1937* 3:613.
76. See Richard J. Walter, *The Province of Buenos Aires and Argentine Politics, 1912–1943* (Cambridge, England, 1985), 134–41.
77. *La Fronda*, February 16, 1937.
78. Embassy Dispatch, March 30, 1938, 835.00F/3.
79. *La Fronda*, July 7, 1939.
80. Arturo Jauretche, *F.O.R.J.A. y la década infame* (Buenos Aires, 1962), 116.
81. See Walter, *Province of Buenos Aires*, passim. For his membership in the Liga see Sandra McGee Deutsch, *Counterrevolution in Argentina, 1900–1932: The Argentine Patriotic League* (Lincoln, NE, 1986), 237.
82. *La Nación*, July 8, 1936.
83. Manuel A. Fresco, "Mensaje leído el 11 de mayo de 1937," in *Conversando con el pueblo: Discursos del Dr. Manuel A. Fresco*, ed. Luis M. Balesta, 3 vols. (Buenos Aires, 1938), 1:275–76.
84. Manuel A. Fresco, *La instrucción primaria en mi gobierno* (Buenos Aires, 1940), 76. See also Deutsch, *Counterrevolution in Argentina*, 91, for a parallel with the Liga Patriótica's teachers' brigades.
85. Manuel A. Fresco, "Discurso en la capital federal, el 17 de agosto de 1936," in Balesta, *Conversando con el pueblo* 1:73.
86. Fresco, *Instrucción primaria*, 53–54.
87. Text in Manuel A. Fresco, *Cómo encaré la política obrera durante mi gobierno*, 2 vols. (Buenos Aires, 1940), 1:118–46.
88. *La Fronda*, July 19, 1937.
89. Term used by Zuleta Alvarez, *Nacionalismo Argentino* 1:423–99, to characterize what he saw as the most significant group in the Nacionalista movement.
90. *La Fronda*, April 12, 1938.
91. Ibid., April 19, 1938.
92. Cámara de Diputados, *1939* 1:133–34.
93. *Noticias gráficas*, March 30, 1939. Newton, "Myth of the Fourth Reich," 87, indicates this plot was a hoax.
94. *Noticias gráficas*, April 5, 1939.
95. *La Fronda*, June 17, 1939.
96. Enrique Dickmann, *La infiltración nazi-fascista en la Argentina* (Buenos Aires, 1939), 90, 94.
97. Silveyra, *Cuestión nazi*, 45.
98. Senate speech reported in *La Fronda*, July 7, 1939.
99. Alejandro Ruiz-Guiñazú, *La Argentina ante sí misma: Reflexiones sobre una revolución necesaria* (Buenos Aires, [1944]), 185.
100. *La Prensa*, May 13, 1937.
101. Cámara de Diputados, *1937* 1:1210.
102. *La Prensa*, January 14, 1939.
103. See text in "La intervención en Buenos Aires," *Revista Parlamentaria* 8 (March 1940): 35.
104. See text in Balesta, *Conversando con el pueblo* 3:32–41.
105. This interpretation derives from Ronald H. Dolkart's conclusions in "Manuel A. Fresco, Governor of the Province of Buenos Aires, 1936–1940: A Study of the Argentine Right and Its Response to Economic and Social Change" (Ph.D. diss., University of California—Los Angeles, 1969), 291–98.
106. *La Fronda*, May 30, 1939, see also Buchrucker, *Nacionalismo y Peronismo*, 209–14.
107. Ray Josephs, *Argentine Diary: The Inside Story of the Coming of Fascism* (New York, 1944), 23.

108. Navarro, *Los nacionalistas*, 148–50. Bonifacio Lastra, *Bajo el signo nacionalista* (Buenos Aires, 1944), 185, estimates fifty thousand attended an Alianza march in 1943.

109. Potash, *Army and Politics*, 128–29.

110. Rennie, *Argentine Republic*, 273. The author states that "nobody knew the exact circulation of *El Pampero*, which was estimated between 15,000 (probably too low) and 80,000 (probably too high)," 277.

111. *El Pampero*, January 8, 1940.

112. Waldo Frank, *South American Journey* (New York, 1943), 210–20.

113. Enrique P. Osés, *Medios y fines del nacionalismo* (Buenos Aires, 1968), 90 (a collection of Osés's articles from *El Pampero*).

114. Cámara de Diputados, *1940* 1:251.

115. See Cámara de Diputados, *Comisión Investigadora de Actividades Antiargentinas, Informe 1-4* and *Formas y medios de penetración totalitaria* (Buenos Aires, 1943). Adolfo Lanus used the commission's results and his own research to expose the efforts of the Third Reich to organize Germans in Argentina. Although much of the evidence was anecdotal, Lanus, a partisan of the pro-Allied Argentine Action concluded that Nazi and Nacionalista organizations of the early 1940s were closely linked. See Adolfo Lanus, *Campo Minado* (Buenos Aires, 1942). Waldo Frank states that "*Campo Minado* was immediately suppressed" (*South American Journey*), 206.

116. *El Pampero*, February 11, 1943.

117. Matías G. Sánchez Sorondo, "El espíritu militar," *Revista Militar* 469 (February 1940): 193–200.

118. Buchrucker, *Nacionalismo y peronismo*, 214–24.

The Right and the Peronists, 1943–1955

Richard J. Walter

On June 4, 1943, the Argentine military overthrew the civilian government of President Ramón S. Castillo and instituted an authoritarian regime that lasted until 1946. The coup, in which Nacionalista military officers were prominent, provided the Argentine right with its best opportunity yet to wield influence and exercise real power at the national level. At the same time, one of the officers involved in these events, Colonel Juan D. Perón, used the circumstances created by the military takeover to prepare his own way to power. In the process the interests of Perón and the Nacionalistas occasionally coincided. More often, Perón and the Nacionalistas worked at cross purposes. In 1946, Perón captured the nation's presidency. During his nine years in power he co-opted the Nacionalistas and their program and relegated the right to minor roles within his administration. By the early 1950s many Nacionalistas had become critics of Perón and joined the movement that ousted him from office and the country in September 1955.

The purpose of this essay is to trace the course of these developments by focusing on the role of the Nacionalistas in the various military administrations that followed the June coup, on the Nacionalistas' relations with Perón during this period, and on the role of the right in Perón's election and subsequent administration. In so doing, the essay will address to some extent the question of the relationship frequently made between Perón and fascism.

The "Revolution" of 1943

In the early 1940s, Argentina's Nacionalistas appeared to be a growing and significant force within the nation. Nacionalista spokespersons, mostly intellectuals and professionals, were increasingly active and visible in public life. Their thoughts were transmitted to the public through frequent speeches and a variety of publications. Two of the most important Nacionalista newspapers were *El Pampero* and *Cabildo*, both based in Buenos Aires. *El Pampero*, founded in 1939, was funded by the German embassy and soon became a pro-Nazi propaganda sheet. Estimates of its circulation ranged from a low of fifteen thousand copies to a high of eighty thousand.[1] *Cabildo*, which was founded in 1942 by former Buenos Aires Governor Manuel A. Fresco, aimed for a popular audience through an attractive format and features on entertainment, social life, and sports. Other publications, with more limited circulation, included *Crisol, El Fortín, La Voz del Plata*, and *Sol y Luna*.[2]

The largest and most important Nacionalista group in the 1940s was the Alianza Libertadora Nacionalista (ALN). Organized in the previous decade by individuals associated with the Legión Cívica Argentina, the Alianza especially appealed to and sought to recruit from high-school and university students.[3] By the early 1940s the ALN claimed to have some eleven thousand members, three thousand of whom were women.[4] Members were organized in local units in the city of Buenos Aires and in major towns and cities in the provinces. Judging from the ALN's success in recruiting students and scattered information about some of its leaders, the Alianza included a mix of persons from middle- and upper-class backgrounds.[5]

Like the other Nacionalista groups, the ALN attacked liberalism, "corrupt" democratic politicians and practices, and the conservative oligarchy that ruled the country in the 1930s. It was also virulently anti-Semitic. Rejecting both capitalism and communism, the Alianza proposed an authoritarian corporate state and national control over major economic activities. Setting itself apart from many other right-wing groups, the ALN called for agrarian reform and social justice, arguing that earlier Nacionalistas had been too elitist in their approach, ignoring the justifiable concerns and obvious needs of the working classes and abandoning the workers to anarchists and communists. The ALN, holding rallies in working-class districts such as La Boca in Buenos Aires, sought to develop a broader base of support than had been the case for other Nacionalista organizations.[6]

In addition to numerous publications and the increased visibility of groups such as the ALN, there were also signs in the early 1940s of substantial and growing Nacionalista influence in two of the nation's most important institutions, the Catholic church and the army. And, of course, the Nacionalistas' growing strength occurred within the context of what was for them a favorable international climate. The early military victories of the Axis made it appear that those sympathetic with them were riding a rising historical tide about to crest. Most Argentine Nacionalistas, although careful not to identify themselves too closely with fascism for fear of tarnishing their own nationalist standing, nonetheless did not hide their admiration for the European dictators and the impressive military power they represented. Accordingly, they strongly favored Argentina's adherence to a position of neutrality in the world conflict and reacted fiercely against any show of support for the Allies. Their harsh criticism of Great Britain's role in the nation's past reinforced this position on the war.

Although the early 1940s seemed to present the Argentine right with many favorable conditions for further growth and influence, there were also certain continuing basic weaknesses in its position. Even though it is impossible to quantify with exactitude, it is doubtful whether the Nacionalistas represented more than a significant minority within the church and the army, where numerous leaders continued to identify with the moderate conservatism of the oligarchy and to express support for liberal democracy. In the larger civilian society where they were vocal and active and included in their ranks many prominent figures, the Nacionalistas nonetheless represented only a relatively small group within the nation's political structure. Unable and unwilling to organize into a coherent and cohesive single organization, and lacking a dynamic and charismatic leader to bring them together, the Nacionalistas remained divided, fragmented, and often at odds with one another. Moreover, although certain aspects of Nacionalista thinking had the potential for widespread popular appeal, other features, particularly elitism and authoritarianism, produced little support. Finally, the Nacionalistas' association with fascism and the German embassy probably did more harm than good. Most Argentines, while favoring a policy of pragmatic neutrality with regard to World War II, were essentially pro-Allied, and, even though unhappy with the fraud and corruption of the Década Infame, still preferred a democratic system of popular elections and constitutional government to the alternatives offered by the Nacionalistas.[7]

The main problem for the Nacionalistas in the early 1940s, then, was how to gain power in order to enact their program. With little popular support and no cohesive political organization, their only possibilities seemed to lie in some sort of national crisis that would open the way for revolutionary action. And on June 4, 1943, such an opportunity did present itself, apparently somewhat to the surprise of the Nacionalistas, when a coup dislodged President Castillo and instituted an authoritarian military rule, which lasted three years.

The basic motive for the military coup was the concern on the part of Nacionalista officers that Castillo's handpicked successor, Robustiano Patrón Costas, would succumb to external pressures and lead the country away from neutrality and toward a pro-Allied position. Underlying the move, too, was general disgust with, as the military saw it, corrupt and inept civilian politicians, and a desire to implement a variety of items on the Nacionalista agenda, particularly to develop a strong and unified Argentina which could resist external pressures and threats and wield a leadership role of its own in hemispheric affairs.

Instrumental in the coup was a Nacionalista-inclined group within the army, the Grupo Organizador y Unificador, or GOU, including among its leaders Colonel Perón.[8] The influence of the GOU and Perón in developments following the coup was extremely important for the Nacionalistas. During the months after the overthrow of Castillo, Nacionalista officers and Nacionalista civilians were appointed to a number of important administrative positions. They carried out at the national, provincial, and local levels measures that bore a clear Nacionalista stamp. For the first time since the military coup of 1930, many Nacionalistas believed that they had a golden opportunity to bring about the spiritual renovation and national revolution they had been championing for two decades.[9]

At the same time, however, Juan Perón was beginning his own drive to power. Initially an apparent pro-Axis Nacionalista, Perón seemed to have the potential to provide the movement with the charismatic national leader it had lacked. And to many, especially to Perón's contemporary opponents, that seemed to be what Perón eventually became—Argentina's version of a European fascist dictator, a spokesperson for the Nacionalista ideology with a broad popular base. Closer examination of the record reveals, however, that from the beginning Perón sought to neutralize and then to eliminate Nacionalista influence from the military government. Riding with, and often helping to direct, the shifting currents of events in these years, Perón soon abandoned any firm commitment to Nacionalista principles and goals (presuming that he had had any such commitment in the first place) in a pragmatic campaign to gain dominance for himself. In the process, Perón captured, used, or discarded the Nacionalistas as it suited his own purposes.

Nacionalista influence was clear in the military governments that followed the coup. General Arturo Rawson, the first provisional president, named a cabinet that mixed civilians and generals and that the U.S. embassy perceived as dominated by "several persons who have hitherto been known as holding Nationalist or even pro-Axis sentiments."[10] When Rawson was replaced as provisional president by General Pedro Ramírez two days after the coup, a reshuffled cabinet made up almost entirely of military officers (the one civilian was Jorge Santamarina, an oligarch of the highest standing, as minister of finance) seemed to be more balanced between Nacionalistas and moderates, between those who favored either the Axis or neutrality and those who favored the Allied position, than its predecessor had been. The struggle between these two forces—pro-Axis and pro-Allied—underlay much of the political activity in Argentina during the months following the coup. Ramírez himself seemed to side with the moderates until October 1943 when he shifted closer to the Nacionalista position.

More important for the Nacionalistas than occupying upper-level cabinet posts were the many positions to which they were appointed within the middle layers of the bureaucracy. Between June 1943 and the end of the year, Nacionalistas assumed such crucial posts as interventors (federal administrative officials with almost unlimited power) in large provinces such as Córdoba and Buenos Aires and mayor and chief of police of the federal capital as well as filling various positions in the national universities of the republic. A cabinet crisis in October, stemming in part from the resignation of pro-Allied

Foreign Minister Admiral Segundo Storni, who was publicly embarrassed in an exchange of notes with U.S. Secretary of State Cordell Hull, produced a cabinet that clearly was dominated by Nacionalistas. The most notorious appointment went to Gustavo Martínez Zuviría, a well-known author (under the pseudonym Hugo Wast) of anti-Semitic novels, as minister of justice and public instruction. Probably more important was the appointment of Nationalista General Luis Perlinger as minister of the interior, a post controlling most matters of internal security.[11]

From the beginning the military government was authoritarian. Ruling by decree, it extended the state of siege (thereby effectively suspending constitutional guarantees) that had been imposed by Castillo in late 1941, canceled elections, dissolved Congress, and occasionally censored the press. Following the cabinet realignment in October, the authoritarian character of the regime became even more pronounced. Opponents, most notably among Argentina's university students, were subjected to considerable repression, as were those groups that actively supported the Allied cause. At the same time the government sought to implement various aspects of the Nacionalista program. It began investigations into various concessions made to foreign capital during the Década Infame, nationalized some foreign-owned properties, and sought to build up defense-related industries. It also attempted to "purify" Argentine moral behavior, a constant concern of the Nacionalistas, by prohibiting the use of *lunfardo* (slang) in public and restricting the playing of certain tangos, measures that produced more ridicule than adherence. In December 1943 and January 1944, the Ramírez government attacked the oligarchy by lowering land rents in the country's major agricultural provinces, sought the support of the church by establishing compulsory religious education in all public schools, and, perhaps to prepare the way for a corporate state, ordered the dissolution of all political parties and groups.[12]

At the same time as the Nacionalistas seemed to be winning the battle against the moderates, another struggle was going on within the Ramírez administration that would have serious consequences for the Nacionalistas' long-range plans and position. This struggle involved the junior officers of the GOU, who tried to gain predominance within the new government. Four GOU members held particularly important positions under Ramírez: Colonel Emilio Ramírez served as chief of police of the federal capital; Colonel Enrique P. González was secretary to the president; Colonel Eduardo Avalos was commander of the vital Campo de Mayo garrison; and Colonel Juan D. Perón was secretary to Minister of War Edelmiro Farrell. Within this powerful quartet, González and Ramírez appeared to seek the support of the Nacionalistas, whereas Avalos and Perón were initially more inclined toward the popular Yrigoyenista Radicals (those associated with the legacy of former president Hipólito Yrigoyen), especially the Fuerza de Orientación Radical de la Joven Argentina (FORJA).[13]

From his position as secretary to Minister of War Farrell, Perón began to develop a web of allies within the military. In October 1943 he survived the threat of removal from the government and saw his sponsor, Farrell, promoted to the post of vice president while retaining the war ministry. Later in that same month Perón was named head of the Labor Department, a position from which he would develop the working-class backing that would propel him to the presidency three years later.

Perón's populist social welfare policies and his embrace of the Argentine lower classes—and their embrace of him—disturbed many Nacionalistas. According to the memoirs of one, the signs of estrangement between the Nacionalistas and Perón were evident early on. Mario Amadeo, who held a post in the Ministry of Foreign Affairs during the Ramírez regime, recalled first meeting the personable Perón on July 7, 1943, and being quite favorably impressed by the colonel's abilities. He saw in Perón, at that time, "an authoritarian leader." In the ensuing weeks, as Perón made clear his intention to reach out to Argentine labor, Amadeo noted his own uncertainty that a military person "could become the 'leader' of the proletarian masses" but acknowledged that he generally approved of such an effort if it could be accomplished with continued adherence to the Nacionalista goals of the June Revolution. Although Amadeo does not give a precise date, the hopes of the Nacionalistas in this regard were soon dashed, and the separation between them and Perón was produced "by the concurrent will of both parties." "For Perón's part," Amadeo wrote, "this can be explained by his decision to focus his action on the masses and within his simplistic scheme we were useless 'theorists' and 'intellectuals' without common sense. . . . For our part, we were not long in realizing that personal ambition and the will to power occupied in his spirit a much more important place than the ideals of which for a moment we considered him to be the expression and symbol."[14]

The press of external events provided Perón with further opportunities to strengthen his own hand, although at the same time straining further his relations with the Nacionalistas. A series of defeats for the Axis in Europe, combined with continued pressure from the United States, including U.S. shipments of arms and other favors to its wartime ally Brazil, a matter of great concern to the Argentine military, forced the Ramírez government to reconsider its international stance. Finally, on January 26, 1944, Argentina broke diplomatic relations with Germany and Japan. This decision immediately touched off a major crisis. The GOU, which in September 1943 had threatened to remove the provisional president if he abandoned Argentine neutrality, on February 24, 1944, forced Ramírez's resignation. General Farrell became the new provisional president, and four days later he selected Perón to succeed him as minister of war.

The break with the Axis, a decision that came as a surprise to many, was a severe blow to the Nacionalistas, who reacted angrily and bitterly.[15] Perón, who tried to play a carefully ambiguous role in these events but was seen as a supporter of the break, became a target for Nacionalista ire. For many Nacionalistas, Perón now represented a traitor to their cause, someone who had been willing to sacrifice the principle of neutrality to advance his own ambitions. An April 1, 1944, dispatch from the U.S. embassy in Buenos Aires reported the open hostility that had developed between Perón and "important elements" among the Nacionalistas, underscored by publications that attacked the government and its actions.[16]

Within the new regime the Nacionalista officers rallied around the minister of the interior, General Luis Perlinger. Although shaken by the events of the past few months and increasingly concerned about the activities of Perón, the Nacionalistas remained a potent force within the government. Perón, in turn, sought to eliminate Perlinger from the cabinet as the principal obstacle to the strengthening of his own influence.

The ensuing struggle between Perón and Perlinger lasted through the first half of 1944. It occurred within the context of a continuing crisis over Argentina's position with regard to the world war. The U.S. government, viewing the Farrell regime as uncooperative, unfriendly, and very much under the control of pro-Axis elements, withheld recognition throughout the year and applied whatever pressure it could to force Argentina to take more aggressive actions against the Axis at home and abroad. In March, Perón, through an emissary, made an overture to the U.S. embassy, painting himself as "an opponent of the Nacionalistas" and promising to move toward a restoration of civilian, constitutional government if recognition were granted. The embassy rebuffed the overture, but it showed that Perón was someone with whom it could deal if circumstances should so dictate.[17]

When it became clear by mid-1944 that Perón could not expect much support from the Radicals he was trying to woo, he shifted to a somewhat different direction. On June 10, 1944, he presented a speech at the University of La Plata entitled "The Significance of National Defense from a Military Point of View." In this address, he emphasized the importance of developing a strong national defense based on the ability of the nation to produce its own armaments. The U.S. government interpreted this speech, coming just four days after the Normandy invasion, as "nothing less than the blueprint for the creation of a totalitarian state."[18] This response, plus the content of the speech itself, probably helped to restore partially Perón's own Nacionalista credentials.

In the meantime, the Perón-Perlinger battle continued. In May, Nacionalista Alberto Baldrich became minister of justice and public instruction, an apparent point in Perlinger's favor. At the same time, General Orlando Peluffo, a Perón supporter, became foreign minister. Perón himself became the permanent, as opposed to interim, minister of war. The struggle reached its climax in July, when, in a vote among leading military officers, Perón defeated Perlinger by a narrow margin in a contest to select the person who would fill the vacant vice presidency under Farrell. With this victory, Perón forced Perlinger's resignation, Perlinger taking with him many Nacionalista supporters.[19]

By mid-1944, then, Perón had emerged as the clearly dominant figure within the military regime. In the eyes of the U.S. embassy, his triumph over Perlinger had broken "much of the extremists' power" within the government.[20] Nonetheless, Nacionalistas still held important posts within the Farrell regime and still represented a potent group within the military. Perón, for the moment, had gained the upper hand, but the "extremists" still remained a force with which to be reckoned.

Perón and the Farrell government's relations with the United States were important factors affecting the developments in late 1944 and early 1945. The United States continued to press the regime to take a more definitive pro-Allied position, to move more actively against pro-Axis elements within the country, and to prepare the way for a restoration of democratic government. In support of this effort, the United States held out the promise to Argentina of military equipment and of backing for Argentine participation in the postwar international conference despite the nation's neutrality during the global conflict. Within this larger context, Perón maneuvered to win U.S. favor by continuing his efforts to remove Nacionalistas from crucial government positions and to replace them with his own allies. In late 1944, for example, former GOU member and Nacionalista General Juan Carlos Sanguinetti was replaced by Perón's ally Dr. Juan Atilio Bramuglia as federal interventor in the key province of Buenos Aires. Shortly thereafter, Foreign Minister Peluffo, who Perón now described as "pro-Nazi," submitted his resignation. Later in the year, Perón's ally Juan I. Cooke filled this position. The head of the national gendarmerie and the interventor in the province of Corrientes, both Nacionalistas, were also removed.[21]

In the eyes of the U.S. embassy, Perón at this time was positioning himself to work for a democratic election wherein he would win the presidency "with a genuinely popular majority."[22] This was a desire Perón wished to keep discreetly hidden so as not to stir military opposition, and it is also clear that he considered the Nacionalistas as both an obstacle to and a convenient target and useful tool for the fulfillment of this ambition. Perón's own views on the Nacionalistas are revealed in two separate pieces of diplomatic correspondence. On March 10, 1945, when the British chargé d'affaires Sir Andrew Noble met with Perón to discuss the possibility of an Argentine declaration of war on the Axis, the vice president responded that such a move could be made with little opposition from the army and that the Nacionalistas "were not capable of much more than shouting in the streets."[23] Earlier that month, U.S. chargé Edward Reed, reporting on the general political situation, relayed a conversation with a former officer friend of Perón's who stated that Perón had won "great popularity" in the country at large for his opposition to the Nacionalistas and quoted Perón as saying that if the Nacionalistas "had not existed, he would have been forced to invent them."[24]

On March 27, 1945, the Farrell-Perón regime declared war on Germany and Japan. Nacionalista reaction, fueled by a photograph of a smiling Perón announcing the decision, surrounded by a somber, grim-faced cabinet, was predictably negative. Nacionalista Máximo Etchecopar, for example, writing on March 30, 1945, observed that "the recent declaration of war has been received with undisguised shock. . . . The men of the June Revolution, tireless seekers of popularity, have carried out the most unpopular act possible."[25] But, as Perón himself had predicted, reactions such as Etchecopar's were generally limited to some hostile editorials and street demonstrations. The U.S. embassy pointed out that the measure probably further strengthened Perón, making a possible Nacionalista coup against "a nation already at war with Germany unlikely."[26] Once again Perón had accommodated himself to the reality of the situation and had turned matters to his own advantage, a characteristic that would bring him to power but do little to endear him to the more ideological and inflexible Nacionalistas. As Perón's biographer Joseph Page has remarked, "expediency always enjoyed first priority in Perón's scheme of things. He would never sacrifice practicality on the altar of ideological coherence."[27]

The Peronist Policy Toward the Right

By mid-1945, Perón was poised to assume total control. He had eliminated potential Nacionalista rivals, continued to gain support in the army and among the working classes, and helped to dissipate some of the hostility between Argentina and the United States. He continued, too, to seek links with various Radical party sectors, albeit with mixed results. Responding to external and internal pressures, the Farrell regime gradually began to loosen the authoritarian controls that had been in place from the time of the June 4 coup. The government restored autonomy to the universities, lifted restrictions on press and other freedoms, allowed political parties to reorganize and resume normal activities, and scheduled elections to return Argentina to constitutional and democratic rule.

With the return to normality, Perón sought to position himself for a future election victory. At the same time, however, greater political freedom presented Perón with opposition, which included most of the major established parties and the press, that now could seize opportunities to attack publicly the military government of which Perón was the most prominent figure. The main thrust of their criticism was that while the world at large, due to the Allied military victory, was entering a new period of democratic freedoms, Argentina still suffered under a regime that smacked of the discredited and defeated fascist dictatorships. The efforts of the opposition culminated on

September 19, 1945, in a massive public demonstration in Buenos Aires for the restoration of "The Constitution and Liberty."

Aiding the opposition was the new U.S. ambassador, Spruille Braden, who viewed Perón as a fascist anachronism and who feared that Argentina under Perón would serve as a haven for fugitive Nazis and as a launching pad for a new Nazi try at world conquest. In a July 11, 1945, telegram from Buenos Aires, for example, Braden noted that "Perón as the one outstanding leader now on the Argentine scene is the embodiment of present Fascist military control."[28] When Braden was recalled to Washington later in the year to serve as assistant secretary of state for inter-American affairs, his successor in Buenos Aires, John Cabot, took some issue with Braden's assessment. In dispatches to the State Department, Cabot argued that Perón and the situation in Argentina were too complex to be labeled in simple terms. In one communication, Cabot argued that "there is a fairly impressive amount of evidence to indicate that Argentina is not and can never become truly fascist," and in another he claimed that to see Perón merely as a fascist demagogue was to oversimplify matters and to ignore his cleverness, opportunism, and widespread support from the working classes.[29] Cabot's advice notwithstanding, Braden continued to consider Perón to be Argentina's version of Europe's deposed dictators and to try to influence Argentine affairs so as to deny Perón the power he sought.[30]

The growing public opposition to the Farrell-Perón regime resulted in a major crisis in October 1945. A combination of Nacionalista and liberal army officers, aided by certain civilian elements, managed to force Perón from office on October 9. After a dramatic and chaotic few days, a mass demonstration of working-class support on October 17 led to the release of Perón from military arrest and the announcement of his presidential candidacy in elections scheduled for February 1946.

The ensuing election campaign quickly polarized Argentine society. Opposed to Perón was a coalition of the established political parties, most importantly the Radicals, the Democratic Progressives, the Socialists, the Communists, and some Conservatives, united under the banner of the Unión Democrática. In general terms, the Unión represented the interests of the upper and middle classes and some established labor unions. Perón, for his part, organized his own party, the Partido Laborista, virtually from scratch, although it benefited greatly from labor union structures already in place. Perón's party, also in general terms, was based essentially on the working classes, although some middle-class elements, including dissident Radicals, joined its ranks as well. Also crucial to Perón's efforts was the backing he received from the Catholic church due to his promise to retain religious instruction in the public schools if elected.[31]

The U.S. embassy, reporting on the swearing in of a new cabinet on October 22, 1945, indicated that the Nacionalistas now appeared to back Perón.[32] This backing continued throughout the election campaign, which culminated in Perón's victory. However, Nacionalista support for Perón was neither especially visible, enthusiastic, nor influential. Nacionalistas had serious reservations about and objections to Perón's strategy of developing a mass base of popular support among the laboring classes. They also had been disappointed by his apparent betrayal of their position with regard to foreign policy and had suffered serious losses of personnel and influence as he had maneuvered for his own advantage in the various administrations that followed the June coup. Moreover, they were unhappy with aspects of his personal life, especially the open relationship he enjoyed with Eva ("Evita") Duarte, who became his second wife, and her increasing prominence in his public life as well. This relationship clearly clashed with the kind of high-flown moral standards that the Nacionalistas preached as essential elements of Argentina's national and spiritual salvation.[33]

On the other hand, Perón was a powerful candidate with a good chance to win, perhaps in the process opening the way for renewed Nacionalista influence. His stance on certain issues, especially his flailing of the oligarchy and foreign capital and his support for religious instruction in the schools, was certainly compatible with Nacionalista thinking. In Nacionalista eyes, Perón was obviously preferable to his opponent, José Tamborini of the Unión Democrática. Tamborini, a longtime Radical party stalwart, represented for the Nacionalistas all the discredited policies of a past dominated by democratic liberalism. To make matters worse, the Unión included the Socialist and Communist parties. Also it bore a clear stamp of approval from the United States, which tried to influence the election. In February 1946 the U.S. government, in the person of Spruille Braden, issued the famous *Blue Book*, which attempted to link Perón to Nazis inside and outside of Argentina. Named as well in the *Blue Book* were various Nacionalistas, who quickly denied that they had any links to the Axis.[34] The ultimate result of Braden's efforts was to strengthen Perón's own nationalist position.[35]

The Nacionalistas were not particularly noticeable in the Perón campaign. Perón depended for advice and support primarily on his labor and military allies. According to Marysa Navarro Gerassi, the Perón campaign offered Nacionalistas the chance for twelve seats in the Chamber of Deputies, but only two individuals—the historian Ernesto Palacio of the federal capital and Joaquín Díaz de Vivar of Corrientes—accepted positions on the Partido Laborista slates in their respective districts.[36]

An exception to this generally low Nacionalista profile was the Alianza Libertadora Nacionalista. On the one hand, the ALN engaged in a variety of violent actions against Jewish and Communist groups, serving as a kind of paramilitary force against opponents of Perón. For example, in late December 1945 the Alianza held a large rally in the Luna Park Stadium in the capital, where various speakers extolled the virtues of former dictator Juan Manuel de Rosas and strongly attacked the diplomatic representatives of Great Britain and the United States, especially Braden, for their efforts to influence

Argentine internal affairs. Following the meeting, members of the ALN
marched through the streets of Buenos Aires, shouting their opposition to
Jews and the democratic press and throwing rocks against the buildings of
various political groups affiliated with the Unión Democrática. The pro-Perón
police did little to restrain these activities.[37]

On the other hand, although the ALN ceremoniously installed Perón as its
symbolic leader and generally backed his presidential campaign, it also determined to break with Nacionalista tradition and enter its own congressional
candidates for the federal capital and in the province of Buenos Aires in the
February elections. The candidate list selected in the capital was headed by
Juan Queraltó, the principal leader of the Alianza, and included intellectuals,
professionals, and retired military officers, several of whom had been appointed to positions in the various administrations of the recent past, and a
Jesuit priest, Leonardo Castellani. The attempt by this particular Nacionalista
group to achieve a presence of its own in the new national congress proved
futile in the extreme. In the February elections the Alianza list polled less than
4 percent of the vote in the capital and less than 1 percent in the province of
Buenos Aires.[38] There could be no more eloquent testimony of the failure of
"pure" Nacionalismo to develop its own base of popular support.

The Nacionalista Response to Peronism

Although the Nacionalistas were not prominent in the Perón campaign itself,
an argument could be made that their activities prior to 1946 did contribute to
his triumph. They had attacked the oligarchy, the British, the North Ameri-
cans, the established political parties, and foreign investment, in sum, the
status quo ante, and had helped to establish the background for many of
Perón's arguments. Nacionalista calls for national greatness, greater sovereignty, and the leadership of a new generation were also themes of which
Perón took advantage.

Whatever their contributions to his triumph, either direct or indirect, once
in office Perón paid little attention to the Nacionalistas. A few were given
posts within the new regime, but the people closest to Perón and most
influential within his government were labor and military allies of the same
pragmatic persuasion as their chief. Although Nacionalistas struggled for
greater influence, by the end of 1947 whatever leverage they once had enjoyed
seemed to have withered away as several appointees lost out in bureaucratic
infighting and resigned from the government.[39] Under Perón, various
Nacionalista publications ceased to appear, and many groups either dissolved
completely or engaged in only sporadic meetings. The ALN, described in
1954 by the U.S. State Department as "the country's principal ultranationalist
organization," did retain something of a presence and continued to support
Perón.[40] In 1948, however, the ALN again put forth a list of candidates in the

national congressional elections and again received only a scattering of votes.[41] This was the last time the ALN entered the electoral arena.

During the first half of the Perón regime, the Nacionalistas could find little to which they might object. Indeed, in certain areas it seemed as though Perón was adhering strictly to the agenda they had helped to set. His moves with regard to economic nationalism, for example, notably the nationalization of the British-owned railroads in 1948, met with general approval from the Nacionalistas, although some believed that the terms of settlement were too generous. Perón's foreign policy, based on a strong military, which sought to establish a leadership role for Argentina in Latin America while adopting an independent "Third Position" vis-à-vis the evolving confrontation between the United States and the Soviet Union, also met with Nacionalista approval. Perón, too, was very much a nationalist in the broad sense of the term. He constantly emphasized the importance of the *patria*, the homeland, to whose greater interests, he argued, all individual concerns should be subordinated. He also seemed to bridge successfully the gap between Buenos Aires and the provinces, amalgamating the interests of the *porteños* and the *provincianos*, particularly as represented by the old immigrant and the new migrant working classes, not only by providing concrete benefits but also by appealing to nationalist, criollo traditions. An anti-Marxist, he stressed the need for national unity through class conciliation rather than through class struggle.

Perón also was a strong, charismatic, and authoritarian leader, ruling with firmness and relegating the "liberal" opposition to minor roles in the management of national affairs. The great international tide of fascism and fascist leaders of the 1920s, 1930s, and early 1940s that had encouraged and sustained many Nacionalistas had been beaten back by the mid-1940s, with only Perón's friend Francisco Franco of Spain a surviving vestige of that era. New circumstances and new forces, both domestic and international, forced the Nacionalistas to adapt to a new reality where the overall climate was less favorable to them than it had been previously. Given these new circumstances, Perón and Peronism seemed acceptable alternatives to many associated with Nacionalismo.

Nonetheless, there were aspects of Perón and Peronismo that bothered the Nacionalistas. Most obvious, if perhaps less openly stated, was that they enjoyed little prominence or influence within either the government or the Peronista party. Where they had been major actors in the events of 1943 to 1946, with, at that time, real opportunities to take and wield power, under Perón they had become minor and inconsequential figures. Their only remaining important presence was in various university positions, where they spent much of their time trying to counter student opposition.[42] On another level, many Nacionalistas had been always less than enthusiastic about Perón's social policies and the benefits that grew significantly in size and scope in the early years of his government. The increasingly visible and important role of

Evita, now Perón's wife and principal political ally, also evoked their displeasure. The Nacionalistas distrusted Perón's pragmatism. They had seen him abandon principle to expediency many times in the 1943–1946 period and in the process, while reaching for power for himself, running roughshod over any Nacionalista who got in his way. Moreover, for some Nacionalistas, Perón was too democratic, too concerned with majority rule than with what they felt should be the proper direction of the state. Some believed also that Perón should have developed a competent elite to manage the nation's affairs and direct its destiny rather than surround himself with what they regarded as unqualified and incompetent bureaucratic hacks. It does not take too much imagination to guess who the Nacionalistas believed should constitute this directive elite.[43]

Perón's attitude toward Argentina's substantial Jewish community also reflected the basic pragmatism that Nacionalistas distrusted. Although he did little to restrain the anti-Semitic attacks of groups such as the ALN during his rise to power, Perón as president, seeking to incorporate all the nation's groups into his coalition, reached out to the Jews of Argentina with a mixture of conciliatory rhetoric and concrete benefits. For example, positions were opened to Jews in areas from which they previously had been excluded, such as the diplomatic service and the army, and a few rose to prominent status within the Peronist party. "With all his flaws," Robert Weisbrot has concluded, "Perón . . . evolved into a president who was one of the most benevolent toward the Jewish community in modern Argentine history."[44] Although the horrors of the Holocaust caused the Nacionalistas to downplay their anti-Semitism in the postwar years, it can be presumed that Perón's "benevolence" toward the Jews was still one more disappointment for them.

Some Nacionalistas made public their concerns with and criticisms of Perón rather early on. A leading figure in this regard was the Catholic priest and philosopher Julio Meinvielle. In 1946, Meinvielle and several Nacionalista intellectuals published a periodical entitled *Balcón*, from which they expressed their objections to certain aspects of Perón's policies and his behavior. Two measures on the international front received particular criticism: the negotiation in 1946 of a trade and financial agreement with Great Britain (Miranda-Eady) and Perón's decision in 1947 to urge congressional ratification of the Treaty of Chapultepec. Both of these moves, the Nacionalistas argued, cast serious doubts on Perón's commitment to economic nationalism and his reputation as a defender of Argentine sovereignty in the face of U.S. pressure and influence.[45]

In 1949, Meinvielle founded another periodical, *Presencia*, which appeared regularly until mid-1951. In various editorials in *Presencia*, Meinvielle noted his admiration for certain of Perón's accomplishments, particularly the advances for the working classes. Nevertheless, he became increasingly critical of what he saw as the excesses that accompanied Peronism, most notably the massive growth of the state, the cult of personality, and Perón's penchant for surrounding himself with mediocre sycophants of little real ability. From the beginning, Meinvielle saw Perón's economic policies as unsound, leading to a persistent inflation that undermined working-class benefits and gravely weakened the nation as a whole. With regard to foreign policy, although he admitted the virtues of the "Third Position," he argued that the new international context created by the Cold War made it incumbent on all American nations to support the United States in its battle against the Soviet Union and atheistic communism. By the time of Perón's presidential reelection in 1951, Meinvielle had concluded that Perón was in danger, perhaps unwittingly, of leading the country toward some kind of communistic dictatorship of the proletariat. In the last analysis, according to Meinvielle, the Perón regime had failed to achieve a thoroughgoing Nacionalista revolution because of its obsession with material concerns and its failure to incorporate Catholic spiritual values into its overall framework of state organization and direction.[46]

The argument that Perón had failed to seize the opportunity to bring about a true revolution in Argentina was one repeated by several Nacionalista critics. Máximo Etchecopar, who had accepted a diplomatic post under Perón, writing in the journal *Quincena*, which he had founded along with several other Nacionalistas and which appeared between 1953 and 1954, noted that "Peronism did not propose seriously to change the institutions in place up to 1943, nor even to renovate them; it limited itself to displacing the Argentine problem from the political to the social; it believed that it was sufficient to inject into the old democratic hulk a growing dose of social justice. No, Peronism is not a revolution. Its greatest ambition consists in convincing, in persuading and adding converts to its justicialist [the official Peronist ideology] creed."[47] Much the same argument was put forth by other Nacionalistas who expressed their opinions in writing after the ouster of Perón in 1955.[48]

Another prominent Nacionalista critic of Perón was Julio Irazusta, a well-known revisionist historian. Irazusta, according to a leading student of Argentine Nacionalisimo, represented a current called "republican nationalism," which had as its main object "*National emancipation* from the plutocratic regime placed at the service of the interests of foreign imperialism, particularly British."[49] A contributor to *Presencia*, Irazusta repeated the claim that Perón had failed to carry out a successful "nationalist" revolution. In works published after Perón's fall, Irazusta especially faulted the former president for not going farther in nationalizing the Argentine economy and severely criticized the various arrangements Perón had made with Great Britain, arguing that despite their apparent advantages, they really operated to the detriment of the nation's best interests. Detailing these measures, he claimed that, overall, Perón's "supposed economic nationalism was always found in words, never in deeds."[50]

These critics and their criticism, while articulating Nacionalista disillusionment with Perón, represented for most of this period isolated and not very significant voices in the opposition wilderness. Many Nacionalistas either kept their peace or, like the "republican nationalist" historian Ernesto Palacio, maintained their support for Perón. By the early 1950s, Perón had co-opted most of the Nacionalistas' ideas he found suitable for his own purposes and had reduced their organizations and publications to either little-noticed opponents or, as in the case of the ALN, obedient supporters of his regime.

At the same time, however, Nacionalista criticisms of Perón began to become part of a larger tide of opposition. As Argentina's favorable postwar economic situation began to deteriorate, a decline that was aggravated, according to critics, by the regime's poorly conceived and managed economic and social policies, a broader opposition began to build. In late 1951, Nacionalista General Benjamín Menéndez organized a coup that proved unsuccessful but that also served as a sign of discontent and of things to come. As economic conditions worsened, Perón was forced to negotiate loans from the United States and to allow American companies, particularly oil companies, greater access to Argentine markets and resources. These concessions angered nationalists of both the left and the right. Following the death of Evita in 1952, Perón embarked on a course of personal conduct, including relations with teen-age girls, that offended not only the moralistic sensibilities of the Catholic nationalists but also the many supporters who cherished the image of the deceased first lady. This overall economic and moral decline also made the excessive bureaucratic growth and governmental corruption of Perón's regime, which critics like Meinvielle had noted earlier, less acceptable than they had been when times were good and popular support was widespread.

The final break between Perón and the Nacionalistas—and many others—came when the caudillo turned against the church in 1954. In the course of this struggle, Perón legalized divorce and lifted restrictions on prostitution, measures that directly attacked the Nacionalistas' view of the importance of the family and the appropriate moral climate for the nation. Writing after the fact, Nacionalista Bonifacio del Carril claimed that the church's support of Perón had been a mistake from the beginning because "the Catholicism of Perón was always merely superficial, the Catholicism of a taxi driver who places the image of the Virgin of Luján in his vehicle, but basically is quite ignorant about the role of priests in society!"[51] In other words, Perón again had proved to be an unprincipled politician who cut his cloth to suit his own purposes and who once more had betrayed those who had placed their faith in him.

In the struggle to overthrow Perón, the Nacionalistas found themselves again allied with sympathetic military officers, as they had been in 1943, as well as with—probably to their discomfort—representatives of the Unión Democrática such as the Radicals and Socialists. Some of the themes were familiar; once more they were opposing a government that had become corrupt, demagogic, and weak to the point where external influences might threaten national sovereignty. On the other hand, many Nacionalistas also criticized Perón for his excessive concentration of power, his antidemocratic proclivities, and the general "loss of public liberties" in the latter stages of the regime.[52] Several Nacionalistas, including Mario Amadeo and Bonifacio del Carril, were active participants in the movements and events that led to the military ouster of Perón in September 1955. Among the last-ditch defenders of the government, however, was the Alianza Libertadora Nacionalista, whose resistance to the coup ended only when army tanks destroyed its headquarters.[53]

Conclusion

The debate over the nature of Peronism is an extensive and continuing one. Those who see Perón as a fascist and Peronism as fascism point to his European experiences and the influence of the examples of Mussolini and Franco on him, the authoritarian and centralized nature of his rule, the development of a strong, personalized political party that he tightly controlled, the attempts to use public education and the means of propaganda to develop a cult of personality, the elaborate ritualistic character of the regime, and the aggressive nationalism that Perón articulated and promoted.[54] Critics of this view emphasize the differences between Peronism and examples of European fascism, especially the retention of most democratic institutions, including elections, the tolerance of often more than just a token opposition, the support of the working class (as opposed to the disaffected middle class) as the principal popular foundation of the movement, and an overall historical context much different from that which prevailed in Europe in the 1920s and 1930s.[55]

Although this debate continues, it is certain that those elements in Argentina most closely associated with fascism, namely the Nacionalistas, did not see Perón as one of their own, nor did he consider himself part of their movement. Whereas at first Perón seemed to some Nacionalistas to be the answer to their prayers, it soon became clear to them that Perón was most concerned with his own ambitions and his own agenda, not theirs. As Perón maneuvered for power between 1943 and 1946, he used the Nacionalistas and their ideas when it suited his convenience and ignored or discarded them when they did not. Once in power, Perón did adopt certain aspects of the Nacionalista program, although it could be argued that he borrowed as much from left nationalism as from the right.[56] But he depended on a very different set of allies and advisers than had his immediate predecessors, and the considerable influence the Nacionalistas had enjoyed from time to time after 1943 dwindled conspicuously after 1946. Eventually, most Nacionalistas came to oppose Perón and to participate, along with sectors of society and the political structure that they had long vilified, in the movement to overthrow him. Throughout this period, as before, they failed to develop any real popular base of their own and only enjoyed a chance for power through the intervention of others or due to chance circumstance. Their disillusionment with and

distancing from Perón only underscored and magnified the Nacionalistas'
own failures to provide the Argentine people with a convincing political
alternative to realize the profound national renovation they sought to lead.

Notes

1. Ysabel F. Rennie, *The Argentine Republic* (New York, 1945), 273–74, 277–79.
2. Marysa Navarro Gerassi, *Los nacionalistas* (Buenos Aires, 1969), 155; Oscar Troncoso, *Los nacionalistas argentinos* (Buenos Aires, 1957), 62.
3. Argentine sociologist José Luis de Imaz joined the ALN when he was a sixteen-year-old high school student. He recalls his impressions of that experience in his *Promediados de los cuarenta (no pesa la mochila)* (Buenos Aires, 1977).
4. Marysa Navarro Gerassi, "Argentine Nationalism of the Right," *Studies in Comparative International Development* 1, no. 12 (1965): 182.
5. Navarro, *Los nacionalistas*, 173. Arturo Jauretche recalled that the leaders of the ALN were the "poor relations" of the oligarchy, that is, people with aristocratic names but not much money (Arturo Jauretche, interview by Luis Alberto Romero, April 1971, Instituto Torcuato Di Tella, Buenos Aires).
6. The themes that the ALN sought to emphasize are well reflected in Bonifacio Lastra, *Bajo el signo nacionalista* (Buenos Aires, 1944).
7. Rennie, *Argentine Republic*, 266–84.
8. For more on the 1943 coup and the role of the GOU see Enrique Díaz Araujo, *La conspiración del '43: El GOU: Una experiencia militarista en la Argentina* (Buenos Aires, 1971); Marvin Goldwert, *Democracy, Militarism and Nationalism in Argentina, 1930–1966: An Interpretation* (Austin, 1972), 58–93; Robert A. Potash, *The Army and Politics in Argentina, 1928–1945: Yrigoyen to Perón* (Stanford, 1969), 182–282; and Robert A. Potash, ed., *Perón y el GOU: Los documentos de una logia secreta* (Buenos Aires, 1984).
9. *Cabildo* hailed the June 4 coup as the "triumph of the national spirit" (*Cabildo*, June 5, 1943). For similarly favorable Nacionalista reactions see Lastra, *Bajo el signo nacionalista*, 163–76; and Marcelo Sánchez Sorondo, "Discurso a los militares," in his *La revolución que anunciamos* (Buenos Aires, 1945), 251–59.
10. Ambassador Norman Armour to Secretary of State Cordell Hull, June 6, 1943, 835.00/1454, U.S., Department of State, *Papers Relating to the Foreign Relations of the United States, 1943*, 6 vols., Washington, DC, 1965, 5:367 (hereafter cited as *FRUS*).
11. For a review of these developments see Díaz Araujo, *La conspiración*, 203–67; and Potash, *Army and Politics*, 201–30.
12. Rennie, *Argentine Republic*, 368–83. For a discussion of compulsory religious education see John J. Kennedy, *Catholicism, Nationalism and Democracy in Argentina* (Notre Dame, IN, 1958), 186–201.
13. Díaz Araujo, *La conspiración*, 211–12.
14. Mario Amadeo, *Ayer, hoy, mañana* (Buenos Aires, 1956), 18–21.
15. For the Nacionalista reaction see Díaz Araujo, *La conspiración*, 253–67, and Gontrán de Güemes, *Asi se gestó la dictadura* (Buenos Aires, 1956), 88–89.
16. Armour to Secretary of State, April 1, 1944, 835.00/2769, in U.S., Department of State, *Records Relating to the Internal Affairs of Argentina 1940–1949*, Record Group 59, National Archives, Washington, DC (hereafter cited as Embassy Dispatch, with date and file number).
17. Potash, *Army and Politics*, 242–43.

18. Joseph A. Page, *Perón: A Biography* (New York, 1983), 73–74.

19. Potash, *Army and Politics*, 247–48.

20. "Summary Statement on the Situation of the Farrell Government, October 7, 1944," 835.00/10-744, *FRUS, 1944* 7:287–88.

21. Díaz Araujo, *La conspiración*, 273; Embassy Dispatch, January 20, 1945, 835.00/1-2045.

22. Ibid.

23. Bryce Wood, *The Dismantling of the Good Neighbor Policy* (Austin, 1985), 88.

24 .Embassy Dispatch, March 2, 1945, 835.00/3-245.

25. Máximo Etchecopar, *Con mi generación* (Buenos Aires, 1946), 119.

26. Embassy Dispatch, March 29, 1945, 835.00/3-2945.

27. Page, *Perón*, 89.

28. Spruille Braden to Secretary of State James F. Byrnes, July 11, 1945, 711.35/ 7-1145, *FRUS, 1945* 9:391–93.

29. John Cabot (chargé in Argentina) to Ellis O. Briggs (director, Office of American Republic Affairs), November 17, 1945, 835.00/11-1745, *FRUS, 1945* 9:426–34; Embassy Dispatch, January 9, 1946, 835.00/1-946.

30. For a review of Braden's attitudes toward and actions against Perón see Gary Frank, *Juan Perón vs. Spruille Braden: The Story Behind the Blue Book* (Lanham, MD, 1980).

31. For a detailed description and analysis of these developments see Félix Luna, *El 45: Crónica de un año decisivo*, 3d ed. (Buenos Aires, 1971).

32. Embassy Dispatch, October 24, 1945, 835.00/10-2445.

33. At least one group of "moderate" Nacionalistas, whose chief was Bonifacio del Carril, actively opposed the election of Perón, labeling him a demogogue, hypocrite, and would-be totalitarian dictator—"el primer mentiroso de la República." See "Vote contra el dictador," in Bonifacio del Carril, *Crónica interna de la revolución liberatadora* (Buenos Aires, 1959), 231–36.

34. Amadeo, *Ayer*, 23–24.

35. Frank, *Perón vs. Braden*, 95–108.

36. Navarro, *Los nacionalistas*, 193.

37. *La Prensa*, December 23, 1945.

38. Darío Cantón, *Materiales para el estudio de la sociología política en la Argentina*, 2 vols. (Buenos Aires, 1968), 1:133.

39. Embassy Dispatch, December 19, 1947, 835.00/12-1947.

40. "National Intelligence Estimate: Probable Developments in Argentina, March 9, 1954," *FRUS, 1953–1954* 6:457.

41. *La Prensa*, April 1, 1948.

42. Bernardo Kleiner, *20 años de movimiento estudiantil reformista: 1943–1963* (Buenos Aires, 1964), 65–139.

43. A leading Nacionalista spokesperson for this point of view was Máximo Etchecopar. See "La clase necesaria (Lo que hoy ha de entenderse por clase dirigente)," in his *Esquema de la Argentina* (Buenos Aires, 1966), 196–208.

44. Robert Weisbrot, *The Jews of Argentina: From the Inquisition to Perón* (Philadelphia, 1979), 240.

45. For more information on these issues see Page, *Perón*, 171, 184–85. For the Nacionalista response see Enrique Zuleta Alvarez, *El nacionalismo argentino*, 2 vols. (Buenos Aires, 1975), 2:527–34.

46. Many of Meinvielle's editorials in *Presencia* were reprinted in his *Política Argentina, 1949–1956* (Buenos Aires, 1956). See also Zuleta Alvarez, *Nacionalismo argentino* 2:534–45.

47. Etchecopar, *Esquema*, 51.

48. For example, see Amadeo, *Ayer*, 96–97, and José María de Estrada, *El legado del nacionalismo* (Buenos Aires, 1956), 76–86.

49. Zuleta Alvarez, *Nacionalismo argentino* 2:478.

50. Julio Irazusta, *Perón y la crisis argentina* (Buenos Aires, 1956), 173. See also Irazusta, *Balance de siglo y medio* (Buenos Aires, 1966).

51. Carril, *Crónica interna*, 38.

52. For example, see Amadeo, *Ayer*, 27–28.

53. Navarro, *Los nacionalistas*, 213.

54. For an argument in favor of the thesis that Perón was a fascist see Paul H. Lewis, "Was Perón a Fascist? An Inquiry into the Nature of Fascism," *Journal of Politics* 42, no. 1 (February 1980): 242–56. For a more general discussion of the problem see Carlos S. Fayt et al., *La naturaleza del peronismo* (Buenos Aires, 1967).

55. Most current scholarship argues that Perón was not a fascist but rather was some kind of a populist. For the latest work in English to make this argument see Robert D. Crassweller, *Perón and the Enigmas of Argentina* (New York, 1987), esp. 220–26. For the latest and most convincing work in Spanish in this regard see Cristián Buchrucker, *Nacionalismo y peronismo: La Argentina en la crisis ideológica mundial, 1927–1955* (Buenos Aires, 1987). For a good theoretical study of the question see Gino Germani, *Authoritarianism, Fascism, and National Populism* (New Brunswick, NJ, 1978).

56. Buchrucker argues that the "populist nationalism" of the FORJA had much more influence on Perón than the "restorative nationalism" of the right. Buchrucker, *Nacionalismo y peronismo*, 208–310.

The Right and Civilian Regimes, 1955–1976*

Leonardo Senkman

[*Editors' Note:* The contemporary period of Argentine history begins in 1955. In September of that year the military overthrew Juan Domingo Perón, who had ruled for a decade. Although Perón was forced to leave Argentina, his movement and his followers were the most powerful political force in the nation and would remain so. The result was that the "Peronist Question" dominated Argentina's politics as well as its economy, society, and culture. The pronouncements of *El Líder* in exile, the divisions among his lieutenants in Argentina, the reactions of his enemies, and the attempts to return the Peronists to office remained the overwhelming issues of concern to Argentines, even after Perón's death.

The fixation on Peronism controlled the right's programs and actions just as it did those of other sectors. The right believed that the Revolución Libertadora, which had overthrown Perón, was once again the military uprising that was meant to install it in power, because the nation had no other alternative to continued Peronist chaos. Argentina fell into a dreary cycle of military regimes forced to give way to weak civilian administrations, that in turn were unable to fend off new army takeovers, all in an effort to prevent the return of Peronism. The right played significant roles in both the military and civilian governments, but the ultimate power to achieve its objectives, which changed little through a half century, remained elusive.

The most important development for the right after Perón involved another pattern characteristic of its history in Argentina, the appearance of a new group that challenged the old leaders. In this case the return of Peronism to power in 1973 caused the Peronists themselves to split into two major factions: a Peronist left that called for socialist-leaning nationalist politics and in the name of "true" Peronism turned to guerrilla warfare against the government, and a Peronist right that declared itself loyal to Perón and the

---

*Translated by Donna Mellen, University of Texas at El Paso; edited by Sandra McGee Deutsch and Ronald H. Dolkart.

established unions. This Peronist right soon found itself making common cause with the old, or "liberal," right and with the Nacionalistas to suppress leftist violence. Equally significant, the Peronist right soon adopted many of the principles of its predecessors and came to consider itself the primary force within the right.

Thus, the history of the right has continued unremittingly to dominate—and to mirror—Argentine politics in the twentieth century. As the nation's politics increasingly became fragmented and complex after 1955, so too did the right.]

The alternation of civilian and military governments during the post-Peronist period demonstrated Argentina's political instability. This instability, in turn, indicated the failure of the military, with its authoritarian concepts, to reorder, remedy, and control Argentina's society and economy. Most researchers have concentrated on investigating Peronism and its role, from 1955 on, as the principal arbiter in determining the nation's political divisions and alliances. Recently, historians and political scientists also have analyzed what has come to be called the "bureaucratic-authoritarian state," in an effort to understand how the military could take over government from civilians and restructure society through drastic and repressive economic measures. But little research has been done on the participants, particularly on the adherents of rightist factions, in the transitional phases of the redemocratization process.[1] This essay will analyze two important periods leading toward democracy in Argentina, 1955 to 1966 and 1973 to 1976, and the part that rightist factions played in this process.

During these years the traditional sectors of the Argentine right often played a legislative role in the guise of centrist parties characterized as anti-Peronist and antileftist but not allied with the old Radical forces. In reality, these parties were disjointed factions, each with a small electoral base obsessed primarily with banning, later with neutralizing, Peronism. Ultimately, they sought to control organized labor, in which they recognized only the infamous power of the strong Peronist unions. Moreover, the old Conservatives formed an alliance with the traditional provincial parties that had a broader base of support. Their votes had sustained the first Peronist administration, and the groups' leader, Vicente Solano Lima, was vice president during the third Peronist administration (1973–74).[2]

The legislative performance of these rightist factions, however, does not show their true political influence during the democratic transitions. Thus the focus in what follows is on the actions and rhetoric of the "extraparliamentary" right, on its connections, particularly with the Peronist right, on the recurrent motives for its actions, and on its ideological influence.

The Right in the Transition to Democratization (1955–1966)

After the Revolución Libertadora overthrew Perón in September 1955, questions of a return to democracy, constitutional reform, and revival of republican institutions immediately arose. However, the armed forces, as well as the civilian political blocs supporting the revolution, were divided by their attitudes toward Peronism. The liberal so-called Gorillas—that is, the extreme anti-Peronists—forced Perón's successor, General Eduardo Lonardi, to resign, accusing him of complicity with the Nacionalistas and of tolerating Peronism and the workers' movement. Eventually, however, the Gorillas would have to face the social and labor consequences of banning Peronism and persecuting the masses.

The sociopolitical problem of Peronism was not resolved by the military, which surrendered its tutelary intervention by allowing elections to take place in 1958. The succeeding civilian administration had as much difficulty as the military had had in governing because the powerful Peronist unions had been able to grow and advance even under repression and political proscription. After 1955 the right realized that the strength of Peronism was increasing outside the government, from which it had been proscribed, and that it was necessary to neutralize or limit the movement's growing operations and coalitions. Yet the attitudes and policies of the various rightist factions—the liberal Gorilla right, the Peronist right, the Nacionalista antiliberal right—differed markedly.

The Liberal Right

The old right of classical liberalism continued to exist after 1955 as an alliance of business organizations, small conservative parties, and anti-Peronist military contingents. They coalesced not only in reaction against Peronism but also, eventually, against the two factions of the Unión Cívica Radical (UCR). The Unión Cívica Radical del Pueblo (UCRP), headed by Ricardo Balbín, shared the Gorilla position of the liberal right and thus until the early 1960s favored banning Peronism at the polls. Balbín's UCRP championed a revision of the union system that would atomize the corporative organization of the Peronist working class. Yet at the same time the UCRP's redistributionist economic policies resembled those of Peronism.

The UCRP's rival, the Unión Cívica Radical Intransigente (UCRI) of President Arturo Frondizi (1958–1962), stood for *desarrollismo*, or developmentalism, which meant government efforts to promote industrialization. As an advocate of the free market and opponent of state intervention, the liberal right suspected that developmentalism threatened its interests. Nevertheless, until 1962 the liberal right supported Frondizi, particularly once he had implemented a stabilization program involving steep monetary devaluation and a wage freeze and had demonstrated that he had renounced his previous pro-Peronist "national and popular" program to attract foreign capital to the energy, transportation, and communication sectors of the nation. However, his approval of the Law of Professional Associations, which extended legal recognition to only one union within each branch of industry and established a collective-bargaining system under state intervention, strengthened the hand of the Confederación General del Trabajo (CGT) and therefore outraged the liberal faction of the right.[3] Indeed, the president's reluctance to abolish the CGT, and his vacillation over banning Peronism in legislative and provincial elections, exacerbated the conflict between the liberal right and Frondizi.[4]

In 1962 and 1963 the liberal right switched its allegiance to the UCRP because of UCRP stands against Peronism and the consolidation of unions, and even though President Arturo Illia (1963–1966) of the UCRP adopted an economic policy opposed to the free-market concept. Yet as Illia's administration progressed, the liberal right realized that it was failing to achieve its fundamental strategic objectives: eradication of Peronism and modification of Peronism's state-controlled industrial policy. The liberal right's eventual repudiation of both of the UCR factions indicated its failure to create a political regime based on an alliance of anti-Peronist parties and a return to the republican parliamentary system. Ultimately, the bourgeoisie's increasingly rightist tendencies would lead it to choose the antidemocratic option of military *golpismo* (coups) to increase the likelihood of success for its socioeconomic programs, in disregard of the parliamentary and institutional democratization that had been attempted after 1955.

The liberal right, then, accepted that there was a need for military intervention in Argentina's politics between 1955 and 1966. Like the military, it wished to hinder the advancement of Peronist unions and, after 1959, the mobilization of the radical left, whose extraparliamentary operations were perceived as dangerous threats to the restricted participatory democracy that had been established in 1955. This right blamed both the UCRI and the UCRP administrations for not repressing these leftist movements. Mainly for this reason the liberal right backed the takeover of the Argentine government by the military, headed by General Juan Carlos Onganía, in 1966. This support also was due in part to the right's realization during this period that it would be impossible to recover a significant electoral base within the process of redemocratization.

The Peronist Labor Right

The Peronist unions' tactics after 1955, as devised by the unions' new leaders, managed to overcome the electoral restrictions that had been placed on this movement. Successful union strategies for collective bargaining and industrial relations obliged representatives from business associations and the state to negotiate with these unions. The proletarianization of the Peronist movement during Perón's prolonged exile indicated the relative power that unions attained after 1955. They replaced the outlawed political wing of Peronism as the main agent for pressure and negotiation. As a consequence, when bans against Peronism at the polls were lifted, union leaders and members played an influential role in politics, often in a way separate from Perón's own strategies. Such was the case of Augusto T. Vandor, secretary general of the powerful Unión Obrera Metalúrgica (UOM), who led the CGT. With his leadership, an entirely distinct current of Peronist unionism, Vandorismo, emerged, which favored the independence of that movement from *El Líder*. Vandor's tactic, used frequently during Illia's administration, was to strengthen the union bureaucracy and to employ aggressive tactics in bargaining with big business and military groups. His concept of corporative unionism—labor as a partner within a system of power based on economic growth and stability guaranteed by a strong state, large industries, and army officers—legitimized this Peronist syndicalism sans Perón, and it would be further developed by other Peronist union leaders after Vandor's assassination by his leftist Peronist adversaries in 1969.[5]

The power of the Peronist union movement, which grew after 1955, depended on two synchronized strategies: an economistic one and a political one. These activities were exercised in the extrainstitutional areas during the repressive years and later, once the legal ban was lifted in 1965, also in Congress. Both defensive and offensive measures neutralized economic stabilization policies and the resulting negative effects on salaries and wages. The additional advantage of these tactics was their ability to employ other social actors—politicians, businesspeople, and officers—to achieve Peronist political objectives; but this situation alarmed the liberal right, who denounced these forces as a cover for Peronist subversive activities. The liberal right indicted the ruinous nature of Peronist unions, led by self-serving bureaucrats despised by the workers but still able to obtain concessions. However, these accommodations undermined the unity of the army, which divided into two antagonistic factions, the Azules and Colorados.

The most reactionary Peronist unions agreed to a plan proposed by the dominant faction of the army, the Azules, which since 1955 had played a tutelary and paternalistic role. They particularly supported the plan's next stage, when the Azules established an alliance between the armed forces and unions. Vandor believed that the time had come both to get the ban on Peronism lifted by incorporating Peronism into General Onganía's authoritarian military regime (1966–1970) and to restructure the economy and civilian society. Thus the organizational strategies and tactics of Vandorismo, as the most powerful faction of Peronist syndicalism between 1962 and 1966, were compatible with the Azules' growing desire during those years for a new authoritarian political order along the lines of the right: corporativism, anticommunism, Catholicism, hierarchy, and state direction.[6]

The Nacionalista Right

The Nacionalistas, who hoped for so much from the Revolución Libertadora, were given important positions in the revolutionary government that overthrew Perón in September 1955. But the November 13, 1955, coup d'état that deposed General Lonardi uprooted these Nacionalistas from the government. Realigned in opposition, then, to the provisional administration of General Pedro Aramburu, the Nacionalistas, especially the important segment that now formed around the publication *Azul y Blanco*, under the direction of Marcelo Sánchez Sorondo, adopted Lonardi's slogan "Neither victors nor vanquished" and endorsed a policy for national reconciliation. *Azul y Blanco* appeared in June 1956 and included articles by Mario Amadeo, Federico Ibarguren, Máximo Etchecopar, and other traditional Nacionalistas. The issue also contained contributions from new figures such as Ricardo Curutchet and Mariano Montemayor. Amadeo advocated the formation of a new rightist movement, freedom of speech, and reestablishment of dialogue and mutual respect among adversaries. He also recommended electoral freedom, as opposed to the banning of political parties, but he attacked the concept of free unionization. Four months after its appearance, *Azul y Blanco* had a circulation of more than a hundred thousand, proving that it voiced the opinion of a very important Nacionalista faction.[7]

Two groups of Nacionalistas participated in the 1957 election: the Unión Federal, led by Amadeo, and the Azul y Blanco party, headed by Sánchez Sorondo and Juan Carlos Goyeneche. The party's newspaper of the same name was shut down by the government in 1957; it reappeared later as *Segunda República*. During the February 1958 presidential elections, Amadeo's group strongly backed Frondizi's "national and popular" program, and Sánchez Sorondo remained the Frondizi supporter he had been since the latter part of 1956. Frondizi took office on May 1, 1958, and appointed a representative number of Nacionalistas as cabinet members and close advisers. Among the well-known members of this group were Carlos Florit, Mario Amadeo, and Santiago Estrada.

Eventually, Frondizi's economic developmentalist program disillusioned and split many of his supporters, including most of the left, the liberal bourgeoisie, and some of his Nacionalista backers. Amadeo's group continued to support the president, but Sánchez Sorondo's faction began a vituperative campaign against the government's "antinational" economic policies and accused Frondizi of being a "Menshevik politician" who was paving the way for communism in Argentina by having "infiltrators" in his administration.[8]

The Peronist triumph in the gubernatorial elections of nine provinces, including Buenos Aires, precipitated the military coup that in March 1962 overthrew Frondizi, who had been hounded by unions, the Nacionalistas (especially the *Segunda República* group), liberal rightist factions, and the military, which feared the unpredictable consequences of a Peronist resurgence. After this institutional shift, the president of the Senate, José María Guido, became interim president but was a virtual hostage of the military. The Azul-Colorado split now degenerated into armed confrontations between these two very different military coalitions and threatened to plunge the country into full-scale civil war, particularly after the Azules defeated the Colorados in September 1962 and April 1963. The question of attitudes toward Peronism continued at the core of their political differences. Both factions were anti-Peronist, but whereas the Azules preferred a political solution to the crisis (excluding Peronism but respecting republican institutions), the Colorados accused Peronist union leaders of subversion and saw no alternative but to "save the homeland" through a coup and a dictatorship capable of eliminating Peronism completely. The factions defined themselves ideologically through their mutual opposition, though their attitudes and positions changed over time. At any rate, it was the Colorados who, in June 1962, unequivocally justified the "state of revolutionary war" as a means to combat communism and Peronism in Argentina.

Like the military, the Nacionalistas split over Peronism. *Segunda República*, Sánchez Sorondo's mouthpiece, espoused an end to the liberal cycle and the installation of a "national dictatorship." To this end, it envisioned a broad-based front, grounded in "social Christianity" and capable of establishing a popular regime, based on consensus, without divisions between "left and right," that would support an authoritarian government. The foundation of this program would be an alliance made up of the Peronist masses, Solano Lima's Popular Conservatives, the UCR parties, and the most militant Christian Democrats.[9] During these months *Segunda República*, therefore, gave much coverage to the political leaders of Peronism, of the UCRP, and of the Popular Conservatives.[10] But this national front was defeated before it even began, for the liberal right, the UCRP, and other Nacionalistas strongly opposed this concept. Moreover, the presentation of candidates as electors for president and vice president from the Unión Popular—a neo-Peronist group— was vetoed by government decree. Parties that included Peronists or former Peronists on their lists of electors also were denied participation.

Through another newspaper, *La Grande Argentina*, Nacionalistas such as Father Julio Meinvielle backed the Azules' repressive measures. In reality, despite their rhetoric, the Azules' policy, implemented by President Guido's Minister of the Interior General Enrique Rauch, differed little from that of the Colorados. *La Grande Argentina* also approved of Rauch's critique of Frondizi's economic and political program. The banning of Peronism by the Azules allowed Dr. Arturo Illia, the UCRP candidate, to win the election of July 1963 with only 25.2 percent of the votes.[11]

The Nacionalista Paramilitary Bands

During the period of 1958 to 1965, the Nacionalistas promoted a vituperative press and organized paramilitary squads that used terror tactics and violent, xenophobic, and authoritarian rhetoric. These gangs mobilized forces of various types. They were divided with regard to strategy and immediate goals but were unified in their common aim of putting an end to the process of constitutional redemocratization. Three groups emerged as especially important for their influence on political parties, labor, the church, and the army during these years.

1. THE MOVIMIENTO NACIONALISTA TACUARA (MNT). The Movimiento Nacionalista Tacuara (MNT) appeared after the 1955 revolution and gained notoriety during the many student mobilizations that occurred over the question of secular education and Frondizi's proposal in favor of church-supported "autonomous" education in state high schools and universities. The MNT's debut marked it as the paramilitary band representing the most violent clerical sectors in Catholic secondary schools. This group, headed by Alberto Ezcurra Uriburu, a Nacionalista from a traditional upper-class family, immediately perpetrated a number of physical attacks on leftist, reformist, and Jewish students. The MNT's most notorious assault was against a young student, Graciela Sirota, whom it kidnapped in June 1962 and tattooed with a swastika.[12] The MNT recruited its militants from young high-school students of traditional, declassé, fervently Catholic, anticommunist, and anti-Semitic families. The recruits underwent military training, used heavy weapons, and terrorized student meetings, independent theaters, and Jewish institutions.

A parliamentary investigation by the Chamber of Deputies found that the persistent heinous acts of the MNT and its racial and political crimes went unpunished. The few actions initiated by the judiciary against the MNT were impeded by the leniency of the intelligence services and law enforcement officials. The MNT, in reality, was used as a paramilitary force not only by the Nacionalistas but also by the same repressive state mechanisms that had been created to combat suspected communists and student and mass movements.[13] It also had formal ties with neo-Nazi international organizations in the United States and in other parts of Latin America, and it was the principal anti-Semitic organization of the right between 1962 and 1965. The MNT unsuccessfully tried its hand at the polls. In the legislative elections of March 1963, it put itself at the head of a group called the Unión Cívica Nacionalista to consolidate the splintered forces of Nacionalismo. The MNT's electoral failure clearly indicated that its sphere of activities could be only extraparliamentary.[14]

Their nationalist-syndicalist ideology enabled leaders of the MNT to penetrate the similarly inclined Peronist movement. This penetration was supported by Juventud Peronista publications such as *Huella*, as well as by some of the union leaders from the Peronist right. The question of support for and solidarity with Peronism and its most populist wings caused splits within the MNT. The first division that the MNT underwent, during November 1960, gave rise to the Guardia Restauradora Nacionalista (GRN). Indeed, it was differences in the MNT over Peronism, rather than differences over the group's supposed "Castroism, Trotskyism, and atheism," that the GRN used to justify the split. MNT leaders, such as Joe Baxter, accused the new organization of being reactionary—of continuing to believe only in the fascist and Catholic ideals of the 1930s generation of Nacionalistas—and of having misunderstood the changes within Peronism.[15]

The MNT suffered another internal rift toward the end of 1963, one that reflected the ideological polarizations within the contradictory Peronist movement. The principal group, which continued under the leadership of Alberto Ezcurra Uriburu and Juan M. Collins, retained the title Movimiento Nacionalista Tacuara. This faction's publication was *Tacuara*, the "Voice of the Nacionalista Revolution." But a leftist group, Movimiento Nacionalista Revolucionario Tacuara (MNRT), headed by Joe Baxter and Amílcar Fidanza, split off. It advocated a communitarian national revolution, though an anti-imperialist and antioligarchic struggle. The goals of this revolution included state capitalism, diplomatic neutrality, and educational policies based on Catholicism that "would not permit the teachings and propaganda of unassimilated ethnic and cultural groups, who will not be allowed to enter the country." The MNRT linked itself to the leftist faction of the Juventud Peronista, under the leadership of Héctor Villalón, which published *Compañero*.[16]

The MNRT's first appearance was its March 1964 terrorist act of robbing the Policlínico Bancario de Buenos Aires, a sensational guerrilla operation that shook the entire country and provoked bloody retaliation. It was after this incident, which demonstrated the group's revolutionary leanings, that the security and police forces decided to suppress the MNT once and for all.

Meanwhile, Villalón's wing of the Juventud Peronista was expelled from Peronism by the Comando Superior Justicialista, headquartered in Madrid. This expulsion was a result of Villalón's espousal of violent means for confronting the local oligarchy. The weekly *Compañero* had advocated this policy in news articles from Baxter's MNRT. Several of these editorials criticized the racist attitudes of the MNT. In one of these articles, Baxter denounced the older group's complicity with repressive state agencies in an antipopular struggle that infiltrated Peronist unions and student groups. According to Baxter, this complementarity of purpose explained how the MNT came to enjoy immunity, as well as the political value of the group to the leaders of the anticommunist struggle.

The MNT demonstrated its influence in the ranks of Peronist unionism when some of its leaders became members of the board of directors of the CGT general assembly in March 1964. It exercised control despite having been violently repelled during a bloody encounter in the Rosario brewery union that killed and wounded several MNT members. Because of this same influence, Ezcurra Uriburu was the keynote speaker at a ceremony held in Santa Fe, in the same week as the general assembly, to support the CGT's strategy.

The MNT attempted to implement its nationalist-syndicalist ideology through a ruthless anti-Semitic and anticommunist campaign. Shortly after the CGT meeting, Ezcurra Uriburu denied allegations that he was a neo-Nazi, explaining that his anti-Semitism was due to the Jews' supposed "Zionist disloyalty to Argentina."[17] Toward mid-1964, however, the MNT faction headed by Ezcurra Uriburu was no longer openly involved in Peronist union activities. Instead, it adhered to the anti-Zionist strategies of an ultra-right Peronist group linked to the Arab League in Argentina, whose members included people such as the national deputy J. C. Cornejo Linares.[18]

Perhaps the reorganization of the Alianza Libertadora Nacionalista (ALN) at the end of 1963 could explain the MNT's retreat from Peronism. The reorganization was headed by Patricio Guillermo Kelly, who was released from prison in August 1963 after serving a sentence that began in 1958 and once again began recruiting Peronist youth. Inclined toward anti-imperialism, Kelly had attracted Peronist followers who did not agree either with the syndicalist conservatism and Catholic anti-Semitism of Ezcurra Uriburu or with the guerrilla adventurism of the Baxter group. There is no evidence as to the potential of the ALN and its recruiting abilities. However, the irrefutable fact is that Kelly, a well-known Nacionalista and Peronist (who during his exile in Caracas took Perón and Rogelio Frigerio, future economics minister under Frondizi, into his home to sign an electoral pact backing Frondizi for the 1958 elections), opposed attempts to commit Peronist groups to the anti-Semitic and anti-Zionist racism fostered by the Peronist (Justicialista) ultra-right sectors, such as those of Raúl Jassem, editor of the *Patria Bárbara*, and of the followers of Hussein Tricki, the Arab League representative in Argentina.[19]

2. THE LEGIÓN NACIONALISTA CONTRARREVOLUCIONARIA (LNC). Unlike the MNT, the Legión Nacionalista Contrarrevolucionaria (LNC) was not a youth organization but an ideological paramilitary group made up of civilians and active and retired military personnel. Its leader was Commodore (Ret.) Agustín H. de la Vega. Some brigadier generals on active duty openly taught cadets and officers at the Escuela de Aviación at Córdoba the LNC credo against three principal enemies: communism, Freemasonry, and Judaism. Its ideologue and principal theorist was a professor, Jordán Bruno Genta, who preached his doctrine of "counterrevolutionary war" at a number of conferences. He also pointed out the urgent need to eliminate liberal *partidocracia*, a long-standing rightist denunciation of parties and politicians, as well as the threat of populism in any of its manifestations.[20]

The LNC was founded at the end of November 1964, on the anniversary of Juan Manuel de Rosas's 1845 victory over France and Britain at Vuelta de Obligado—an important event in the Nacionalista calendar. De la Vega, together with the notorious Colorado officers, retired Brigadier Generals Cayo Alsina and Gilberto Oliva, released a document entitled "Government Plan for a Counterrevolutionary War Policy," written by Genta.

Genta's document was based on the premise that foreign communism had subversively infiltrated all ranks of the Argentine state, society, culture, and economy. A state of war was necessary to combat this enemy, whereupon a military dictatorship would assume power and would change the entire judicial, economic, and cultural structure of the liberal state. To this end, the country needed a unifying doctrine with which to mobilize unions, workers, businesses, the military, and the church and take the offensive. This doctrine would clearly define the positive principles that Argentines should know, love, and serve, and the negative principles that they should recognize, repudiate, and combat. This Manichaean view posited the following notions: 1) Roman Catholicism should be publicly and officially professed in Argentina, and non-Catholic religions should be permitted only as long as they did not offend public morality and did not proselytize in Argentine territory; 2) the only legitimate Argentine traditions are those inherited from Roman Catholic hispanidad; 3) public schools at all levels should abolish secular teaching; 4) Argentine youth should be prepared to serve God and Country in the schools and in mandatory military and national work services; 5) national universities should be converted into autonomous corporations of professors and students, and the University Reform, comprised of a tripartite administration, should be abolished; 6) private property should be used socially in keeping with Pope John XXIII's *Mater et Magistra* encyclical; 7) Catholic morals and the social doctrine of the church should guide a reformed judiciary; and 8) international capitalism and worker movements, as well as their ideological weapons—communism, Freemasonry, and Zionism—should be declared incompatible with the very essence of the nation; and their agents and activities should be nullified, as should those of occultist, spiritualist, and theosophic sects.[21]

Before the release of this document, Genta, according to his own statements, had been invited by the air force intelligence service to teach his concept of counterrevolutionary war. This indoctrination was extended to include the army forces stationed at the Campo de Mayo. However, the Azules' victory over the Colorados also translated into the short-term domination of the principles of military professionalism and legalism over those of the counterrevolutionary war and *golpismo*. Nevertheless, Genta's document, which went practically unnoticed at the time, would be, in later years, the basis for the national security doctrine of the army factions who would take power in 1976.

3. LA GUARDIA RESTAURADORA NACIONALISTA (GRN). The Guardia Restauradora Nacionalista (GRN) was organized in a military fashion by regional commands—federal capital, Greater Buenos Aires, Bahía Blanca, and Cuyo—and was headed at the national level by Augusto Moscoso. Moscoso's ideological mentor and spiritual confessor was the well-known

Nacionalista Catholic theorist, Father Julio Meinvielle. Meinvielle made his public statements from the altars of the churches of Buenos Aires, despite his being at odds with the Catholic hierarchy.[22] Unlike supporters of the MNT, GRN members were from the patrician upper class, and they had no intention of catering to the nation's popular sectors.

From an ideological point of view, the GRN advocated a national revolution to halt the "advance of Marxist materialism and the failure of bourgeois liberalism." Restoration of the Catholic faith was indispensable to combat the so-called materialist subversion, "whose two fronts—capitalism and communism—were instruments of International Judaism." The GRN defended the family and indissoluble marriage as the bases of the new Catholic social order. It favored the creation of corporations made up of representatives of the state, capital, labor, and technology to protect the common good. Because the Catholic church was the "evangelizing and civilizing agent of our Nation," the GRN demanded that the state establish a concordat with the papacy to guarantee the exclusive involvement of the church in the spiritual life of the Argentine people. On the international level the GRN allied itself with militant anticommunist policy and opposed the United Nations, which it considered to be the "instrument of dissociation of all nations, used by International Judaism to increase its universal control."[23]

The National Front and Rightist Cooperation

As Peronism returned to the parliamentary scene in 1965, the CGT gathered strength, and the reformist student movement was winning the streets; in response the Nacionalista paramilitary groups such as the MNT, GRN, and LNC, despite their political differences, agreed to work together to halt student activism and the radicalization of Peronism. Guillermo Mac Green, an MNT leader, publicly advocated unification around a National Front with the strategic objective of "permitting the masses to count on military and clerical backing to confront communism, Judaism, and Free Masonry." At times in collaboration with one another and at times independently, during the first half of 1965 these groups perpetrated a series of physical attacks that cost the lives of militant leftist university students. These attacks had as their primary targets Jews, such as Daniel Grinblack, and were carried out with total impunity.[24]

The Radical government of Arturo Illia remained paralyzed in the face of this rising tide of violence. Moreover, the multifaceted Peronist strategy resulted in parliamentary victories and confrontations with the government through vigorous labor actions; the possibility of a Peronist return to power in the next election loomed large. Meanwhile, the Radical government feared *golpista* sectors of the army and extreme right-wing militants. Toward the end of 1965, an antiliberal and fiercely anticommunist National Front, comprised of Peronists from the right and anti-Peronists, coalesced around a basic goal: to support a military coup in order to end Illia's democratic government.

During 1964 the National Front could not express itself openly because of the initiative launched by the Justicialista movement to bring Perón back to Argentina. Once this initiative had failed, however, at the end of 1965, the way was clear for agitation in favor of an army coup. Their commitment to a military solution was strong enough to cause members of the Front, traditionally anti-Semitic and anti-Zionist, to downplay their racist rhetoric in order to elevate a message of anticommunist dangers and military salvation as the only hope.

Peronism's right wing went on a crusade against those it considered to be "Trotskyite and Marxist infiltrators" within the Justicialista movement. This effort began particularly after the reorganization of the movement, which displaced the leftist youth groups. It replaced as well, temporarily, the coalition of unions headed by Augusto Vandor, who had taken credit for the successful CGT strategy. The groups that benefited from the polarization of forces resulting from Perón's tactics to maintain power over his volatile multiclass movement were principally those of the Peronist right, particularly those who favored a military coup. One exponent of this trend was the newspaper *Retorno*, headed by Pedro Michelini (former editor of the anti-Semitic Peronist newspaper *Huella*) until his appointment as head of the Partido Justicialista of Buenos Aires province, and then headed by Raúl Jassem, former editor of the *Nación Arabe* and *Patria Bárbara*. *Retorno* considered itself Hispanist and Catholic and admired the ideology of José Antonio Primo de Rivera, a leader of the Spanish fascists in the 1930s, as the basis for a Peronist revolution, hailing the intervention of the armed forces to put an end to "Masonist and stateless liberalism." During the first months of 1966, Jassem refrained from attacking the "Argentine Zionists": his principal adversary was the liberal democracy of President Illia.

At the same time, communism and liberalism were the enemies displacing "Jews" and "International Zionism" in the political rhetoric of the LNC through its newspaper *Combate*, edited by Alberto R. Torre. Other publications followed the same political line—the need for a military coup to save the country from crisis and to fight communism. These newspapers included *Nuevo Orden* of the Guardia Restauradora Nacionalista as well as *La Voz Nacional*, edited by Juan C. Vestre, the organ of the Confederación de Organizaciones Anticomunistas de la República Argentina (COARA). These publications traded lists of supposed communists and even published similar editorials advocating the anticommunist crusade and urgently calling on the military to save the country from "social and economic chaos." Other, lesser-known, Nacionalista publications that followed the identical anticommunist and pro-coup lines, including *El Aliancista* of the Alianza Libertadora Nacionalista, *El Federal*, and *Malón*, suspended their anti-Semitic preaching to support the anticommunist and *golpista* positions. Nacionalista agitation, however, was only one factor that helped lead to the coup against Illia in June 1966.[25]

Thus, the years between the overthrow of Juan Perón in 1955 and the coup against Arturo Illia in 1966 witnessed a determined attempt to revive democratic government in Argentina. But the right proved a stubborn adversary to this effort, fearing, as ever, that elections would bring to power the left or would bring the return of populist Peronism; and so it continued to oppose civilian regimes. This right had become a complex network, for it included not only the old liberal conservatives and the Nacionalistas but also the Peronist right, which formed an important part of the active and violent paramilitary bands and of the anti-Semitic pro-Palestinian elements. These groups worked diligently to convince the extreme elements of a divided military to join them in establishing once again the armed forces' control of Argentina. The bleak period of army rule that followed, from 1966 to 1973, only created the conditions that would bring an aged Perón back to the presidency.

The Political Culture of the Third Peronist Period and the Right's Activity in the Process of Redemocratization (1973–1976)

Unlike the process of democratic transition (1956–1958 and 1962–63) when the military opted to cede control to civilian society, the triumph of the redemocratization process and the Peronist electoral victory in 1973 took place through the action of political, union, and student organizations during the turbulent period that started with Lieutenant General Alejandro Lanusse's administration (1971–1973). The middle and lower classes' role in the defeat of the bureaucratic-authoritarian state between 1971 and 1973 aroused an aggressive response from both the Peronist right and the anti-Peronist Nacionalista right.

Political action along the entire ideological spectrum focused outside of the partisan framework, and even those affiliated with political structures such as the Justicialista movement concentrated on "winning" the universities, factories, streets, and squares as their privileged spheres. These years witnessed the mobilization of many groups to a degree never seen before. The CGT and the more combative "base" syndicalism conducted offensives on behalf of workers. Small- and medium-sized businesses grouped themselves in the Confederación General Económica (CGE). Students held large demonstrations, and, in general, intellectuals and academics involved themselves in politics in new ways. Residents organized political and mutual aid activities in urban barrios and rural areas. And, of course, there was the violence of the urban leftist guerrillas and of the Peronist and paramilitary ultra-rightist action guards.

This scale of mass participation overwhelmed the regime established with the Peronist electoral triumph of 1973. The contradictions between heterogeneous political forces and powerful social actors within the Peronist alliance ultimately made it impossible for the regime to govern. In the center of the Peronist social base of support were the labor unions and the CGT, flanked on the left by a large group of middle-class youths and intellectuals and on the right by the national business bourgeoisie. Over time these forces polarized between an extreme right and an ultra left. As this process took place, the Congress was displaced from any role other than political negotiations and transactions. Confrontations between the disputing forces were resolved corporatively through extraparliamentary means, resulting in the deterioration of institutional republicanism.

In 1974 the death of Perón, the indisputable arbitrator between the antagonistic forces within his multiclass movement and government, accelerated the violence of the struggle over the distribution of wealth and power. His death also meant the loss of control over the unions, whose sectoral interests led them to neutralize official economic initiatives and, thus, to paralyze government economic policy. In this crisis of authority, the ultra-right wing of Peronism, which was centered around José López Rega, Perón's minister of social welfare and the editor of *Las Bases*, the official Justicialista mouthpiece, and Perón's third wife, Isabel, took power. This regime unleashed violent repression against leftist guerrillas, unions, students, intellectuals, and popular movements at the same time it confronted the CGT.[26] The political violence that accompanied this Peronist regime—a method of policymaking legitimized by a political culture that subordinated respect for institutional norms to partisanship—led not only to a short-term political and economic crisis but also, ultimately, to the hegemonic crisis of the entire democratic system. The resulting chaos only further catalyzed the right.

The right, both within and outside of the Peronist movement, was the first to perceive the warning signs of this crisis of hegemony. It noted the emergence of a counter power that was not limited to the unions, student groups, and the extensive fringes of the radicalized middle classes. Aside from its fear of guerrilla violence, this right also felt threatened and even spurned by the position that the national business sector had managed to secure through the CGE as part of the Peronist coalition and government.

The former president of the CGE, José Ber Gelbard, had become Juan Perón's minister of economics. As such, Gelbard designed and implemented the *Pacto Social* (Social Pact), the key to Perón's economic and political strategy. By freezing wages and prices, the Social Pact was intended to control inflation and, in turn, attract investment, spur industrial growth, and create prosperity for all sectors of Argentine society. As part of this class conciliation plan, the administration accepted the CGE and CGT as active partners. Gelbard's enforcement of the Social Pact unleashed a chain reaction from the liberal right, which was frightened by a policy that affected its traditional agricultural exports and financial interests. The crisis was worsened by the inability of the political and union actors who supported the Social Pact to defend it adequately through institutional mechanisms against their rightist enemies within and outside of Peronism. The CGE, for example, was incapable of confronting the double attack by the liberal and Peronist right at the extraparliamentary level.

The Peronist Right and Its Shock Troops

The Peronist right had established a powerful organization and accumulated resources during the years prior to the Peronist victory. It had been forming paramilitary groups since 1969 to confront the radicalized Peronist youth movement (Juventud Peronista), as well as the union "base" activists who emerged out of the bureaucratic ranks of the union hierarchy. The union, youth, and university sectors all provided personnel and weapons to the rightist shock troops in the Peronist movement. Coordinated by López Rega, these armed groups first sought to restrain but then to unleash a civil war against the base organizations and the leftist guerrillas—the Montoneros, the Fuerzas Armadas de Liberación (FAL), and their allies. Against the leftist rhetoric of national liberation through an evolution toward socialism, or the "Patria Socialista," the Peronist right proclaimed its devotion to traditional Justicialismo and verticalism, or the "Patria Peronista."

The events at Ezeiza Airport on June 20, 1973, demonstrated the lengths to which the Peronist right would go to impose its own conception of the Patria Peronista and terminate the revolutionary mobilization around the Patria Socialista. On that day Perón was due to land at Ezeiza, ending his long exile and assuming the presidency from his underling, Héctor Cámpora. Lieutenant Colonel Jorge Osinde, a subordinate of López Rega in charge of security for Perón's reception at Ezeiza, opted to protect the official stage with armed civilians instead of plainclothes officers from the Federal Police. Osinde's collaborators were important figures from the rightist Peronist union and political factions: Norma Kennedy, Manuel Damiano, and Alberto Brito Lima, who was head of the armed ultra-rightist Comando de Organización. These three ensured the recruitment of people from the different right-wing Peronist groups that had been defeated in internal elections and that were anxious to halt the wave of revolutionary activism. Members of such groups, then—the Juventud Sindical, Concentración Nacional Universitaria, Alianza Libertadora Nacionalista, and Comando de Organización—guarded the stage. The metallurgical workers' (UOM) and mechanics' unions (Sindicato de Mecánicos y Afines del Transporte Automotor, SMATA) also took part, and the intendants of Quilmes and Avellaneda supplied arms and personnel. These groups, which, along with parapolice, answered to former Undercommissioner Juan Ramón Morales and former Deputy Inspector Rodolfo Eduardo Almirón, received orders to stop the activities of the Juventud Peronista, Juventud Universitaria Peronista, Juventud Trabajadora Peronista, and the Montoneros and other armed leftist organizations. In the midst of the enormous crowd that had come to the airport to welcome Perón, estimated at five hundred thousand, the right fired on the left and provoked a battle. Dozens, perhaps hundreds, died.[27]

The Ezeiza Massacre was significant for several reasons. First, it symbolized the extreme polarization between the left and right wings of Peronism. Moreover, it indicated the willingness of various Peronist sectors—the unions; shock troops such as the Comando de Organización; *El Caudillo, Patria Peronista, Consigna, Nacional,* and other periodicals; public officials such as López Rega and Osinde; Kennedy and other leaders of the movement's Superior Council—to work together to halt the swelling wave of mass mobilization, guerrilla activity, and class warfare. After the Ezeiza bloodbath, they cooperated with the parapolicial Alianza Anticomunista Argentina (AAA), the notorious death squad organized by López Rega, as well as with the anti-Peronist right, to create a fascist climate of indiscriminate terror and repression.

The Peronist Right and the Use of Anti-Semitism

As in the earlier period, anti-Semitism emerged as an important tactic of the right. The union and Lópezrreguista factions used anti-Semitism first to combat and then to displace the CGE from the government and end Gelbard's policy of social conciliation. Workers easily could have faulted the latter policy for its restrictions on collective bargaining and strikes, but this was not the ultra-right's main reason for opposing the CGE and the Social Pact. Instead, it visualized the Social Pact as having imposed on Perón an economic and social policy designed by upstart social actors from the CGE who did not belong to historic Peronism and were attempting to corrupt the movement. The Jewishness of these social actors—Gelbard; President Julio Bronner of the CGE; Jacobo Timerman, the influential journalist; and the financier David Graiver—was the pretext for filling the populist anti-Social Pact discourse with anti-Semitic language. Gelbard, Bronner, Timerman, and Graiver were accused of being "infiltrators" from the "Sinarquía," or Synarchy, the supposed union of capitalism, communism, and Zionism, in the popular government.[28]

While Perón was alive, the assault on the Social Pact had been covert: it was easier to accuse the Synarchy of infiltrating the ranks of the government than to confront directly an economic and social plan backed by Perón himself. The confrontation between López Rega and Gelbard stimulated the rejection of Perón's economic plan. The Lópezrreguistas simplified the complexities of Perón's alliance to the point of parody; for example, it was demagogically simple, and useful, to attribute difficulties in negotiating trade and financial agreements with Libya to the "interference of Jewish officials in the Argentine Government," alluding to Gelbard.

The Peronist administration, on the one hand, backed Gelbard's measures but, on the other, abstained from publicly disavowing the anti-Semitic campaign of ultra-rightist Peronists.[29] Thus even the official CGT communiqués equivocally used the term "International Synarchy" to repudiate crimes against its leaders, such as the assassinations of its militants.[30]

General Perón's reaction to the accusations of the organized Jewish community was politically ambiguous. Representatives of the Delegación de Asociaciones Israelitas Argentinas (DAIA), an important Jewish organization, spoke with Perón to express their concern regarding the increase in pamphlets and publications that twisted "the concept of Synarchy to apply it inappropriately to the Jewish community," a community that had become, in the DAIA's opinion, "the target of aggressive and unjustified attacks." In reply, Perón noted that "the application of the concept of Synarchy to the country's Jewish community is absurd, given that this statement has an entirely different meaning." Significantly, Perón's resounding "clarification," as defined by the DAIA, was not made public by the government but was released by the DAIA to the press in October 1973. Nevertheless, this clarification complemented Perón's known pro-Jewish and pro-Israeli statements, which had been collected by the DAIA and published in book form in 1954.[31]

At the same time, Perón did not disqualify or exclude from his multifaceted and contradictory national movement the ideas of any sector. Even Perón could not deprive anyone of the condition of being a Peronist; he could only withdraw his official blessing from Peronists who promulgated opinions, including anti-Semitic ones, that the Leader, or leaders that Perón himself authorized, had not expressly pronounced. His interest was in preserving his exclusive position as the Voice, not to be intruded upon by any sector of his movement. Although Perón sacralized his oracular political discourse, he allowed other Peronists from the right or the left to take complete personal responsibility when they offered a variation on his rhetoric. This discursive logic did not permit disciplinary sanctions or public repudiation. As long as they did not represent themselves as speaking for the leadership of the movement, the Peronist militants, then, were free to say, albeit at their own risk, whatever they wanted about the Jews; in doing so they did not compromise either the doctrine or the national movement.

Moreover, in the past Perón himself had resorted to using the term "Synarchy," although he denied any racist or anti-Semitic intent. For example, in an interview with *Primera Plana* in July 1971, Perón affirmed that "the great International Synarchy is manipulated from the United Nations, where communism, capitalism, Judaism, the Catholic Church . . . and Masonry are found." Perón expressed similar thoughts to a group of priests in December 1972, but this time he substituted Zionism for Judaism; in his opinion, Zionism, together with the other forces mentioned in his *Primera Plana* interview, had been responsible for ending "Argentine sovereignty." These ideas received some clarification in Perón's prologue to Enrique Pavón Pereyra's book, *Coloquios con Perón*. Here he attempted to explain the tactical alliances of the "Great Internationals," such as "Communist Imperialism and Capitalist Imperialism," to attain world domination and their systems of alliances "with other Internationals, such as Vaticanism, Masonry, and Judaism."[32] Thus, the Peronist right could invoke Perón's own words when condemning Zionism, the left, or liberalism.

Given Perón's equivocations on Synarchy and other questions, his death left the Peronist identity open to appropriation by all of the contenders who disputed with the right to inherit the divided movement. Never before had the lines that differentiated the Peronist "traitors" and "loyalists" become so important in the political struggle. The Peronist right's strategy to claim the ideological legacy and political identification of Peronism without Perón involved the deliberate use of anti-Semitism to end the Social Pact.

The right attempted to explain to the Peronist masses the magnitude of the infiltration within the movement by partisans of the Patria Socialista and the Synarchy. It pointed an accusing finger at the specter of Gelbard and the CGE. Between August and October 1974, *El Caudillo* and *Primicia Argentina* (linked to Lorenzo Miguel's Sixty-two Organizations, the political arm of the union movement) used the myth of Synarchy to fight the Social Pact. At the same time, Jews were insulted in public gatherings, anti-Semitic graffiti appeared on the streets, and the slogan *Fuera Gelbard, Judío Vende Patria* (Out with Gelbard, Jewish Traitor) was coined.[33]

This offensive against the Social Pact, however, did not come only from the Peronist right and the allies of the CGT. The rightist sectors of the liberal agro-exporting and financial bourgeoisie also attacked the CGE by using xenophobic arguments. An illustration of this approach appeared in the editorial of *La Prensa* on August 27, 1974. The editorial criticized Julio Bronner for defending the Social Pact. His defense of national interests over short-term sectorial interests seemed intolerable to the representatives of the liberal press and the Sociedad Rural, made up of prominent ranchers and landowners, and his origins resulted "from those who, coming from foreign countries so dissimilar to ours and unfamiliar with our history, had incorporated themselves into national life just a short time ago. . . . Such persons had no right to give lessons on patriotism to the Argentine people."[34] It is significant that, although they may not have coordinated their attacks, the Peronist and non-Peronist right shared the same opinion of the Social Pact and directed similar rhetoric against it.

Between October 1974—after Gelbard's fall from power—and March 1975, an extremely violent political war was unleashed between two contenders within Peronism, each attempting to impose its own economic plan. The Lópezrreguista right, which filled the power vacuum after Perón's death, was confronted by the unions of the CGT, which resisted being marginalized from power. López Rega's offensive focused on President Isabel Perón (1974–1976) and was strengthened by an attempt to set up a national rightist front, including anti-Peronist Nacionalistas, such as Julio Irazusta, who agreed on the need to prepare for the serious hegemonic crisis that threatened the dominant classes. This front, the Acción Nacionalista Argentina, following the slogan "For the National, Popular, and Christian Revolution," launched an assault against "Judeo-Marxism and International Zionism" in the rightist press, Peronist as well as anti-Peronist. One of the recurring topics of this campaign in the press was a warning of the imminent Synarchic takeover of Peronism. Another topic was the Plan Andinia—the supposed Zionist plan to set up a Jewish state in Patagonia. Such varied organs as the Nacionalista *Cabildo* and the Peronist *El Caudillo, Consigna Nacional, Patria Peronista,* and *Semana Política* disseminated the Plan Andinia widely, linking it to Argentina's social and economic crisis after Perón's demise.[35]

During this critical stage—from September 1974 to July 1975—Lópezrreguismo's offensive was able to take power away from the unions and to focus the violence of the AAA squadrons against "Judeo-Marxism." The discursive prototype appeared in March 1975 in *El Caudillo,* which threatened to go from violent rhetoric to armed action by inciting a pogrom against the Jewish Barrio Once, or the *"Barrio de la usura,"* as the poet Gabriel Ruiz de los Llanos put it. At the same time *Patria Peronista* published "Memorandum on the Jewish Question and Argentinism," in which it declared another war, this time against the media, controlled supposedly by the Synarchy "in Jewish and Zionist hands." *El Fortín,* a publication that replaced the Nacionalista *Cabildo* (temporarily closed for criticizing the government), protested the showing of the anti-Nazi movie *QB VII* on television, alleging that "the Jew has become shameless and is capable of showing his corruption on the T.V. screens of thousands of homes in our Catholic Argentina for five consecutive nights."[36] This same "insolence of the Synarchy" was a crime against the state, according to the new interventor of the University of Buenos Aires, the ultra-right Peronist Alberto Ottalagano, who had been chosen to restore order and eliminate "Judeo-Marxist" penetration. To accomplish these tasks he appointed anti-Peronist Nacionalistas to university positions,[37] again demonstrating the collaboration between the Nacionalista and Peronist right.

In this same interregnum, in June 1975, López Rega appointed Celestino Rodrigo as minister of economics. His massive currency devaluation and austerity plan created popular discontent. Attempting to divert attention from Rodrigo, Norma Kennedy blamed spiraling inflation and shortages on Jews and threatened to "expel those unscrupulous merchants of Barrio Once who were sabotaging the country." The same merchants were objects of her attack when she expressed her desire "to seize those who were hoarding basic goods now that we can count on the support of the new Minister of Economics." DAIA protested this anti-Semitic stratagem before the vice president of the

Justicialista party. In response, Kennedy, using intimidation and threats, forced the president of the DAIA, Nehemías Resnitzky, to publish a joint communiqué with her in which he denied his own group's accusation that Kennedy had anti-Semitic intentions and attributed the accusation to a lamentable misunderstanding. This joint communiqué, however, did not neutralize the anti-Semitic campaign during the months of June and July 1975.[38]

A CGT counterattack succeeded in removing Rodrigo from office and deposing López Rega from government. Yet the Lópezrreguistas refused to give up and continued fighting against their political enemies. The increased political violence, the intersectorial struggle in the business area, the failure of economic conciliation, and the radicalization of the workers' base in several important industrial centers accelerated the process of political deterioration, which became even more severe after September 1975. It seemed that public decision making no longer took place through democratic political channels, but in the battlefield of a grueling civil war whose most visible contenders were the parapolice squads and the guerrillas.[39] Through such groups as the AAA, the right wing employed brutal methods including outright murder. It attributed any criticism of these terrorist methods to the Synarchy. Thus, when AAA commandos assassinated the Poujadas, a leftist family in Córdoba, they "warned" the people in a public communiqué not to be "fooled by the attempts of the Jewish-Synarchic newspapers to distort and misconstrue our patriotic objective." Perhaps more subtle but just as clearly racist were the AAA's other sinister activities, not published in the press and only brought to light by recent interviews. One such activity was the particularly severe torture that Jewish prisoners received in clandestine prisons; another was the AAA's particular preference for blackmailing powerful and wealthy members of the Jewish community.[40]

In this environment of civil war, where the violence of fascist and racist rhetoric prepared the way for criminal violence, ideological clichés expressing hatred of Judaism and Zionism played a major role. It is important to note the degree to which this widely spread discourse required anti-Semitism to justify the crimes and acts of terror. The right condemned the "Judeo-Marxist" enemy both to accuse the guerrillas and to fight "economic subversion," or the corrupt official dealings investigated by Congress. It even used anti-Semitism to fight unionists who condemned the terrorist tactics of the death squads. Just before the military coup in March 1976, the daily *El Cronista* published a communiqué from the AAA that defended López Rega as a "nationalist and Christian patriot" and threatened to execute those union leaders who "were being closely watched because of their contacts with International Zionism." The communiqué also alerted the country against deception "by the psychological ploys of the media controlled by *judeomarxismo apátrida*."[41] Marxist subversion, economic delinquency, and cultural subversion were the three areas targeted for state terrorism after the military coup. The purpose was to confront what General Ramón Camps called the Graiver-Timerman-Gelbard group's tactic of *"entrismo,"* meaning its "infiltration in the economic, cultural and political organizations."[42]

Conclusion

Rightist activity under civilian regimes between 1955 and 1976 exhibited certain basic continuities. During this period the right was divided into four factions: the liberal right, the Peronist right, the Nacionalistas, and sectors within the military. The right's main preoccupations were government economic policy and the suppression of mass political movements. Nevertheless, the most consistent ploy, particularly of the Peronist and Nacionalista right, was to cloak their concerns with the mantle of anti-Semitism. These groups used anti-Semitic rhetoric and violence in an attempt to mobilize the nation's middle- and lower-class sectors, diverting them from reformism, whether of the Frondizi, Balbín, or Peronist left varieties.

The right during the transition to democracy between 1958 and 1966 basically operated as a reaction against the resurgence of Peronism and the radicalization of student and popular sectors. The parliamentary liberal right favored outlawing and later violently repressing the perceived subversive danger of the Peronist base-level organizations and the mobilization of the left, granting leniency to different Nacionalista shock troops operating during these years to confront these threats. The Nacionalistas used xenophobic, anticommunist, and anti-Semitic discourse to justify their violence. They acted with impunity because they were protected by state security services. Ironically, despite the anti-Peronism of the rest of the right, the Peronist unions were an important partner in the stratagem of the Azules to implant the bureaucratic-authoritarian state. Their experience in negotiating the demands of a workers' movement hierarchically organized with the state and with business associations predisposed them to accept the 1966 Argentine revolution.

A serious crisis in the bureaucratic-authoritarian state forced the military to initiate the transition to democratization after 1972 and permit the Peronist triumph in 1973. This crisis, in turn, prompted a violent struggle for power within and outside of Peronism between the left and the right. Once in power in October 1974, the Peronist right sought to eliminate the Peronist left-wing unions and guerrillas, unleashing a civil war that spread into civilian society and profoundly weakened the democratic parliamentary mechanisms after Perón's death. The unmanageable process of democratization alarmed the armed forces, the Nacionalista right, and the anti-Peronist liberal bourgeoisie. They perceived the consequences not only of the political and socioeconomic crisis caused by Peronism but also of the threat against the entire system of power posed by the guerrillas and the attempts of the CGT and the CGE to defend their sectorial interests in a time of hyperinflation, recession, and wage freezes. Despite their disagreements on other issues, all factions of the right supported the AAA's efforts to physically eliminate their political enemies.

The implantation of military dictatorship after the March 1976 coup meant the institutionalization of state terrorism, in which the state reabsorbed (and, in effect, clothed in uniform) the anarchic repressive mechanisms of the threatened Peronist government as well as the Peronist vigilantes. Both the Nacionalista and liberal right backed implementation of the so-called Process of National Reorganization, or Proceso, whose bloody "national security" doctrine justified the antisubversive war on civilian society, the academic world, culture, unions, and intermediate socioeconomic associations. As previewed by the right during the period under study, the military and its civilian allies used violence and xenophobic, Nacionalista, Catholic, and anti-Semitic discourse to punish brutally this so-called subversion at all levels of the devastated civilian society.

Because the military governments in these years collapsed and gave way to democracy, albeit fragile, one could argue that the right failed. The divisiveness of the right also could lead one to this conclusion. Both of these points are explored in this volume by Paul Lewis in "The Right and Military Rule, 1955–1983." Nevertheless, the historical experience of the regroupings and alliances between sectors of the Argentine right, on the eve of and during military coups, demonstrates in some ways the right's viability as a powerful social and political force. The right prepared its economic and political strategies during the periods of democratization, which served as testing grounds for policies of subsequent authoritarian governments. The latter, particularly the Proceso, indeed managed to eliminate the "subversion" feared by the right. Yet rightist activities and discourse under the civilian regimes deserve to be studied not just in terms of the final product's appearance in the military dictatorships but also for their less explicit, more hidden, behavior during the redemocratization processes.

Notes

1. The writer uses the following authors for conceptual guidelines: Liliana de Riz, "Argentina: Ni democracia estable ni régimen militar," and D. R. García Delgado, "Nuevos patrones de participación política en procesos de transición a la democracia: El caso argentino," in *Proceso, crisis y transición democrática,* ed. Oscar Oszlak, 2 vols. (Buenos Aires, 1984), 2:7–28, 88–132; and Oscar Landi, "Cultura y política en la transición democrática" in Oszlak, *Proceso* 1:102–23. On authoritarianism in Argentina see Guillermo O'Donnell, *El estado burocrático autoritario, 1966–1973* (Buenos Aires, 1982); "Las fuerzas armadas y el estado autoritario del Cono Sur de América Latina," in *Estado y política en América Latina,* ed. Norbert Lechner (México, 1981); and *Notas para el estudio de procesos de democratización a partir del estado burocrático autoritario* (Buenos Aires, 1979). Also see Marcelo Cavarozzi, *Autoritarismo y democracia, 1955–1983* (Buenos Aires, 1983). On the military in

Argentine politics see Robert A. Potash, *The Army and Politics in Argentina, 1945–1962: Perón to Frondizi* (Stanford, 1980); Alain Rouquié, *Poder militar y sociedad política en la Argentina*, vol. 2, *1943–1973* (Buenos Aires, 1981); Rubén M. Perina, *Onganía, Levingston, Lanusse: Los militares en la política argentina* (Buenos Aires, 1983); Eduardo Viola, "Democracia e autoritarismo na Argentina contemporánea" (Ph.D. diss., University of São Paulo, Brazil, 1982). The military officers, administrations, and movements mentioned in this chapter are treated in detail by Paul Lewis in "The Right and Military Rule, 1955–1983," in this volume.

2. De Riz, "Argentina," 25; Cavarozzi, *Autoritarismo*, 73 n. 9; Marcelo Cavarozzi, "Elementos para una caracterización del capitalismo oligárquico," *Revista Mexicana de Sociología* 78, no. 4 (January–March 1978): 123–24; Roberto Azaretto, *Historia de las fuerzas conservadoras* (Buenos Aires, 1983), 129–55.

3. Alfredo Allende, *Historia de una gran ley* (Buenos Aires, 1963); *La Prensa*, August 8, 29, 1958; Nicolás Babini, *Frondizi, de la oposición al gobierno: Testimonio* (Buenos Aires, 1983), 241, 244–45.

4. For information on this and the following paragraphs see Cavarozzi, *Autoritarismo*, 20–25; and Guillermo O'Donnell, *Un juego imposible: Competición y coalición entre partidos políticos en Argentina, 1955–1966* (Buenos Aires, 1970), 8–19.

5. Cavarozzi, *Autoritarismo*, 26–30; Marcelo Cavarozzi, *Consolidación del sindicalismo peronista y emergencia de la fórmula política argentina durante el gobierno frondizista* (Buenos Aires, 1979); Marcelo Cavarozzi, *Sindicatos y política en Argentina, 1955–1958* (Buenos Aires, 1979).

6. Cavarozzi, *Sindicatos*, 62; Gilbert W. Merkx, "Los conflictos políticos de la Argentina post-peronista," in *Argentina conflictiva: Seis estudios sobre problemas sociales argentinos*, ed. J. F. Marsal (Buenos Aires, 1972), 136–69; Santiago Senen González, *El sindicalismo después de Perón* (Buenos Aires, 1971); O'Donnell, *El estado*, 130–38.

7. Marcelo Sánchez Sorondo was the son of Matías Sánchez Sorondo, thus continuing rightist proclivities across generations. This pattern was not unique, as other sons of well-known rightists followed their parents in the political tradition. For data in this and the following paragraph see *Azul y Blanco* 12 (August 1956); and Comisión de Estudios de la Sociedad Argentina de Defensa de la Tradición, Familia, y Propiedad, *El nacionalismo: Una incógnita en constante evolución* (Buenos Aires, 1970), 85–89.

8. Daniel Rodríguez Lamas, *La presidencia de Frondizi* (Buenos Aires, 1984), 71–122. For various critiques of Frondizi see Francisco Hipólito Uzal, *Frondizi y la oligarquía* (Buenos Aires, 1963); Mariano Montemayor, *Claves para entender un gobierno* (Buenos Aires, 1963); Ismael Viñas, *Orden y progreso* (Buenos Aires, 1960); Isidro J. L. Odena, *Libertadores y desarrollistas* (Buenos Aires, 1977), 207 ff.; and Rouquié, *Poder militar*, 2:201–23. On the pre-1966 political crisis see O'Donnell, *El estado*, 65–85.

9. See the following articles in *Segunda República*: "Un programa institucional," April 18, 1962; "Bases teóricas," August 18, 1962; "Política de apertura," May 16, 1962; "Hora de decisión," July 25, 1962; "El pueblo pide una dictadura nacional," August 22, 1962. On the National Front see Enrique Ghirardi, *La democracia cristiana* (Buenos Aires, 1983), 122–27.

10. "Convivencia Nacional," *Segunda República*, April 24, 1962. Vicente Solano Lima published an article, "Salgamos de los errores," in *Segunda República*, May 21, 1962.

11. For the history of the relationship between the Azul and Colorado wings of the army during Guido's interim administration see Rouquié, *Poder militar*, vol. 2, chap. 5, esp. 212–28.

12. On the repercussions of the assault on Graciela Sirota see Leonardo Senkman, ed., *El antisemitismo en la Argentina*, 2d ed., 3 vols. (Buenos Aires, 1989), 1:37–55.

13. República Argentina, Cámara de Diputados, *Diario de Sesiones*, 36th meeting, 18th ordinary session (August 20, 1965), 2352–60. Also see Senkman, *El antisemitismo* 1:60–65.

14. On the connection of the MNT with security agencies see the declaration of Minister of Defense Leopoldo Suárez in Mar del Plata, in Senkman, *El antisemitismo* 1:50. To analyze the connection of the MNT with foreign groups see "Argentina, el antisemitismo y los Judíos," *Nueva Sión*, special edition (November 1974).

15. *Usted*, November 19, 1960, cited by Marysa Navarro Gerassi, *Los nacionalistas*, trans. Alberto Ciria (Buenos Aires, 1968).

16. Movimiento Nacionalista Revolucionario Tacuara, in report to *Compañero* (September 8, 1964): 3.

17. *Leoplan* (March 20, 1964): 18.

18. Peronist Deputy J. C. Cornejo Linares unsuccessfully asked the Chamber of Deputies to investigate anti-Argentine activities and to denounce the subversive infiltration of Zionism in Argentina. See his *El nuevo orden sionista en Argentina* (Buenos Aires, 1964) and his statements in *La Luz*, July 1, 1964; *Nueva Sión*, July 4, 1964; and *Crónica* June 18, 1964, 6.

19. *Primera Plana* (February 11, 1964): 5; Horacio de Dios, *Kelly cuenta todo* (Buenos Aires, 1984), 7–60.

20. *Combate*, June 1964.

21. This preliminary document was written by Genta in the form of a doctrinal book. See his *Acerca de la libertad de enseñar y de la enseñanza de la libertad. Libre examen y comunismo: Guerra contrarrevolucionaria* (Buenos Aires, 1976), 351–65.

22. For an analysis of Meinvielle's Nacionalista and anti-Semitic doctrine see Cristián Buchrucker, *Nacionalismo y peronismo: La Argentina en la crisis ideólogica mundial, 1927–1955* (Buenos Aires, 1987), 123–84. The archbishop of Buenos Aires closed *Presencia*, Meinvielle's publication, because of its editorial, "Puede un comunista ser presidente de los argentinos?" cited in Comisión, *El nacionalismo*, 91. On the GRN's recruitment activities see A. García Lupo, "Los jóvenes fascistas," *Marcha* (Montevideo), February 16, 1962.

23. "XXVII puntos programáticos de la Guardia Restauradora Nacionalista," March 1964, File on Nationalist Organizations (1964), Delegación de Asociaciones Israelitas Argentinas (hereafter DAIA) Archive, Buenos Aires.

24. *La Nación*, May 20, 1965; Senkman, *El antisemitismo* 1:48ff.

25. Confidential memorandum, File on Nationalist Organizations (1965), DAIA Archive, Buenos Aires. Also see *Nueva Sión*, April 7, 1965. To understand the coup environment, see *La CGT en marcha hacia el cambio de estructuras juzga el pasado, analiza el presente y proyecta el futuro* (Buenos Aires, 1965); Juan E. Miguens, "Morfología y comportamiento de la opinión pública urbana argentina" in Marsal, *Argentina conflictiva*, 170–90; Samuel Baily, "Argentina: Search for Consensus," *Current History* 51 (1966): 301–6; Marcelo L. Acuña, *De Frondizi a Alfonsín: La tradición política del radicalismo* (Buenos Aires, 1984), 156–94.

26. I follow the lines of interpretation found in the following studies of Peronism, 1973–1976: Liliana de Riz, *Retorno y derrumbe: El último gobierno peronista* (México, 1981); Viola, "Democracia"; Cavarozzi, *Autoritarismo*, 51–60; Marcelo Cavarozzi, "Los partidos y el parlamento en la Argentina: Un pasado de fracasos y un futuro cargado de desafíos," in *Democracia, orden político y parlamento fuerte*, ed. Hilda Sábato and Marcelo Cavarozzi (Buenos Aires, 1984), 136–52; Juan Carlos Torre, *Los sindicatos en el gobierno, 1973–1976* (Buenos Aires, 1983); Adolfo Canitrot, *La viabilidad de la democracia: Un análisis de la experiencia peronista, 1973–1976* (Buenos Aires, 1978), 23–38.

27. On the evolution of the parapolice organizations and the other groups that led to the AAA, and their participation in the Ezeiza Massacre, see Horacio Verbitzky, *Ezeiza* (Buenos Aires, 1984), 30–34. Claudio Díaz and Antonio Zucco, in *La ultraderecha argentina* (Buenos Aires, 1986), indicate the international connections between the Peronist and non-Peronist parapolice gangs during and after the Ezeiza Massacre and the Black International and neo-Nazi New European Order, 95–100, 104–13.

28. I use the theoretical analysis of political discourse offered by Oscar Landi in *El discurso sobre lo posible* (Buenos Aires, 1985). For examples of rightist Peronist discourse and the anti-Semitic thematic clichés as related to Jacobo Timerman, see *El Caudillo*, especially the following issues: (March 8, 1974): 2; (March 22, 1974): 2, 23; (March 29, 1974): 8, 9, 10, 11; (April 5, 1974): 23; (April 12, 1974): 13; (May 10, 1974): 5, 16; (May 24, 1974): 23; (June 14, 1974): 8, 9, 16; (June 28, 1974): 14; (July 12, 1974): 4, 5; (October 11, 1974): 21; (October 18, 1974): 10, 19; (November 8, 1974): 21, 23; (November 10, 1974): 15; (November 10, 1974): 10, 11; (December 3, 1974): 4, 10, 23; (December 17, 1974): 13, 15; (January 8, 1975): 9, 16; (March 19, 1975), 2. On previous Peronist usage of Synarchy and related concepts see Senkman, *El antisemitismo* 1:109–20.

29. On the anti-Semitic campaign to undermine Gelbard see *Prensa Confidencial*, May 5, 1974, reproduced in *Servicio Informative OJI* (May 29, 1974): 10.

30. See "La Sinarquía internacional no conseguirá sus objectivos," signed by the CGT and published in all the daily newspapers on April 7, 1974.

31. *Boletín Informativo DAIA* 60 (May 31, 1973): 10; *El pensamiento del Presidente Perón sobre el Pueblo Judío* (1974; reprint ed., Buenos Aires, 1954).

32. *Primera Plana* (July 23, 1971): 16; *La Razón*, December 13, 1972; Juan D. Perón, "Prólogo," in Enrique Pavón Pereyra, *Coloquios con Perón* (Madrid, 1973), 9, also see 146, 220.

33. Leonardo Senkman, "Los usos políticos del antisemitismo bajo el Peronismo, 1974–1975," in Senkman, *El antisemitismo* 1:117–26, 2:129–35.

34. *La Prensa* (August 27, 1974): 8. For an analysis of the relationship between the new businesspeople organized in the CGE and the traditional Argentine industrialists see John Freels, *El sector industrial en la política nacional* (Buenos Aires, 1970); Jorge Niosi, *Los empresarios y el estado argentino* (Buenos Aires, 1974).

35. For the reasons for a Nationalist Front see *Semana Política* (2da. quincena, September 1974): 2. On the formation of Acción Nacionalista Argentina, see *La Razón*, September 27, 1974, 7. José Enrique Miguens is not willing to recognize the possibility that Peronism in 1973 could have recruited its social and intellectual base from the fascist right; see his *Los neo-fascismos en la Argentina* (Buenos Aires, 1983), 73–91. On the Plan Andinia see, for example, *Consigna Nacional* (2da. quincena, September 1974): 24–25.

36. See *El Caudillo*, March 1975, and *El Fortín* (April 1975): 30–31.

37. On Alberto Ottalagano's views see his "Concepción doctrinaria del nacional justicialismo," *Retorno*, 98 (April 15, 1966), and his *Soy fascista* (Buenos Aires, 1984). His appointment as "normalizer" of the UBA was hailed by the Nacionalista organ *Cabildo* (November, 1974): 7, and by all of the rightist Peronist press. See *El Caudillo* (November 1974): 4–5; *Consigna Nacional*, 17 (la quincena, November 1974): 10–12.

38. *Boletín Informativo DAIA* (September, 1975): 6. The joint communiqué, dated June 23, 1975, was released to the press. See the letter of protest by the Unión Revisionista Jerut against the joint communiqué, August 1, 1975, that accused the president of the DAIA of "political defection . . . that affected the political neutrality of the community," DAIA Archive, Buenos Aires. In a personal interview, August 1986, Dr. Resnitzky gave me details of Kennedy's actions and of the pressures she

imposed to secure the communiqué. Kennedy's ideological transition from the Peronist left to the Peronist ultra-right, and her boldness and armed intervention in several operations and assaults, is related by Verbitzky in *Ezeiza*, 65–69.

39. Torre, *Los sindicatos*, 123–26; Guido De Tella, *De Perón a Perón* (Buenos Aires, 1983), 266–72, 320–29; Pablo Kandel and Mario Monteverde, *Entorno y caída* (Buenos Aires, 1976), 48–53; Santiago Senen González, *El poder sindical* (Buenos Aires, 1978), 104–6.

40. On the AAA see Ignacio González Jansen, *La Triple A* (Buenos Aires, 1986); Verbitzky, *Ezeiza*. The Peronist right recognized the AAA's contribution to free Peronism from the union and political left. See, for example, *Semana Política* (September 17, 1974): 3: "We do not know who the organizers of the AAA are, but it is obvious that their activities have in a few days dismantled the leadership of the extreme left groups." For the AAA communiqué cited in the text see *Nueva Sión*, 574 (September 3, 1975): 3. See Jacobo Timerman, *El caso Camps, punto inicial: Preso sin nombre, celda sin número* (Buenos Aires, 1983), chap. 5, on the AAA's propensity to kidnap wealthy members of the Jewish community. Personal interviews with several Jewish leftist militants revealed information on the AAA's kidnappings and imprisonments in clandestine jails.

41. *El Cronista* (March 15, 1976): 6. The Argentina Actors' Association, faced with death threats to some of its members from the AAA, released a communiqué denouncing the "supposed Judeo-Marxist conspiracy" used by the terrorist group "to claim the right to condemn to exile or to death any persons it chose." See *Nueva Sión*, 571 (2da. quincena, December 1974).

42. Ramón Camps, *El poder en la sombras: El affaire Graiver* (Buenos Aires, 1983), 211–14.

The Right and Military Rule, 1955–1983

Paul Lewis

> Politically the armed forces suffer from two crippling weaknesses. These pre-
> clude them, save in exceptional cases and for brief periods of time, from ruling
> without civilian collaboration and openly in their own name. Soldiers must either
> rule through civilian cabinets or else pretend to be something other than they are.
> One weakness is the armed forces' technical inability to administer any but the
> most primitive community. The second is their lack of legitimacy: that is to say,
> their lack of a moral title to rule.

So concluded Samuel Finer in his classic study of military politics, *The Man on Horseback*.[1] This essay will show how military governments in Argentina demonstrate the truth of Finer's thesis by the way they recruit civilian personnel from the political right to elaborate legitimizing ideologies and to provide technical expertise. To begin, it is important to emphasize the continuing split in the right, which has remained constant. In this period from the fall of Perón to the end of the military dictatorship, as before, there are two principal rightist tendencies: 1) the Nacionalista, which is authoritarian, corporativist, and militantly defensive about Argentina's Hispanic heritage; and 2) the right-liberal, which believes in authoritarian capitalism. Right-liberals may be subdivided further into ultras and moderates, with the former in favor of long-term military rule to keep down populism and the latter favoring a restricted version of democracy. In both cases they differ from Nacionalistas in their desire to link Argentina to the world economy, their willingness to sacrifice cultural tradition to technological and commercial innovation, and in recent years their admiration for the United States. Also, right-liberals are more likely to be economists, engineers, or administrators, in contrast to the generally literary orientation of the Nacionalistas. Indeed, right-liberal *técnicos* are attracted to military regimes because under them they are free to plan and execute their policies without interference from politicians or interest groups.[2]

The Nacionalista and right-liberal are not the only types of rightist activity, but they are the ones that have influenced Argentina's military governments most in recent years. Below them lies another stratum of sinister and

violent elements: storm trooper formations, "death squads," and counterintel-
ligence operatives whose activities border on—indeed, sometimes blend into—
outright criminality. This essay then will deal mainly with the right's public
participation, as cabinet ministers, in the formulation of policy under military
regimes, but it will bring in the rightist "underworld" also, to the extent that its
activities are identifiable. It is important, first, to make some general observa-
tions about the Argentine military's participation in politics and how the
military comes to recruit the kinds of civilians it does to its cabinets. The main
effort will be to describe particular military regimes, the individuals they
recruited, and the rivalries between the rightist groups for predominance.

The Military-Civilian Nexus

The military ruled Argentina for nineteen of the twenty-eight years between
the fall of Juan Perón in September 1955 and the inauguration of Raúl
Alfonsín in December 1983. Nine generals occupied the presidency: Eduardo
Lonardi, Pedro Aramburu, Juan Carlos Onganía, Roberto Levingston, Alejandro
Lanusse, Jorge Videla, Roberto Viola, Leopoldo Fortunato Galtieri, and
Reynaldo Bignone. One civilian, José María Guido, acted as a flimsy constitutional facade for de facto military rule. During that same period, three demo-
cratically elected civilian presidents were overthrown by coups: Arturo Frondizi
in 1962, Arturo Illia in 1966, and Isabel Perón in 1976. Another, Héctor
Cámpora, "resigned" in 1973 in the face of threats from his own party as well
as from the military.

The military always intervened on the grounds that the incumbent government either had failed to maintain order or was pursuing policies that
threatened the country's social and economic well-being. The officers arro-
gated to themselves the role of guardians of the national interest, inspired by a
belief that they were an elite that stood above petty politics, alone in their
readiness to make hard, unpopular decisions when the nation's permanent and
transcendental interests required them.[3]

This self-image of the military of being above politics did not square with
reality. Five of the nine military presidents just named (Lonardi, Onganía,
Levingston, Viola, and Galtieri) were overthrown by their fellow officers for
the same reasons that civilian presidents were deposed, and more than once
during the twenty-eight years of military governments units of the armed
forces were ranged against each other in battle to determine which faction
would dominate. Far from being a monolith, the military was split by service
rivalries as well as by certain functional loyalties, such as to the cavalry or to
the infantry. Military officers came from different social backgrounds and
different regions of the country, and although their military education instilled
in them certain common professional values, it did not furnish them with
precise guidelines for making political decisions. Whether in power them-

selves or seeking to influence those in power, officers frequently disagreed over what was to be done.

Factional cleavages were inspired, up to about 1972, by a fear of Perón's return to power and the revenge he might take for the 1955 coup. After 1972 the military's chief concern was with left-wing terrorism. In both cases, however, officers felt obliged to achieve economic growth to reunify the country. Given the military's professional values, in which order, hierarchy, discipline, solidarity, and sacrifice were emphasized, it is hardly surprising that the thinking of most officers about society was inspired by the right. But the ideologies of the Nacionalistas and right-liberals appealed to different officers, and, frequently divided over ends as well as means, the officers fought each other almost as often as they fought the military's opponents. Soldiers and civilians who embraced the Nacionalista position distrusted the secularism and "cosmopolitanism" of the right-liberals, whom they accused (often with good reason) of having links to foreign corporations. They blamed economic liberalism for dividing the nation into antagonistic classes and thus giving the left its opening. The right-liberals, on the other hand, dismissed Nacionalista ideology as "medieval" and accused its proponents of wanting to perpetuate Argentina's economic isolation and technological backwardness. Such factional struggles were responsible for the falls of the Lonardi, Onganía, Levingston, and Viola governments. Under Guido the factionalism led to several dramatic military confrontations, and they served to weaken the determination of the remaining military governments to retain power. In the end, the military proved no more able than were elected politicians to stake out a policy and stick to it.

Before describing specific factional battles, it is necessary to explain how, in general, the military selected civilian intellectuals and technocrats from the right wing to participate in governing Argentina. There was no one particular avenue. In many cases Catholic lay organizations were the point of contact between the military officers and Nacionalista intellectuals. Prestigious social institutions such as the Jockey Club brought together civilians and officers from Argentina's leading families—as did the Sociedad Rural Argentina (Argentine Rural Society, SRA), the Cámara Argentina de Comercio (Argentine Chamber of Commerce, CAC), the Bolsa de Comercio (stock exchange) and the Unión Industrial Argentina (Argentine Industrial Union, UIA). In fact, retired military officers frequently became landowners or business executives. Many civilian cabinet ministers got their positions through contacts they had made as professors at the various military schools. Others, especially the *técnicos*, had served in junior-level positions in previous military governments. Some civilians were recruited because they were prominent in their professions and some owed their posts to the fact that they were related to important officers. But whatever the route civilians took to reach the cabinet, as either Nacionalistas or right-liberals they had in common that both were elitist groups with almost no prospect of coming to power through elections. They owed their offices exclusively to their co-optation by the military.

The ratio of Nacionalistas to right-liberals in the cabinet differed from regime to regime. Lonardi and Levingston clearly favored the former; Aramburu, Lanusse, and Videla the latter. Onganía's government was dominated by Nacionalistas in the beginning, but a balance was struck later on as more liberal elements were brought in. In most cases, military governments contained representatives of both these rightist tendencies. As a very rough, general rule, right-liberals were recruited for the more technical posts, such as the minister of economy, the secretary of finance, the secretary of industry, or the secretary of agriculture. Nacionalistas tended to get the more political jobs, such as the minister of interior or the minister of foreign affairs. Such generalizations, however, must not obscure the complex web of military–right-wing civilian relations.

The First Military Period: Lonardi and Aramburu

On the morning of September 20, 1955, crowds cheered the triumphal procession through Buenos Aires of General Eduardo Lonardi from the downtown airport to the presidential palace. Against all odds, Lonardi had led a successful coup to overthrow the increasingly dictatorial regime of Juan D. Perón. In his first public speech, Lonardi promised there would be no persecution of the defeated Peronists. The revolution was nonpartisan, he said, and aimed only at restoring democratic liberties, such as freedom of the press, fair judicial processes, and university autonomy. The working class and its trade unions should not be penalized for Perón's misdeeds. All interests and parties, Lonardi continued, including the Peronist party, would be invited to cooperate in restoring the rule of law.[4]

Such a conciliatory course left most of Lonardi's supporters dissatisfied. Anti-Peronist trade union leaders, who had been ousted and jailed under the previous regime, wanted to abolish labor legislation that put the labor movement under government control. They also called for the removal and trial of the notoriously corrupt Peronist labor bosses. Military officers, anxious to prevent Perón's return to power, demanded the dissolution of the Peronist party and public exposure of the corruption and brutality of the previous government so as to "desanctify" Perón and his wife Evita. Businesspeople demanded new labor contracts on the grounds that the Perón regime had forced them to agree to stipulations that hindered productivity. Militant liberals wanted a return to the 1853 constitution, with its emphasis on property rights, as well as the dissolution of all the corporativist organizations Perón had set up to control labor, business, and the professions. In addition, restoration to its original owners of the daily newspaper *La Prensa*, which Perón had expropriated in 1951 and given to the Confederación General del Trabajo

(CGT), became a symbolic issue around which all the anti-Peronists rallied. Nor were the feelings of anti-Peronists mollified by Lonardi's freeing of political prisoners, dissolution of the Peronist-dominated Congress, or restoration of the original nomenclature of places that had been renamed in honor of Juan and Evita Perón. His refusal to intervene with the CGT, cancel labor contracts, or act on the *La Prensa* case because these acts would seem to be "punitive" cost him much of his original support as the suspicion grew that he secretly favored continuing the Peronist system, but with himself in Perón's place.[5]

Lonardi's appointments to high government posts confirmed this suspicion. His appointment of his brother-in-law, Clemente Villada Achával, as presidential secretary emphasized that he himself had married into an old aristocratic and Catholic family from Córdoba, which had a long tradition of right-wing activism. Tristán Achával Rodríguez, one of the family's progenitors, had been a violent Catholic reactionary, and Manuel Villada Achával, Clemente's father, had used his position as minister of education under the 1943 military government of General Pedro Ramírez to impose Catholic religious instruction on the public schools. Clemente himself was a Nacionalista activist, having been head of Acción Católica (Catholic Action) youth in Córdoba. Not only did appointments like that of Clemente threaten the kind of liberal reforms that many anti-Peronists were demanding but because the Catholic hierarchy had supported Perón for so long liberals might justifiably fear that the Nacionalistas intended to use Lonardi to replace Perón's labor-based corporativist dictatorship with a clerical-corporativist one.[6]

Even more alarming than Villada Achával's appointment was Lonardi's choice of Mario Amadeo as his minister of foreign relations, Atilio Dell'Oro Maini as his minister of education, and Juan Carlos Goyeneche as his press secretary. All three were open admirers of fascism and veteran activists in Nacionalista movements. Amadeo and Goyeneche had edited a Nacionalista journal, *Sol y Luna*, during the late 1930s and the war years, and Dell'Oro Maini had edited the right-wing Catholic journal *Criterio*, which had been favorable to the regime of José Uriburu and to Francisco Franco's Spain. Amadeo had been so enamored of the Axis cause that he twice resigned from the diplomatic corps, once when Argentina broke relations with Germany and again when the nation declared war on Germany and Japan. Goyeneche, who had been invited to Madrid during the war and had come to know Franco and the leading officials of his regime, was an enthusiastic supporter of Franco's "counter-revolution, or Christian Restoration." Dell'Oro Maini's career began with his participation in the Liga Patriótica Argentina in the years following World War I. All three men had held minor posts in the Perón government but had become disillusioned by Perón's shallow demagoguery and attacks on the Catholic church.[7]

Other Nacionalistas in Lonardi's cabinet were Luis B. Cerruti Costa, a former Peronist lawyer for the Metallurgical Workers' Union, who hoped to attract the proletariat to Nacionalismo, as minister of labor; César Bunge, who had served as Perón's representative to the Inter-American Economic and Social Council but resigned when Perón began to attack the church, as minister of commerce; General Justo León Bengoa, who also had served Perón faithfully until the break with the church, as minister of the army; and General Juan José Uranga, as minister of transportation. Another influential Nacionalista military figure in Lonardi's government was Colonel Juan Guevara, who, as a liaison between Lonardi and the navy, had played a pivotal role in the revolt against Perón. He now served as a special advisor to the president.[8]

The Nacionalistas were not entirely in control, however. Ranged against them was a group of anti-Peronist "liberals," most of whom were military officers: Admiral Isaac Rojas, a leading figure in the September revolt, who was Lonardi's vice president; Admiral Teodoro Hartung, minister of the navy; Captain Arturo Rial, undersecretary of the navy; and Colonel Bernardino Labayrú, head of the president's military staff, who owed his position more to his personal friendship with Lonardi than to his political views. In addition, there were two prominent civilians: Eduardo Busso, the minister of interior and justice, and his undersecretary, Carlos Muñiz, an anti-Peronist student activist. As a group, they not only opposed Lonardi's conciliatory policies but also were convinced that an extensive purge of the country's social institutions was necessary before democratic rule could be restored.

To placate these liberals Lonardi appointed a National Investigating Committee to look into charges of scandal and treason in Perón's regime. Such sensational revelations emerged about his luxurious life and escapades with teen-age girls and the uncontrolled graft that went on behind the scenes that Perón was tried in absentia and stripped of his rank and honors as an army officer. Many of his close collaborators were sent to jail, and some Peronist CGT officials were dismissed from their posts. Lonardi also appointed a National Consultative Council, composed of representatives of all parties except the Peronists and the Communists, to advise him on public policy.

Even these concessions did not satisfy the right-liberal military officers, who suspected General Bengoa of dragging his heels on the question of purging the army of pro-Peronist elements. In early November the rumor began to spread that Lonardi was preparing to raise Villada Achával's position to ministerial status and that the latter was plotting with Amadeo and Bengoa to establish a Nacionalista dictatorship. Accordingly, on November 8, Lonardi was presented with an ultimatum forcing him to dismiss General Bengoa. Although the liberals demanded that Bengoa be replaced by General Pedro Aramburu, Lonardi insisted upon filling the post with an old friend and co-plotter, General Arturo Ossorio Arana. Arana was vehemently anti-Peronist, however, and as predicted by General Uranga, the other Nacionalista officer in Lonardi's cabinet, Arana could not be trusted to stay loyal in a showdown.[9]

Immediately, the Nacionalistas sought to recover lost ground. Villada Achával prepared a decree for Lonardi to sign that divided Busso's ministry of interior and justice into two cabinet posts. A second decree designated Luis María de Pablo Pardo, a well-known Nacionalista and friend of General Bengoa's, as minister of interior. This move touched off a political explosion. Not only had it been taken without consulting Busso but also Pablo Pardo was a particularly objectionable Jew-baiting Nacionalista who had collaborated closely with Julio Meinvielle, the right-wing priest and wartime editor of the anti-Semitic, profascist journal *Crisol*.[10] Despite an outcry from the liberal military officers, Lonardi, pressured by the Nacionalistas, proceeded to swear in Pablo Pardo on November 12. With that, Busso resigned and so did all the members of the National Consultative Council except for the representatives of Amadeo's nationalist party, the Unión Federal. That night a junta of fourteen armed forces officers from all three service branches removed Lonardi as president and replaced him with Aramburu. The junta also issued a declaration of principles calling for the Peronist party's dissolution, the disqualification of leading Peronists from voting or holding office, and the early scheduling of elections.

The Many Faces of Liberalism

Only two Nacionalistas survived Lonardi's fall: Atilio Dell'Oro Maini, who resigned a few months later, and Commodore Julio César Krause, the air force minister, who was replaced in 1957 by Brigadier Eduardo McLoughlin, a liberal. The bulk of Aramburu's cabinet was drawn from Argentina's elite pressure groups representing the business and landowning classes. They were liberal in matters of private enterprise and free trade but cautious about extending political participation to groups they considered irresponsible and demagogic. Government officials such as Eduardo Busso, the first interior minister, whom Aramburu carried over from the Lonardi cabinet; Pedro Mendiondo, the public works minister; Luis Podestá Costa, the foreign affairs minister; Alberto Mercier, the agriculture minister; and Laureano Landaburu, the later interior minister, and his brother, Commodore Jorge Landaburu, who became air force minister in August 1957, were connected to Argentina's large landed interests, as represented by the SRA. All four of Aramburu's finance ministers were successful businesspeople with links to the UIA or the CAC: Julio Alizón García, Eugenio Blanco, Roberto Verrier, and Adalbert Krieger Vasena. So too were Alvaro Alsogaray, the industry minister, a former army officer whose brother, Julio, was still in the cavalry; Julio César Cueto Rua, the commerce minister; Luis María Ygartua, the communications minister; Juan Llamazares, the trade minister, who represented the Bolsa de Comercio; and Raúl Migone, the labor minister. Adolfo Lanús, the press secretary, had been editor of *La Prensa* at the time Perón expropriated it.[11]

Ideologically, these men were committed to classical liberalism's beliefs in free enterprise and constitutional government. Two events during 1957 were to strain the latter belief, however: the division of the middle-class Unión

Cívica Radical (UCR) into two antagonistic and independent parties in January, and the Peronists' strong showing (as revealed by the great number of blank ballots cast in protest) in the July elections for a constitutional convention. The Radicals' split was fatal for the hopes of those who saw in the UCR a way of restoring a stable middle-class democracy. The Unión Cívica Radical Intransigente (UCRI), led by Arturo Frondizi, sought to attract working-class votes with a populist program hardly distinguishable from Peronism. The old-line Radicals, grouped under Ricardo Balbín's Unión Cívica Radical del Pueblo (UCRP), showed slightly greater strength, winning 24.2 percent of the vote in the July elections to the UCRI's 21.2 percent; but with the blank ballots reaching 24.3 percent it appeared that the Peronists held the balance of power. Either they would support Frondizi and so keep their economic policies in force or they would remain on the sidelines in the general elections and let Balbín assume the running of a minority government. Whatever the outcome, the chances for liberal democracy looked slim.[12]

The prospect of a weak democracy that might provide Perón with an opportunity to stage a comeback convinced many liberals that the military ought to stay in power. From the standpoint of these right-liberals, Argentina needed a thorough purge to cleanse it of Peronism. Aramburu's vice president, Admiral Isaac Rojas, was perhaps the most important right-liberal of all the high military officers. The army minister, General Arturo Ossorio Arana, was as already mentioned another fervent anti-Peronist; nevertheless, he was willing to follow Aramburu's lead out of loyalty to the service. Only a firm promise by Aramburu, whose personal prestige was extremely high among the officers, that the military would never permit the legalization of the Peronist party, could bring these right-liberals to accept an early return to constitutional rule. And even so, it would have to be a limited democracy, like the managed politics of the Década Infame.

So far as the civilians in the cabinet were concerned, the government's highest priority was to return Argentina to a more liberal economic system. They agreed on the need to de-Peronize society, to reduce the power of the trade unions, to link wages to productivity, to diminish the power of the state, and to foster private enterprise, including foreign investment. What is more, they had support for their demands from publication of the so-called Prebisch Report, a study of the state of the economy commissioned by Lonardi but carried to conclusion under Aramburu. According to this study, Argentina was passing through the most severe economic crisis in its modern history and only strong encouragement of the private sector, including foreign capital, could overcome it. The state would have to reduce its expenditures as well as general living standards in order to accumulate savings for investment.[13]

Aramburu's policies pleased the right-liberals at first. Besides abolishing the Peronist party, he intervened the CGT and its member unions, abolished the Peronist Law of Professional Associations so as to permit competing unions, required that new labor contracts contain incentive clauses, reduced the role of shop stewards, made it easier for management to fire or reclassify workers, and restored *La Prensa* to its original owners.[14] This tough line reached a climax in June 1956, when remaining Peronist elements in the army, seconded by Peronist labor militants, attempted to revolt. They were quickly smashed and their leaders were shot without trials.

Paradoxically, this crackdown was followed by a more conciliatory line. Having eliminated any likelihood of Peronism seizing power, Aramburu was free to distance himself from the right-liberals. Within the military, they had been lodged mainly in the navy. Now service rivalries asserted themselves, and the navy ministers in the cabinet saw their influence dwindle. At the same time, the government's more moderate course steered away from any strict application of the Prebisch Report. In an effort to cajole workers away from what he hoped they perceived as Peronism's lost cause, Aramburu "forgot about" tying wages to productivity. The labor ministry awarded 38 percent increases to workers during 1957, whereas productivity rose hardly at all. And to insure that these wage increases were not passed on to consumers, price controls were imposed on a wide variety of essential goods.

In the end, Aramburu's policy resembled the consensus politics Lonardi had advocated: no one was to sacrifice for someone else's gain. Not only was the free market not restored but also the Instituto Argentino para la Promoción del Intercambio (Argentine Institute for the Promotion of Trade) (IAPI), the hated state grain-purchasing and grain-export monopoly, was not even dismantled until the very last days of the regime. By that time the SRA, UIA, and CAC had gone into opposition, and the loss of their support was not offset by any gains from labor. The lifting of intervention and the holding of a "normalizing" congress of the CGT in August 1957 gave the Peronists their opportunity to show that they still dominated most of the industrial unions.

As the time for general elections approached, the most that Aramburu was willing to do was to back Balbín's UCRP. Carlos Adrogué, Aramburu's education minister, Francisco Martínez (health), Carlos Alconada Aramburu (interior, and no relation to the president), Acdeel Salas (justice), and Angel Cabral (communications) all belonged to this party and were extreme anti-Peronists. Tristán Guevara (labor), a member of the orthodox liberal Progressive Democratic party, was another ally on the liberal right.[15] There was little doubt where the military's heart lay in the February 1958 elections, but their hope for a UCRP victory was dashed by an electoral pact between Frondizi and Perón, just as many right-liberals had feared.

Aramburu's regime thus ended in failure. For the next four years military *golpistas*, the UCRP, and other right-liberals would be busy conspiring against Frondizi, painting him both as an irresponsible leftist and a stalking-horse for Perón. Their persistence, coupled with Frondizi's own mistakes, eventually were to give the Argentine right—especially the right-liberals—another chance to take power.

The Guido Interlude

On March 28, 1962, the military deposed Arturo Frondizi as president because he had allowed the Peronists to run in congressional and gubernatorial elections, which they won. Right-liberal officers, having been of the opinion that the return to civilian rule had been premature, wanted to impose a military dictatorship. They were thwarted by their moderate colleagues, who, in collaboration with the Supreme Court, swore in José Maria Guido, president of the Senate, as the first in line to succeed Frondizi under the constitution (the vice presidency being vacant at the time). Although the right-liberals acquiesced in this ploy for the time being, they insisted that the recent electoral results be canceled, that Congress be dissolved, and that all the provinces where Peronists gained victories be intervened. Thus, Guido became provisional president, but he and his largely civilian cabinets were to be merely a facade behind which opposing military factions battled ferociously for power.

Both Nacionalistas and right-liberals helped to form Guido's cabinets, but this was not the main line of political cleavage during the violent twenty months that followed Guido's swearing in. Nor was it Peronists versus anti-Peronists, because all of the military officers and most of the civilians were opposed to Perón. Rather, the principal difference seems to have been between those who opposed return to civilian government and those who favored it. For example, who could be more representative of the right-liberal oligarchy than Federico Pinedo, Guido's first minister of economics? A member of the Sociedad Rural, the Cámara de Comercio, and the very exclusive Jockey Club, Pinedo had twice served as finance minister under conservative governments during the Década Infame and had suffered imprisonment under Perón. Yet his was the voice of moderation. Argentina's troubles were essentially political, not economic, he argued, and no progress toward recovery could be made until stable institutions and procedures were established. Consequently, he opposed demands that Congress be dissolved and the provinces intervened, although he was willing to annul the Peronist victories on the grounds that their party was outside the law and therefore had been ineligible to participate in the elections. Furthermore, he argued, as a totalitarian movement Peronism had no right to participate in future elections. To the claim that Peronism represented the will of the sovereign people, Pinedo answered that even the people must respect the constitution and the laws. Moreover, democracy had no obligation to permit its enemies to use its procedures to destroy it.[16]

Neither the Peronists nor the military's extremists accepted Pinedo's logic. The navy, led by Admiral Gastón Clement, insisted that either all of the elected candidates be seated or none of them. Because the Peronists were unacceptable, this demand meant that Congress must be dissolved. On April 20, 1962, the navy, together with hard-line army elements led by General Raúl Poggi, chief of the General Staff, revolted and presented Guido with an ultimatum. When he gave in, Pinedo resigned as did Rodolfo Martínez, the minister of interior, who had fought to preserve Congress and the provincial governments.

Rodolfo Martínez was a maverick Nacionalista who belonged to the right wing of the Christian Democratic party. He had good military connections, having served under Aramburu as minister of commerce and industry. He also had been recruited by Frondizi, in an act of desperation, as his last minister of interior. After the coup Martínez remained in office but switched to the ministry of defense. Like many other Nacionalistas, he believed in a corporativist order, and he hoped to integrate Peronist labor into the political system rather than exclude them as the right-liberals wished. But he wanted to do so without either bringing back Perón himself or conceding to the unions too much power. His scheme was to return to civilian rule as soon as possible but to prevent any single party from obtaining a majority of the seats in Congress, using a proportional representation that would encourage minor parties and thus require all governments to be formed by coalitions.[17]

Martínez's undersecretary of interior was his friend and a fellow right-wing Catholic, Mariano Grondona, who also had served as his undersecretary in the Frondizi government. Grondona's political education included studies in Franco's Spain at the Instituto de Estudios Políticos. His military contacts were excellent too. In 1959 he became a professor at the Navy War School and since 1961 had taught at the Superior War School, to which all promising young officers were sent.[18] When Martínez left the government, Grondona went with him.

The departures of Martínez and Grondona brought about a more definite shift to the right-liberal position.[19] Jorge Walter Perkins, an old-time Radical who once had been former President Hipólito Yrigoyen's lawyer, took over at interior. Pinedo was replaced as economics minister by the even more laissez-faire Alvaro Alsogaray. Within the army, *golpistas* and moderates reached a compromise by which General Poggi and the war secretary, General Mario Carreras, both *golpistas*, would resign in return for the replacement of General Enrique Rauch, a Nacionalista, who commanded the crucial Campo de Mayo cavalry base just outside the capital. The compromise did not last. On August 8 the *golpistas*, now known as the Colorados, or the "red" faction of the army, revolted. Their leader, General Federico Toranzo Montero, accused the new war secretary, General Juan Bautista Loza, of being too sympathetic to the Peronists. He was equally critical of the next man Guido appointed, General Eduardo Señorans, who had been a major figure in the plot that overthrew Perón.

More cabinet shifts followed as this crisis continued. Perkins resigned as interior minister because of constant military interference. His replacement, Carlos Adrogué, one of the right-liberals in Aramburu's cabinet, resigned too after five days but finally was prevailed upon to stay. Bowing to Toranzo Montero's demands, the posts of war secretary and army commander in chief were separated. The former was given to General José Octavio Cornejo Sarávia, who was from an old landowning family in Salta and who was known as a strong anti-Peronist; the latter was given to General José María Túrolo, Toranzo Montero's close friend. This compromise was upset a few days later, however, when 120 junior officers wrote to Guido, refusing to recognize Túrolo's authority. He was replaced by General Bernardino Labayrú, a Nacionalista who had served as head of Lonardi's military household when he was president. Adolfo Lanús, Aramburu's press secretary, was made minister of defense.

Neither side was satisfied by the latest compromises, so it was only a matter of time before a new armed clash took place. It came on September 18, 1962, and this time the forces favoring a return to civilian rule initiated it. The revolt was touched off when General Cornejo Sarávia attempted to replace General Onganía, who was known to be a "moderate," as commander of Campo de Mayo. Accusing his superiors of plotting to install a permanent military dictatorship, Onganía demanded a complete overhaul of the cabinet and the top military commands.

Fighting broke out on September 20 as Onganía, now heading the Azules ("blue" forces), moved his tanks into the streets of Buenos Aires. Meanwhile, at the Campo de Mayo, a team of Nacionalista intellectuals began to issue manifestos calling upon all Argentines who wanted a return to civilian rule to support the revolt. Besides Martínez and Grondona, one of the more prominent figures among them was José Miguens, a political science professor and head of a polling firm, who had taught at the military school.

At first President Guido went along with the "loyalist" Colorados in his cabinet and ordered the rebel Azules to lay down their arms. However, his new economics minister, Alvaro Alsogaray, who had been in Washington when the revolt erupted, immediately flew back to Argentina and convinced him to switch sides. Although he was a rigidly ideological liberal and very anti-Peronist, Alsogaray was a proponent of limited democracy. Moreover, his brother Julio commanded the First Armored Division at Campo de Mayo and supported Onganía. Guido's change of mind disgusted the authoritarian right-liberals in his cabinet—particularly Adrogué, Lanús, and Admiral Clement—all of whom resigned. After four days of sporadic clashes, the Azules gained a clear superiority over the Colorados. General Toranzo Montero, the latter's principal commander, was forced to surrender and submit to arrest. Afterwards, there was a shuffle of military and cabinet assignments. Onganía took over as army commander in chief and General Benjamín Rattenbach, a respected officer and advocate of apolitical professionalism, was made war minister. Rodolfo Martínez returned to the ministry of interior, with Mariano Grondona as his undersecretary. Carlos Muñiz, a Frondizi supporter, replaced Mariano Drago, a right-liberal, as foreign minister.

Peace was still a long way off, however. Brigadier Cayo Alsina raised a revolt in Córdoba on December 11, 1962, after Guido dismissed him as head of the air force. Alsina had been a major figure in Frondizi's ouster and, although he remained neutral during the September revolt, was considered by Onganía as too "ultra." The uprising was snuffed out after two days. Its real significance, however, may have been its link to certain changes in the cabinet. Only a week before, Alsogaray had been forced to resign as economics minister after a run-in with General Rattenbach. Criticism had been rising against him from the UIA, the SRA, and the CAC because of his harsh austerity measures. Argentina was in the throes of a severe economic recession at the end of 1962, resulting in a record number of bankruptcies. Rattenbach wanted to appoint a five-member committee of independent economic experts to study the situation, but Alsogaray resisted the idea. When the cabinet upheld Rattenbach, Alsogaray resigned, as did the president of the Central Bank and thirteen high officials in the Ministry of Economics.[20]

There were signs that the government might be moving in a direction that would involve conciliating populist opinion. The return of the Nacionalistas and the appointment of Muñiz, the *frondicista*, pointed this way. So did Alsogaray's replacement by Eustaquio Méndez Delfino, who, though a member of the UIA and the Bolsa de Comercio, was known to favor a loosening of credit. Nevertheless, right-liberals still held important posts. Horacio García Belsunce, the treasury secretary, was a strong believer in orthodox economics as was José Alfredo Martínez de Hoz, the agriculture minister, and a descendant of one of Argentina's oldest and richest *estanciero* families.[21]

A large degree of uncertainty and tension was inevitable as Argentina moved toward holding new elections. On November 19 a new electoral law was issued. It contained Martínez's scheme for proportional representation and, also, forbade a party (i.e., the Peronists) from bearing any individual's name. For militant anti-Peronists, this provision seemed to imply that their enemies would be allowed to enter electoral races so long as they enlisted under another title. Their suspicions were confirmed in March 1963 when Miguel Angel Zavala Ortiz, leader of the UCRP's extreme anti-Peronist wing, announced that he had been approached by Martínez with a proposal that he run as vice-presidential candidate on a National Front ticket that would include the Peronist Unión Popular. This revelation produced an uproar. Martínez was forced to admit that he had been busy constructing a broad alliance that would include Peronists, *frondicistas*, the Popular Conservatives, and his own Christian Democrats: in brief, almost all of Argentina's parties—even (it was hoped) the UCRP. By involving all parties in the government, Martínez argued, Argentina might at last achieve political stability and begin the process of incorporating the Peronist masses into the mainstream. The right-liberals were not mollified. Treasury Secretary García Belsunce resigned in disgust. After much heated discussion, the military officers in the cabinet rejected the whole project, whereupon Martínez resigned too.[22]

This cabinet crisis was the signal for the Colorados' last revolt, on April 2, 1963. Led by the retired Generals Benjamín Menéndez and Federico

Toranzo Montero, and backed by the navy under the retired Admiral Isaac Rojas, they launched the most destructive uprising of this tragic period. Much equipment was destroyed and twenty-five people lost their lives. However, with the fall of the Puerto Belgrano naval base, on April 5, the Colorados were beaten for good. There was a thorough purge of the armed forces, which removed all further obstacles to holding elections.

The government's agonies were not finished, however. The new interior minister, General Enrique Rauch, the former commander of Campo de Mayo, soon split the cabinet with his moral crusade against the "economic delinquents" identified with the previous administration. Indeed, government investigations had turned up evidence of widespread graft in the economics ministry and Central Bank under Frondizi, with the result that Rauch ordered the arrest of a score of prominent bankers, businesspeople, and economists, charging them with fraud, smuggling, and misappropriating public funds. Many of those arrested had friends in the cabinet, who now rallied to their aid. Consequently, Rauch demanded the removal of Eustaquio Méndez Delfino (economy), Carlos Muñiz (foreign affairs), Alberto Rodríguez Galán (education and justice), and Rodolfo G. Martelli (labor) as accessories.[23]

Rauch's conduct created a dilemma for his fellow officers. Though sympathetic with his aims, they feared that President Guido would resign unless they overruled him. This would leave them with no alternative but an openly military dictatorship. Their hand was forced, too, by the collective resignation of all the civilian members of the cabinet on May 12. Thus, Rauch was forced to resign, but he was replaced by another Nacionalista officer, General Osiris Villegas, a good friend of Onganía's. At the same time, Rauch's opponents, Méndez Delfino, Muñiz, Rodríguez Galán, and Martelli, were dropped from the cabinet as well. José Martínez de Hoz moved over from the agriculture secretariat to become economics mininster, and his former post was taken over by Carlos A. López Saubidat, a prominent SRA member. It is perhaps symbolic that one of the few officials retained in this shuffle was José Mariano Astigueta, who took over the education and justice ministry in addition to the defense portfolio. Astigueta was a relic from the military's optimistic past, having served as education and justice minister under the dictatorship of General Edelmiro Farrell (1944–1946).

The remaining months of the Guido government were spent in preparing for July's general elections. With the National Front idea dead, the Peronists were unable to run their own candidates or to ally with other parties. Frondizi refused to field a ticket. Ironically, only the UCRP, which had so frequently been associated with *golpista* military elements, was left as a major party in the race. In a three-way race, featuring a rump faction of the UCRI and a personalistic campaign by former President Aramburu, the UCRP's Arturo Illia won the presidency with only a quarter of the total vote. This was hardly a mandate, which meant that the prospect of military intervention hung over Illia's administration from the very beginning.

The "Argentine Revolution"

The sword dangling above President Arturo Illia's head fell at last on June 28, 1966, when the armed forces, critical of his allegedly too-soft handling of the Peronists, once more took control of the government. A junta composed of the three service branches then offered the presidency to General Onganía, who had retired a few months before, and asked him to form a government.

Onganía's first cabinet was composed almost entirely of Nacionalistas, although many different intellectual circles within this general category were represented. One group formed around Enrique Martínez Paz, the minister of interior, a devout Catholic from Córdoba who was a close friend of Onganía's as well as of General Pascual Pistarini, the army commander in chief who had led the coup that ousted Illia. A member of the Popular Conservative party, which frequently allied itself with the Peronists, Martínez Paz considered himself a "social Christian" rather than a traditional right-wing Nacionalista. Martínez Paz and Onganía had come to know each other through their frequent participation in retreats organized by conservative Catholic church leaders for military officers, businesspeople, and professionals.[24]

As interior minister, Martínez Paz ordered state intervention in Argentina's previously autonomous universities, abolishing their internal government and shutting down the Marxist-dominated Federation of Argentine Students. While invading the University of Buenos Aires campus the police used excessive force, beating the students and professors unmercifully. This event, which became known as the "Night of the Long Clubs," created a fateful breach between the government and Argentina's youth, but it secured the "unreserved support" of a right-wing terrorist organization called Tacuara. Tacuara was an outgrowth of the old Alianza de la Juventud Nacionalista, which in turn had been the nucleus for the Peronist storm-trooper Alianza Libertadora Nacionalista.[25]

No believer in civil liberties, the new interior minister issued decrees allowing the police to enter homes without warrants and to hold suspects for up to ten days without charges. His effectiveness was enhanced by the fact that the undersecretary of interior was his cousin, José María Sarávia, another wealthy Catholic from Córdoba. A former professor of sociology, Sarávia frequently outlined his corporativist views at the religious retreats attended by Onganía and Martínez Paz.

Another group of Nacionalistas called itself "Ciudad Católica," after the original French organization Cité Catholique. Fervently anticommunist and antiliberal, it aimed particularly at recruiting military officers through the practice of planting "cells" in various garrisons.[26] Some of the prominent military figures around Onganía had been drawn into its orbit, such as Colonel Juan Guevara, General Eduardo Señorans, and General Francisco A. Imaz. The first two had been deeply involved in the plot that led up to Perón's overthrow. Onganía removed Guevara, a perennial plotter, from the country by an ambassadorship to Colombia, and Señorans was made head of the Servicio de Información del Estado, a secret countersubversion agency. Imaz, a fervent opponent of civilian rule, became Onganía's minister of interior in 1969.

Ciudad Católica also had civilian followers in the cabinet, chief of whom was the minister of economy, Jorge Salimei. Salimei was the president of Sasetrú, an agroindustrial conglomerate in which General Señorans was a director, and he also owned the Banco de Boulogne, which was said to handle a good bit of the Catholic church's finances in Argentina. He brought with him to the government his fellow social Christians Evaristo Piñon Figueiras, vice president of the Banco de Boulogne and secretary of the Sasetrú conglomerate's insurance company, as undersecretary of economy, and Francisco Aguilar, a Sasetrú director, as secretary of finance. Although not an actual member of Ciudad Católica, Felipe Tami, Onganía's Central Bank president, was closely associated with this group as well. Finally, the president of Ciudad Católica, Roberto Gorostiaga, was named to Onganía's cabinet as secretary of state for "the promotion of the community." This portfolio, with its cumbersome title, had the purpose of designing a whole new political constitution that would embody the "communitarian" (i.e., the corporate-state) principles of the Catholic right.

This first phase of the Onganía regime was short-lived. Businesspeople and *estancieros* who had expected a radical shift away from the *dirigiste* style of the Illia years were gravely disappointed to find that social Christians preferred even more state control of the economy. Indeed, communitarianism was hostile to economic individualism and implied not a little income redistribution in order to knit the working classes ever more closely into the national community. The entrepreneurs' disappointment was reflected in their refusal to reinvest, in continued capital flight, and in a stagnant economy. As a result, by the end of December 1966, Onganía was forced to shake up his cabinet, replacing many of the social Christians who held important posts with right-liberals, the sort of bureaucrats who could gain the confidence of both the local business community and foreign capitalists.

Chief among the new appointments was Adalbert Krieger Vasena, one of Aramburu's former finance ministers, who now took over the economics ministry. Krieger Vasena was forty-six, had earned a Ph.D. in economics, and was a board member of several private, including foreign, business concerns. He also had been in government administration, including as a director at the Central Bank in 1957 and his brief stint as finance minister, and he had been Argentina's representative to various international trade conferences. Krieger Vasena was Jewish on his father's side; his mother's family were nouveaux riches manufacturers, although this did not bar him from membership in the exclusive Jockey Club.[27]

Partly because of his Jewish background, but more because of his liberal policies, Krieger Vasena quickly became the Nacionalistas' bête noire. His top priority was controlling inflation, which he aimed to do by cutting government spending, reducing the bureaucracy, increasing revenues through higher taxes and charges for public services, and holding down wages. He also intended to make Argentina's hothouse economy more efficient and competitive by lowering tariffs. Credit would be restricted to those producers whose goods had export potential. Such an approach directly threatened the power of trade unions as well as the security of a great many business enterprises whose existence depended on government subsidies and protection. It could work only under the aegis of a military regime, and it flew in the face of the communitarians' ideal of a closed, harmonious national society.

The first *promoción* of Nacionalistas had been swept from office in December, but an even more formidable group of them had been recruited by Onganía to balance Krieger Vasena's influence. This faction was organized around the Ateneo de la República, a club founded in 1962 by Mario Amadeo and Máximo Etchecopar, which was pledged to work for an end to the "corrupting influence" of liberal democracy and for a "patriotic" government of military officers and high-minded civilians.[28] Amadeo, the energetic force behind the club, had been disillusioned with the military when Aramburu threw Lonardi out of power. He had supported Frondizi in 1958 as the most nationalist candidate in the race, in return for which he was made United Nations ambassador; but three years of UCRP government under Arturo Illia proved so distasteful to him that Amadeo once more was looking for a military hero to restore order. Under Onganía he would receive the ambassadorship to Brazil: a gentle form of exile for a notoriously meddlesome spirit. Etchecopar, who collaborated with Amadeo previously on various right-wing journals, had been in the diplomatic service under both Perón and Frondizi. Onganía made him head of the Foreign Service Institute.

Other Ateneo members were given even more important positions in the government. Guillermo Fals Borda, the new minister of interior, had been a Peronist judge and law school professor but had gone into opposition during the regime's antichurch campaign. Although a member of the Jockey Club, he nevertheless was one of the Nacionalistas considered to have good contacts with the Peronist movement. His principal collaborator at the ministry was Mario Díaz Colodrero, the secretary of government, who was responsible for relations between the federal government and the provinces. A product of the Instituto de Cultura Hispánica in Madrid, Díaz Colodrero was a strong believer in nationalism as defined by Hispanic culture and Catholicism. He also was a member of Opus Dei, a semisecret Catholic lay society that encouraged businesspeople and conservative intellectuals to become active in public life. Díaz Colodrero was one of the younger Nacionalistas and a protégé of Amadeo. Before entering the Onganía government, he had edited Opus Dei's influential journal *Cuadernos del Sur*.

Other Ateneo members operating within Borda's jurisdiction were 1) Ernesto Pueyrredón, his undersecretary of interior, an important businessperson and descendant of an old Argentine *estanciero* family; 2) Enrique Pearson, undersecretary of government, a Nacionalista militant from the mid-1930s, when he helped organize pro-fascist University of Buenos Aires law school students; 3) Ernesto Olmedo, who later succeeded Pearson as undersecretary of government; 4) Fernando Alizón García, a retired general who was appointed governor of Tucumán province; 5) Héctor D'Andrea, governor of Salta province; and 6) Carlos Caballero, the governor of Córdoba province, who as a student in the 1930s had belonged to the Partido Nacional Fascista.

Caballero may be said, in some ways, to epitomize the Ateneo brand of Nacionalismo. After receiving his law degree in 1940 he soon dropped his fascist connections in favor of traditional Catholic conservatism. Perón made him a labor court judge to satisfy the right but later removed him during the church-state struggle because of his pronounced Catholic sympathies. Caballero had good connections within the air force, having taught politics at the School of Military Aviation and served as that institution's advisor on its educational curriculum. Lonardi, whom he supported warmly, appointed him to a labor commission and also got him a professorship at the Catholic University of Córdoba. Caballero was actually Onganía's first choice for minister of interior, but he declined the post on the grounds that he realized that he was too abrasive and controversial, and he suggested Martínez Paz instead. By way of compensation, he was named to Córdoba's provincial supreme court, and when the governorship of Córdoba fell vacant in September 1967 his good friend Díaz Colodrero, a fellow *cordobés*, picked him to fill the vacancy. As governor, Caballero experimented with corporativist schemes of representation by meeting with hand-picked delegates of capital and labor.[29]

The interior ministry was only one area of the government colonized by the Ateneo. Foreign policy also was influenced heavily by this group. In addition to Amadeo and Etchecopar, it was able to claim the minister of foreign affairs, Nicanor Costa Méndez, who was a former ambassador to Chile under Guido, a former president of the Ateneo, and an active member of Opus Dei. Other Ateneo members serving under him were 1) Eduardo Roca, ambassador to the Organization of American States, from an old *estanciero* family; 2) Manuel Malbrán, ambassador to Chile; 3) Héctor Obligado, board member of the National Immigration Service; 4) Jorge Mazzinghi, undersecretary of foreign affairs, a former contributor to Father Meinvielle's *Nuevo Tiempo* and yet another Opus Dei activist; 5) Basílio Serrano, delegate to GATT (General Agreement on Trade and Tariffs, a UN agency), a longtime militant in right-wing nationalist movements, including Perón's nefarious storm troopers, the Alianza Libertadora Nacionalista; 6) Enrique Pelltzer, assistant director of political affairs in the foreign ministry; and 7) Juan Martín Oneto Gaona, ambassador to the Latin American Free Trade Area, a former president of the UIA—to which Mario Amadeo had been an advisor during Oneto Gaona's term of office.

A third focus of Ateneo penetration was in the fields of social and cultural affairs. Prominent among these officials was Samuel Medrano, the secretary of social security, an old journalistic colleague of Atilio Dell'Oro Maini on *Criterio*. Medrano, another Opus Dei member, was a "revisionist" historian, who, in a blistering biography of Bernardino Rivadavia, attacked the liberal tradition in Argentina. His undersecretary was Santiago de Estrada, Jr., a former ambassador to the Vatican, judge, and professor of canon law. Another prominent, albeit unsavory, figure was Raúl Puigbó, the secretary of "promotion and assistance to the community," who once had been an Alianza Libertadora Nacionalista bullyboy. His job was to foster corporativist organizations. Reshaping Argentine culture fell to José Mariano Astigueta, the secretary of culture and education. He was aided by two younger Ateneo members, Gastón Terán Etchecopar and Alberto Ezpezel, both undersecretaries and both from families with long experience in Nacionalista movements.

The Ateneo was not without influence in the economic sphere either. Among its membership it could count Pedro Real, president of the Central Bank, whose background was in industry and banking, and Rafael García Mata, the secretary of agriculture, who had served in that same post under Frondizi. Finally, the Ateneo had one of the most influential of all the members of the "inner core" of Onganía's government: Héctor Repetto, a retired general, who was secretary to the president.

The Ateneo members who held government positions were but a part of the whole organization. Many other Ateneo members held no official post yet were influential as contacts between the public and private sectors of society. Quite a number of them—Ignacio B. Anozateguí, Miguel Angel Echeverrigaray, Guillermo Gallardo, Héctor Llambías, Carlos and Mario Mendióroz, and Ricardo Zorraquín Becú—were right-wing writers and intellectuals who traced their careers back to the pre-Perón era. They had been editors or contributors to journals published by noted Nacionalistas such as Ernesto Palacio, Julio Irazusta, Atilio Dell'Oro Maini, Mario Amadeo, and Julio Meinvielle. Others, like Ramiro de la Fuente and Bonifacio Lastra, were veterans of paramilitary organizations. Lastra had begun as a member of the Alianza de la Juventud Nacionalista, the youth arm of the Legión Cívica, before graduating to the Alianza Libertadora Nacionalista. De la Fuente recently had led a group of hoodlums whose chief notoriety was gained in a series of violent scuffles intended to prevent the showing of a film, *Morir en Madrid*, that purported to expose Nationalist atrocities during the Spanish civil war. Still other Ateneo members were relatively young men who often were carrying on a family tradition of participating in Catholic Nacionalista organizations.

All of the *atenistas* shared certain common characteristics. They were strong Catholics, fervent anticommunists, and haters of liberalism in all its forms. Although the older members had sympathized with fascism (or at least with Francoism) up to the end of World War II, out of hatred for Anglo-Saxon imperialism, the Cold War had forced them to revise their world outlook.

American liberalism now seemed to them to be much the lesser evil compared with Soviet communism, so they supported the United States as the champion of Western civilization. Nonetheless, they remained economic nationalists, believers in autarky and a managed economy as opposed to free enterprise and foreign investment.

In addition to the Ateneo other Nacionalistas and antiliberals found their way into pivotal positions in the Onganía regime.[30] One of these was Federico Frischknecht, secretary of propaganda and tourism, who had been dean of the School of Economic Sciences at the University of Buenos Aires. Another was Roberto ("Bobby") Roth, the legal and technical advisor to the president. A favorite speechwriter of Onganía's, Roth carried on an unrelenting campaign to get Krieger Vasena out of the cabinet. He was a "developmentalist," or a believer in using closely regulated foreign capital to achieve import substitution in heavy industry, and so he employed many former Frondizi supporters in his department. Another "independent Nacionalista" was Carlos Vidueiro, a former army officer, who served as undersecretary in the presidential office, under General Repetto. Charged with the task of "rationalizing" the state administration, Vidueiro spent most of his time as a liaison with the labor unions.

Among the military officers not previously mentioned as nationalists were General Adolfo López, commander of the Campo de Mayo; General Osiris Villegas, general secretary of the Consejo Nacional de Seguridad; and Generals Jorge and Gustavo Martínez Zuviría, the former an air force chief and the latter the commander of the First Army Corps, located in the capital. General Villegas, a close friend of Onganía's, had replaced General Rauch as minister of interior in 1963, in the latter months of the Guido administration. The two Martínez Zuvirías were descendants of the infamous Gustavo Martínez Zuviría, who in the 1930s and 1940s had written scurrilous anti-Semitic novels under the pen name Hugo Wast and had served as head of Perón's official corporativist organization to control literature and the arts. The family was from Córdoba and was related through birth or marriage to the families of both Enrique Martínez Paz and General Eduardo Lonardi.

Although this was a formidable array of Nacionalistas, there were right-liberals in powerful positions too. Among these were General Julio Alsogaray, a central figure in the overthrow of Illia, who succeeded Pascual Pistarini as army commander in chief, and his brother, Alvaro Alsogaray, the ambassador to the United States. A true believer in classical liberal economics, Alvaro had benefited by his military connections to become economics minister under Frondizi and Guido. Onganía passed him over for this post, however, presumably to avoid placing himself too much under the Alsogarays' influence. The assignment to Washington, where Alvaro was said to have excellent contacts, not only kept him safely out of the country but also was designed to attract investors. Another powerful right-liberal officer was General Alejandro Lanusse, commander of the Third Army, in Córdoba. Arrested in 1951 for plotting against Perón, he had supported Aramburu against Lonardi. He favored suppressing the Peronist party and praised Onganía's harsh tactics in February 1967 when the government broke up a general strike planned by the CGT. Unfortunately, Generals Lanusse and Alsogaray were personally at odds, which weakened the right-liberals. Their quarrel was heightened even more when Lanusse's younger brother, Antonio, was forced to resign as minister of defense in January 1967, after quarreling with Alsogaray over the purchase of some military equipment.[31]

General Lanusse did not have to wait long for his revenge. The Alsogaray brothers were combative, and they were determined to dislodge the Ateneo clique from the cabinet. Because they had succeeded in getting Onganía to oust the original group of Nacionalistas, they presumed that the president always would bow to their pressure. Near the end of August 1967, Alvaro Alsogaray gave a press conference in Washington in which he attacked the "bureaucratic" and "statist" mentality of the Nacionalistas in the Argentine cabinet. The next week he was called back to Argentina to face an angry Onganía, who nonetheless was forced to swallow this act of insubordination because Krieger Vasena had supported it as well. At this moment Krieger Vasena's prestige was on the rise in Argentina, because of his success in reactivating the economy, so Onganía did not wish to provoke his resignation by firing his friend, Alsogaray. Nor was he ready to face a confrontation with the army commander in chief.

Emboldened, the Alsogarays stepped up their efforts to pry the Nacionalistas out of power. Federico Frischknecht and Guillermo Fals Borda were the main targets. Finally, on May 5, 1968, General Alsogaray made a public speech in which he attacked Borda's "corporativist" aims. This not only earned him a rebuke from Onganía, but on May 20 the president summoned all the division-level generals to his house and, after outlining his political program, asked for a vote of confidence. They supported him overwhelmingly. Defeated, General Alsogaray and his brother then began contacting Peronists and Radicals with the idea of replacing Onganía with a civilian government. This was going too far. In August, General Onganía, now confident of his position, dismissed the Alsogarays from their posts. General Lanusse took over as the new army commander in chief.

Squabbling among the right-liberals might have been fatal but for Krieger Vasena's immense personal prestige. Under his economic leadership Argentina moved from a stagnant, hothouse economy to one that was more attractive to business. Credit was directed to larger, more efficient industries, and taxes on agricultural exports were abolished. Smaller firms, which had been kept alive by subsidies, were allowed to go under, while at the same time the government's tough measures toward labor unions permitted wages to be frozen. Although there was a record number of bankruptcies as a result of these policies, and much grumbling on the part of workers, inflation began to come down. From an annual rate of 22.6 percent when Krieger Vasena took over in December 1966, it fell to only 4 percent by the end of 1968. Conversely, the gross national product began to climb, by 2 percent in 1967, 4.6 percent in 1968, and 6.9 percent in 1969, with manufacturing leading the way. This achievement of growth without inflation was considered miraculous by the business world, especially because it did not entail any contraction of the money supply.[32]

Krieger Vasena's apparent success only spurred on the Nacionalistas to undermine him. Their strategy developed along three fronts. First, they bitterly resisted any cuts in the personnel or expenditures of the government, for without these any liberal reforms were bound to be ephemeral. Rationalization schemes got lost in bureaucratic red tape, were quietly buried in the bottom drawers of Vidueiro's desk, or—if they got as far as the president—were attacked for their potential effect of increasing unemployment. Second, and related to the first line of attack, the Nacionalistas attempted to discredit Krieger Vasena by arguing that he was polarizing the country and undermining the regime's original popular support. Finally, they moved ahead with drawing up a political plan that would be the basis of a new corporativist order.

The Nacionalistas enjoyed their most splendid moment when, in May 1969, Onganía put his seal of approval on a "Fundamental Charter" drawn up by Borda and Díaz Colodrero. This document, which was to supersede the old constitution, provided for a hierarchical system of advisory councils representing business, labor, agriculture, professional groups, and cultural organizations. At each level officially recognized interest groups would prepare lists of nominees from which the government could choose the representatives it wished to consult. There would be no Congress, provincial legislatures, or municipal councils because the new system would be, in the view of its authors, more truly representative of national opinion. Skeptics had their attention directed to Córdoba province, where Governor Carlos Caballero already was working with a similar system.[33]

A few days later both the Nacionalistas and the right-liberals had their plans blown apart when the worst riots in Argentina's history erupted in Córdoba. Students and workers occupied the factories, overwhelmed the police, threw up barricades in the streets, and called for a revolution against Onganía. After four days of street warfare, a dozen people killed, and enormous property damage, martial law restored order. Afterwards, a badly shaken Onganía changed his entire cabinet, dismissing both Krieger Vasena and the most prominent Nacionalistas. Right-liberals have since accused the Nacionalistas of staging the *cordobazo* as their only way to discredit Krieger Vasena.[34] There is evidence to support this charge, but if the Nacionalistas deliberately used such a scheme to dislodge their right-liberal opponents, they succeeded far too well, because they were ousted too.

Onganía's new cabinet tried to strike the same political balance as the old. Krieger Vasena was replaced by José Maria Dagnino Pastore, whose economic views were very similar. Guillermo Fals Borda was succeeded by retired General Francisco Antonio Imaz, another Nacionalista. The Nacionalistas did receive a setback, however, when the position of secretary of government was abolished. Furthermore, General Lanusse began a purge in July of prominent Nacionalista army officers and pressed Onganía (unsuccessfully, as events were to show) to dismiss Roth, Guevara, and Señorans from the government. Nothing could restore the regime's former confidence, however. It was mortally wounded, and fresh blows aimed from the terrorist left would finish it off over the new next few months. In June, Augusto Vandor, the principal trade unionist favoring cooperation with the government, was assassinated. Then, in May 1970, former President Aramburu was kidnapped and executed. Although it was proved later that this was done by left-wing Peronists, at the time the fact that Aramburu recently had become a vocal critic of the regime aroused deep suspicions within the military. On June 8, 1970, Onganía was forced by the three service heads to resign.

The "Argentine Revolution" Winds Down

Although General Lanusse now had the real power, he compromised with the other service heads and chose General Roberto M. Levingston, a little-known intelligence officer, as the new president. Levingston's choice of economics minister, Carlos María Moyano Llerena, was indicative of his Nacionalista orientation. Moyano Llerena was a veteran intellectual of the right who had contributed to Father Meinvielle's journals and had been an early supporter of Perón. Like other right-wing Catholics, he also broke with the Peronist regime when it attacked the church.[35]

Economic policymaking would also involve the Consejo Nacional de Desarrollo, headed by General Juan Gugliamelli, who was well-known as a "super-nationalist" officer. Indeed, it was largely because of his extreme views that Gugliamelli had been passed over by the service heads in their search for a new president.[36] Even more controversial was the appointment of Luis María de Pablo Pardo—whose inclusion in the Lonardi cabinet had precipitated the downfall of that government—as foreign minister. The defense minister, José Cáceres Monie, who was carried over from the Onganía cabinet, was a moderate. He was retained because his brother was a high-ranking general. Aldo Ferrer, the minister of public works, rounded out the "team," but in many ways he was a maverick. He had served Buenos Aires governor Oscar Alende as economics minister back in the late 1950s and earned a lasting reputation as a "leftist" by a controversial tax plan aimed at forcing farmers and ranchers to produce more by taxing their "eventual profits." Both Ferrer and Cáceres Monie subscribed to Frondizi's developmentalist economics, which sought to use foreign capital to build import-substituting heavy industry under state supervision.[37]

The two liberals in the cabinet were Francisco Manrique, the social welfare minister, and Brigadier Eduardo McLoughlin, the minister of interior. Both had served in high office under Aramburu, both were friends of Lanusse's, and both were in favor of a quick return to civilian rule. As it turned out, neither had much influence in the cabinet because Levingston listened exclusively to the Nacionalistas.

Setting a firm Nacionalista course proved to be more difficult than Levingston first imagined, however. Moyano Llerena, though known as a Nacionalista, apparently became convinced that it was necessary to hold the line against inflation by using orthodox economic policies essentially no different from those of Pastore or Krieger Vasena. He immediately clashed with General Gugliamelli, who was busy drawing up edicts nationalizing bank deposits, raising tariffs, imposing exchange controls, and granting large wage increases. Pressured by Gugliamelli and unable to enlist the president's support, Moyano Llerena resigned on October 13, 1970. Brigadier McLoughlin resigned the same day after learning that his subordinates, with Levingston's encouragement, were negotiating behind his back on the terms of an amnesty for Perón. Manrique, the remaining liberal in the cabinet, did not resign until the following February.[38]

Aldo Ferrer succeeded Moyano Llerena as economics minister and quickly asserted his independence. For General Gugliamelli he was "insufficiently nationalist," but on November 10 it was the general who left the government. Indeed, Ferrer's policies followed faithfully in the ruts of previous economics ministers: government spending rose, more people were put on the public payroll, wages were increased, and the state purchased its supplies only from nationally owned companies. He also had plans to boost agricultural production by breaking up the big *estancias* and turning over the land to medium-sized farmers.

Before much could be done, however, there was a second *cordobazo*, in March 1971, which resulted in Levingston's removal. The military realized that it was dictatorship, not the content of economic policy, that created the fertile ground for discontent. General Alejandro Lanusse now assumed the presidency to begin a process of "political decompression." The "Argentine Revolution" was over and all that was left was to negotiate an orderly retreat to the barracks.

The regime's next two years were filled with bargaining with Argentina's two main parties, the Peronists and the Radicals, and trying to dampen social protest with generous levels of government spending and wage increases. Lanusse's original goal of forming a winning electoral front of democratic parties, which he called the Gran Acuerdo Nacional (the Great National Accord), was completely frustrated by Perón's superior strategizing, however. In the end, runaway inflation brought on by Lanusse's short-sighted economic policies made the regime unpopular and contributed to the Peronists' victory in the March 1973 general elections.

The "Process of National Reorganization"

The Proceso de Reorganización Nacional, or Proceso, as the military liked to call its grim period of rule from March 1976 to December 1983, was a harsher and more terrifying dictatorship than any Argentina had ever seen. Under Isabel Perón law and order had collapsed. At the time she was overthrown it was estimated that the left-wing Peronist Montoneros and the Trotskyite Ejército Revolucionario del Pueblo (ERP) were fielding urban terrorist and rural guerrilla forces that totalled around 30,000 actual fighters, with another 275,000 supporters who supplied them with money, goods, information, and hiding places. Security forces also estimated that, since March 1973, more than 1,350 people had died in armed clashes or from terrorist acts: 445 leftist guerrillas, 236 soldiers or police, and 677 civilian noncombatants, such as businesspeople, politicians, and anticommunist labor union officials. In the last months of the Peronist regime there was an average of one political killing every five hours and a bomb explosion every three.[39] Capital fled the country, production was at a near-standstill, and inflation approached a yearly rate of 1,000 percent.

When General Jorge Rafael Videla, the army's commander in chief, finally removed Isabel Perón from office it was clear to most military officers (and to many civilians as well) that Argentina needed a thorough reorganization. Although, as in previous military regimes, it would be necessary to include civilians, the military was determined to follow its own plan. Rather than serve to connect the government to important social groups, civilians tended to be recruited to General Videla's cabinet for their technical expertise.

This policy worked against Nacionalistas, whose intellectual orientation usually was more literary than technical. Between March 1976 and March 1981 only three Nacionalista civilians sat in the cabinet: Alberto Rodríguez Varela, minister of justice, a member of the Corps of Catholic Lawyers who had been secretary to the Supreme Court under Onganía; Juan José Catalán, minister of education, a high-school teacher from Tucumán who served the provincial government during the Onganía era as minister of economy; and Catalán's successor, Juan Rafael Llerena Amadeo, who once had been Díaz Colodrero's director general of provincial affairs and later served Onganía as undersecretary of education. Catalán was forced to resign when his plan to centralize the public university system's administration caused an uproar. Llerena Amadeo reintroduced Catholic instruction in the public schools.

Two right-liberal economic experts, José Alfredo Martínez de Hoz, the economics minister, and Juan Alemánn, the secretary of finance, were far more powerful under the Proceso. Both had served, in those same positions, under Guido, and both were strong believers in a free-market economy. Martínez de Hoz, as a wealthy *estanciero* and former president of Argentina's largest private steel company, had ties to both the rural and industrial elites. His current task, as he saw it, was to instill efficiency and competitiveness into the economy by lowering tariffs, favoring larger enterprises, privatizing the state companies, and deregulating the banks. Such a strategy was certain to arouse the opposition of small business, labor, bureaucrats, and nationalists as a whole. Only an authoritarian government committed to classical economic liberalism could have dared attempt it.

On the military side of the government there was a shared belief that a full-scale purge of the schools, labor unions, churches—indeed, of every social institution—was needed in order to uproot corruption and subversion. "Unhealthy" elements would be destroyed without mercy. Even under Isabel Perón, Videla had been blunt about the military's counterguerrilla tactics: "As many people will die as are necessary to achieve peace in our country."[40] However, it was still a matter of debate as to how widely repression should be applied. Videla and other, more "moderate," generals, such as Roberto Viola, the new army commander in chief; Carlos Washington Pastor, the foreign affairs minister (and Videla's brother-in-law); and Horacio Liendo, the labor minister, wanted to concentrate on the actual rural and urban terrorists and their support networks. "Hardliners," such as General Albano Eduardo Harguindeguy, the interior minister; General Ramón Genaro Díaz Bessone, the planning minister; General Carlos Suárez Masón, commander of the Campo de Mayo cavalry base; General Luciano Benjamín Menéndez, head of the Third Army; and Admiral Emilio Massera, head of the navy and Videla's vice president, favored more sweeping repression. Not just the left-wing activists themselves, but also those who inspired their beliefs, those who sympathized with their actions, and even those who simply stood on the sidelines as neutrals would have to be eliminated.[41]

The hardliners headed most of the army units from which the antiguerrilla campaign was carried out. Each military district conducted its own antiterrorist raids and ran its own detention camps. No records were kept of victims, who simply "disappeared" along with friends or relatives unlucky enough to be with them when they were seized. Such decentralized operations made it difficult for government officials to exercise much effective control over the repression, which became increasingly widespread and indiscriminate, reaching a peak about 1979. This pattern also enabled top government officials to deny any knowledge of, or responsibility for, what was going on.[42]

The number of "disappeared" can never be known with certainty. Estimates vary from six thousand to twenty thousand. Not all, perhaps not even most, were actual terrorists. The military sought to uproot the guerrillas' underground organization by rounding up suspected sympathizers, such as academicians, journalists, and social workers, and sending them to secret detention camps to be tortured and interrogated. In most cases, no records were kept of the victims. It was, Daniel Lutzky wrote, "the most terrible repression ever known in Argentina throughout its entire history. In reality, it seemed more like a gigantic police operation than a war, since there were hardly any battles—just kidnappings, torture, and assassinations."[43]

Yet the "Dirty War," as the military chiefs called it, had its supporters on the right, including the higher Catholic clergy. Pastoral letters deplored the kidnappings and disappearances but also were careful to note that the guerrillas had brought the country to such a state of disorder that the security forces might easily commit excesses in their zeal to protect the nation from Marxism.[44] One did not have to go that far to recognize that the struggle was indeed a "dirty war" in which the tactics of guerrilla warfare, especially as applied in urban settings, dictated the military's response. The urban guerrillas seemed to have infiltrated everywhere: the clergy, the bankers, even the military itself. A rising chorus of condemnation by foreign governments and international organizations only convinced Argentine security forces that their country was a great battlefield in a worldwide revolutionary war.

This conviction did not prevent factionalism from dividing Videla's government. Within the cabinet, his chief opponents were Díaz Bessone and Admiral Massera. Both concentrated their fire on Martínez de Hoz and, to a much lesser extent, on General Liendo. Díaz Bessone, who hated politics, resigned in December 1977, when it became clear that the economics minister, not he, had the president's ear. Massera, a blustering bully in public and inveterate conspirator in private, continued to try to undermine Videla by posing as an advocate of returning to civilian rule. Naturally, he saw himself in the role of the hero who made such a thing possible, and he was able to line up support from the Peronist movement.

Massera's Peronist contacts always had been good. He had served as navy minister in Isabel Perón's cabinet and once had been a business partner of Lorenzo Miguel, the metal workers' union boss. Not until 1981 was it learned, however, that Massera—as well as General Suárez Masón—had belonged to a secret Masonic lodge called Pro-Patria, which had been organized by José Lopéz Rega, the sinister *éminence grise* behind Isabel Perón and the organizer also of the "death squads" known as the Alianza Anticomunista Argentina (AAA). Pro-Patria was the spin-off of a similar lodge in Italy, called Propaganda-Due (P-2), to which powerful figures in the Italian governmental, military, financial, and clerical worlds belonged. The head of this right-wing "underground," Licio Gelli, apparently had been a major financial backer of Perón, who rewarded him with the "Grand Cross in the Order of the Liberator General San Martín" six weeks after returning to power, for unspecified "important services to the country." Gelli was given an Argentine passport and made an advisor to the Argentine embassy in Rome—favors he continued to enjoy even after the Peronists were out of power, thanks to Admiral Massera's patronage.[45]

Pro-Patria, like its parent organization, P-2, was able to dispose of large sums of "laundered" money through its connections with the international business community, the Catholic church, and the underworld. In the case of Argentina, these funds often were used to buy legitimate businesses that could be used as "fronts," or—in the case of publishing houses—as outlets for right-wing propaganda, or simply for patronage (General Suárez Masón, for example, was made a director of a private oil company). The P-2's enemies claimed that its ultimate aim was to create an anticommunist "international." Whatever the case might have been, the P-2's existence was discovered in March 1981, resulting in the arrest or flight of its leaders and the disruption of all its schemes. Its records were seized, and a list of its members, including those of its Argentine affiliates, was published.

Even before this discovery, however, the military's hardliners had proven ineffective in undermining Videla. Admiral Massera, the most purposive member of the clique, split them over the issue of a return to civilian rule. Generals Menéndez and Suárez Masón totally opposed it. Furthermore, the two generals resented a naval officer's asserting a claim to leadership. Interservice rivalry overcame their ideological sympathies as they rallied behind Videla.[46] Massera's star began to wane as early as 1979, when he retired from the navy and thus from the governing junta. The revelation of his connection to P-2 finished him off, especially when rumor linked that underground lodge to the kidnapping and murder of Elena Holmberg, a foreign service employee at the Argentine embassy in Paris, and to the disappearance of Hidalgo Solá, Argentina's ambassador to Venezuela. Former Treasury Secretary Juan Alemánn alleged in 1981 that Holmberg had been killed because she knew too much about the Gelli-Massera connection, a charge that her brother, Enrique Holmberg, took up, adding that Ambassador Solá might have been murdered for the same reason. Holmberg noted that Solá's replacement as ambassador was Federico Bartfield, whose name appeared in the P-2 codebook. Together, the presumed links between Gelli, López Rega, Massera, and the AAA death squads were too suggestive to overlook. Although never arrested by the regime, Massera quickly faded from prominence after these allegations.

The P-2 connection also tarnished General Suárez Masón. He was removed from the direct command of troops by being promoted to chief of the General Staff, after which he was retired from active duty. General Menéndez self-destructed in a more dramatic way. Angered over the release from detention of the celebrated journalist Jacobo Timerman, he raised a revolt in September 1979, which failed, and he was forced to retire. Thus, step by step, President Videla, though starting from what seemed to be a weak position, outlasted his rivals and was able to finish a full five-year presidential term.

The "Process of National Reorganization" Winds Down

The Proceso de Reorganización began unraveling soon after Videla's successor, General Roberto Viola, took office. The opening up of the economy, which Martínez de Hoz initiated, was reversed by the new economics minister, Lorenzo Sigaut. Not a Nacionalista, Sigaut nevertheless leaned more toward the *dirigiste* position than had Martínez de Hoz. He had been a senior treasury official in the Onganía government and had good links to the military. He was a personal friend of Videla and Viola, and he had taught economics at the Naval War School, where he helped administer its Center for Strategic Studies. He also served as a director on the board of the military-run state steel company, Sociedad Mixta Siderúrgica Argentina (SOMISA). Finally, he had Catholic connections through his teaching at the University of San Salvador.

Sigaut ordered two massive devaluations of the peso, justifying them on the grounds that Argentina needed to attract capital and encourage trade, which it had been unable to do because Martínez de Hoz had overvalued the currency. Instead of improving the situation, however, the devaluations destroyed local investor confidence in the regime, leading to a massive run on the banks and an unprecedented capital flight. It proved impossible to reverse the panic. In desperation, the armed forces removed Viola on December 12, 1981, and replaced him with General Leopoldo Fortunato Galtieri.

Although its existence was fleeting, Viola's government, it is worth recording, was a mixture of Nacionalistas and liberals. Among the former were Foreign Affairs Minister Oscar Camillión and Amadeo Frigoli, minister of justice. Camillión had been a professor of international politics at the National Defense College and of constitutional law at the Catholic University of La Plata. He also had taught at the Argentine Institute of Hispanic Culture. He had served under Frondizi as undersecretary of foreign affairs and been a member of Frondizi's Movement for Integration and Development. Frigoli, a former senator from Mendoza elected from the Conservative Democratic party, had been minister of social welfare under Levingston.

The right-liberals in Viola's brief administration included General Liendo, the only holdover from the Videla government, who moved from the Ministry of Labor to the Ministry of Interior; Eduardo Oxenford, scion of a prominent Anglo-Argentine family that owned the country's largest textile company, who served as secretary of industry; Jorge Rubén Aguado, the secretary of agriculture, who had been general secretary of the Buenos Aires province cattleowners' association, CARBAP; and Carlos García Martínez, the trade minister, who had been an adviser to Martínez de Hoz when the latter was Guido's economics minister and who later was president of the Central Bank in 1963.

The Galtieri government also maintained a balance of sorts. The economics ministry went back to the right-liberals with the appointment of Roberto Alemánn, who had served in the same capacity under Frondizi. Furthermore, Aguado was retained as secretary of agriculture. Oxenford was replaced as industry secretary by another liberal, Livio Guillermo Kuhl, president of the UIA and head of the country's largest paper and pulp company. On the other hand, Camillión was replaced at foreign affairs by an individual even further identified with Nacionalismo: Nicanor Costa Méndez, the *atenista* who had served under Onganía in the same post. Liendo was replaced at interior by

General Alfredo Oscar Saint-Jean, who was considered an extreme hardliner. Frigoli was retained as minister of justice.

Alemánn's appointment did much to restore investor confidence, especially because he promised to return to the free market policies of Martínez de Hoz, but any hopes of economic recovery were dashed a few months later when Galtieri involved Argentina in the Falkland (Malvinas) Islands war with Great Britain. The government fell in the aftermath of the country's humiliating defeat. The military, its confidence shattered, installed the caretaker government of retired General Reynaldo Bignone on July 1, 1982, for the purpose of preparing for the restoration of civilian rule.

Bignone's government was not remarkable for either its makeup or its policies. Its character was more technocratic than ideological. Its two identifiable Nacionalistas were both academicians at the University of Buenos Aires: Lucas Jaime Lennon, the justice minister, a former appeals court judge and currently dean of the law school, and Cayetano Liccardo, the minister of education and culture, who had been Guido's undersecretary of the treasury and Videla's head of the National Budget Office. Right-liberals were represented by Jorge Wehbe, an economist, who was the new minister of economy; Julio Martínez Vivot, the defense minister, an *estanciero* who was prominent in the SRA; and Juan Aguirre Lanari, the foreign affairs minister, a leading member of the Liberal Party of Corrientes and former ambassador to Venezuela. None of these cabinet officials had the authority to make much difference in the course of events; they are interesting only for showing the military's connections to various segments of Argentine society.

Conclusion

Argentina's deep ideological divisions led to frequent military intervention during the thirty-year period from 1955 to 1985. This was not unusual, for as political sociologist José Luis de Imaz has observed, enlisting military support is a "tacit rule of the Argentine game" and one from which "all of the political groups have benefitted at least once." No one admits this openly, of course, but all political parties and pressure groups have, at some time or another, "gone to knock at the barracks doors."[47]

Once in power, the armed forces approached politics from their own particular perspective. The values of any military organization emphasize hierarchy, authority, discipline, and solidarity. Good soldiers obey their officers; good officers look after their troops. Such a system is similar to the Nacionalistas' social model. Nacionalistas also emphasize other values dear to the military, such as patriotism, tradition, and faith. These are the ideals that an army depends upon to inspire troop morale, so it is not surprising that Nacionalistas were recruited by military governments to instill these virtues in the society as a whole.

In Argentina, where religion and Nacionalismo are so intertwined, the Roman Catholic church was often the connection between conservative military officers and the elitist intellectuals of the traditional right. Many Nacionalista cabinet ministers not only taught at military institutions, but they held teaching posts at Catholic universities as well. They tended to be lawyers, writers, or diplomats, and their services most often were employed in those ministries that are especially useful for promoting a particular way of life. The Ministry of Interior, with its control of the police and its authority over local governments, was one avenue by which Argentine institutions could be "purified." The Ministry of Education and Culture obviously lent itself to the propagation of religion and patriotism. The Ministry of Foreign Affairs and Religion not only defended Argentine interests abroad but also was directly involved with regulating the affairs between church and state through its relations with the Vatican.

Social pacification, however, required economic growth, which was also the key to national power. Thus, the military had to look beyond the world of Nacionalista intellectuals for its economists, who were presumed to have the peculiar knowledge needed to lift the economy out of its stagnation. Success here, where civilian governments had failed, would be by itself a sufficient justification of military rule.

In choosing their economic "teams," the military were more pragmatic than ideological. On the whole, their proclivities were *dirigiste*, as befitting their natural approach to politics, but the overriding need to succeed forced the military to recognize that the world's most dynamic economies operated generally on the principles of the marketplace and that *dirigisme* in Argentina had a long, unbroken record of economic failure. Hence, the officers tended to recruit right-liberal economists to head the economics ministry, the Central Bank, the treasury secretariat, the agricultural secretariat, and similar posts.

Right-liberals came from the same privileged social background as many Nacionalistas, but their outlook was more cosmopolitan. Whether or not they approved of military dictatorship in principle, they accepted it as necessary for Argentina in the given context, and their decision-making style was authoritarian. Their economic strategy proceeded from a highly theoretical perspective in which every aspect of the plan was coordinated carefully with every other aspect. Once it was announced, its architects resisted any modifications that might compromise its intellectual coherence. For the same reason, there was little or no consultation beforehand with the groups that were to be affected by these policies. Such a principled approach by right-liberals could be carried out only under a government that was relatively insulated from public opinion; and indeed these economic "experts" shared the military's disdain for populism. For them, popular democracy meant compromise, or the substitution of political criteria for efficiency, a crazy quilt of special-interest legislation for a rationally integrated plan.

Part of the reason that the military regimes in Argentina proved unstable was that Nacionalistas and right-liberals were opposed so deeply to each other. Their rivalry, which extended to the ranks of the military officers themselves, prevented any coherent policy from being applied long enough to make an impact. In the end, the dissension and frequent cabinet turnovers it caused rendered the military governments no more effective than the civilians they replaced.

Notes

1. Samuel A. Finer, *The Man on Horseback* (New York, 1962), 14.
2. Adriana N. Bianchi, "Politics and Economic Policy-Making: A Case Study of Argentina" (Ph.D. diss., University of Texas, 1978), 109, 112, 114, 131–32.
3. For the Argentine military's self-image as the nation's moral guardian see Horacio Verbitsky, *Medio siglo de proclamaciones militares* (Buenos Aires, 1988), which starts with General Uriburu's 1930 coup and ends with the Semana Santa coup of February 1987.
4. *Hispanic American Report* (October 1955), 431.
5. Arthur P. Whitaker, *Argentine Upheaval* (New York, 1956), 48–49, 109; Alain Rouquié, *Poder militar y sociedad política en la Argentina*, 2 vols. (Buenos Aires, 1978), 2:125.
6. Rouquié, *Poder Militar* 2:122–24, 370.
7. Robert A. Potash, *The Army and Politics in Argentina, 1945–1962: Perón to Frondizi* (Stanford, 1980), 217–21; Enrique Zuleta Alvarez, *El nacionalismo argentino*, 2 vols. (Buenos Aires, 1975), 1:183, 188–89, 249–50, 299; 2:502, 549; Marysa Navarro Gerassi, *Los nacionalistas* (Buenos Aires, 1968), 109–12, 123–26, 216; Mario Amadeo, *Ayer, hoy, y mañana* (Buenos Aires, 1956), 19–23, 64–65; Cristián Buchrucker, *Nacionalismo y peronismo: La Argentina en la crisis ideológica mundial, 1927–1955* (Buenos Aires, 1987), 183; Tulio Halperín Donghi, "Crónica del periódo," *Argentina, 1930–1960* (Buenos Aires, 1961), 66–70.
8. Miko Mandilovitch, "Group Conflict and Political Change in Argentina, 1955–1966" (Ph.D. diss., University of Michigan, 1976), 111–12; Potash, *Army and Politics*, 215; Samuel L. Baily, *Labor, Nationalism, and Politics in Argentina* (New Brunswick, NJ, 1967), 165.
9. Potash, *Army and Politics*, 220.
10. Zuleta Alvarez, *Nacionalismo argentino* 1:288.
11. Jorge Niosi, *Los empresarios y el estado argentino* (Buenos Aires, 1974), 42–47; *Review of The River Plate* (November 22, 1955): 21–22.
12. On the Radical party split see Peter Snow, *Argentine Radicalism* (Iowa City, 1965), 71–77.
13. For the text of the Prebisch Report, translated into English, see *Review of the River Plate* (October 31, 1955): 25–35, and (November 11, 1955): 19–30.
14. Daniel James, "Rationalization and Working Class Response: The Context and Limits of Factory Floor Activity in Argentina," *Journal of Latin American Studies* (November 1981): 390–91; Tomás Roberto Fillol, *Social Factors in Economic Development: The Argentine Case* (Cambridge, MA, 1961), 67–68.
15. Potash, *Army and Politics*, 249.
16. *Review of the River Plate* (April 30, 1962): 133–134.
17. Rouquié, *Poder militar* 2: 193–96, 217.
18. Ibid., 193–94.

19. For the many other cabinet changes under Guido see Rouquié, *Poder militar* 2: 196–214.

20. Niosi, *Los empresarios,* 102; *Review of the River Plate* (November 10, 1962): 191, and (December 11, 1962): 369–73.

21. Rouquié, *Poder militar* 2: 221; *Review of the River Plate* (December 11, 1962): 369–73.

22. *Review of the River Plate* (March 22, 1963): 360–61, and (March 30, 1963): 423–24.

23. Rouquié, *Poder militar* 2: 221.

24. Ibid., 259–260.

25. Navarro, *Los nacionalistas,* 225–28; *Primera Plana* (July 12, 1966): 14, and (July 19, 1966): 20.

26. Rouquié, *Poder militar* 2: 260.

27. *Quién es quién en la Argentina* (Buenos Aires, 1968); and Jockey Club, *Nómina de sócios* (Buenos Aires, 1964).

28. On the Ateneo, see Rouquié, *Poder militar* 2: 260, 371; *Análisis* (January 9, 1967): 8–10, (January, 16, 1967): 12–15, and (February 6, 1967): 16–20; *Confirmado* (November 3, 1966): 25.

29. *Primera Plana* (May 14, 1968): 20–22, and (August 27, 1968): 13–15.

30. *Primera Plana* (February 20, 1968): 15–19.

31. *Primera Plana* (August 27, 1968): 15.

32. Juan Carlos de Pablo, *Política antiinflacionaria en la Argentina, 1967–1970* (Buenos Aires, 1970), 119; Carlos Ramil Cepeda, *Crisis de una burguesía dependiente: Balance económico de la "Revolución Argentina," 1966–1971* (Buenos Aires, 1972), 68, 73–74; Niosi, *Los empresarios,* 149, 151; Banco Central, *Boletín estadística,* 1965–1969; *Panorama de la Economía Argentina,* 2d trimester 1970, 278; *Periscópio* (August 4, 1970): 25; *Review of the River Plate* (September 22, 1970): 454, and (January 30, 1971): 138.

33. *Primera Plana* (May 13, 1969): 36.

34. For example, see Roberto Aizcorbe, *The Peronist Myth* (Hicksville, NY, 1975), 222.

35. Zuleta Alvarez, *Nacionalismo argentino* 2:502, 528, 542.

36. Alejandro Lanusse, *Mi testimonio* (Lima, 1977), 145–46.

37. For an overview of the cabinet appointments see *Review of the River Plate* (June 19, 1970): 893–94; and on Aldo Ferrer specifically, *Primera Plana* (October 27, 1970): 19–20. Cáceres Monie had been Frondizi's presidential secretary, undersecretary of defense, and secretary of public works.

38. *Review of the River Plate* (October 23, 1970): 629; *Quarterly Economic Reports* (October 1970): 2.

39. Kenneth F. Johnson, "Guerrilla Politics in Argentina," *Conflict Studies* (October 1976): 15; Richard Gillespie, *Soldiers of Perón: Argentina's Montoneros* (Oxford, England, 1982), 216–17, 223.

40. *Confirmado* (December 3, 1975): 23.

41. For the political orientation of these officers, see Rosendo Fraga, *Ejército: Del escarnio al poder, 1973–1976* (Buenos Aires, 1988), 244–53.

42. Gillespie, *Soldiers of Perón,* 245, 250–51; Charles Maechling, Jr., "The Argentine Pariah," *Foreign Policy* (Winter 1981–82): 72–73.

43. Daniel Lutzky, "La izquierda de los 60," in *La nueva izquierda argentina: 1960–1980,* ed. Claudia Hilb and Daniel Lutzky (Buenos Aires, 1984), 74.

44. Emilio F. Mignone, *Iglesia y dictadura* (Buenos Aires, 1986), 50.

45. Martin Berger, *Historia de la logia masónica P-2* (Buenos Aires, 1983), 31–76; Gerardo Bra, "La P-2 en la Argentina," *Todo es Historia* (February 1985): 8–26; Pino Buongiorno, "La internacional del Venerable Licio," *Todo es Historia* (February

1985): 27–37; *Somos* (May 28, 1981): 16–19, (July 16, 1982): 46, (September 24, 1982): 6–11, and (October 15, 1982): 6–12.

   46. *Latin America* (April 21, 1978): 117.
   47. José Luis de Imaz, *Los que mandan* (Buenos Aires, 1964), 84.

Conclusion

The birth of the modern right in Argentina occurred soon after the nation celebrated its centenary of independence in 1910. This anniversary took place in an atmosphere of optimism and faith in the future. To many contemporary observers, Argentina's export-based prosperity and its ability to attract immigrants seemed unlimited, although in hindsight one can detect flaws in the model of economic development that the nation followed. Most important, the ruling oligarchy projected an image of political unity and consensus, despite the challenges posed by Radicals and Socialists. Yet the country soon plunged into deep political schisms between the right, the democratic center, and the left—schisms from which it has yet to recover.

The forceful, if not preeminent, role of one of these persuasions, that of the right, has been the theme of the six preceding essays. The articles have followed the history of the right from its philosophical origins in the late nineteenth century through its activities in the course of the twentieth. What is striking at the end of this survey is the remarkable consistency that marks the doctrines and evolution of the right.

The right proclaimed, and maintained, an ideology that primarily expressed its antipathy for the modernization process that had begun with the French Revolution. Although writers elsewhere have emphasized the right's antiliberalism,[1] the authors of the preceding essays have tended to highlight the right's opposition to labor and leftism. Sandra McGee Deutsch demonstrated how the workers' mobilizations of the early 1900s spurred formation of the Liga Patriótica Argentina. Succeeding rightist groups, such as the Nacionalistas, as well as the various conservative parties, upheld the Liga's opposition to organized labor—except for the sham unions that they themselves formed—as the immediate source of disorder in the nation. The right claimed that a series of foreign doctrines, beginning with anarchism and followed by anarcho-syndicalism, revolutionary Marxism, and Soviet communism, although inapplicable to Argentina, had infected the Argentine working class. Furthermore, although the right could not describe left-wing Peronism as "foreign," it nonetheless regarded this movement as equally dangerous. Its fear that workers, inspired by one or more of these ideologies, would attempt to overthrow the class hierarchy obsessed the right. Even across its broad factional spectrum, the right never has wavered in this fixation, as Ronald H. Dolkart and Leonardo Senkman in particular have shown.

Another continuity lay in the division between two major doctrines of the right. In Argentina, as in most of Latin America, classical nineteenth-century liberalism, modified by positivism, had become the official ideology of the ruling elite. At the turn of the century, the challenge to the Argentine elite posed by some landowners and members of the middle class who had been excluded from power pushed the oligarchy into a more rigidly defensive posture, prompting it to call itself "conservative," or, more descriptively, "liberal conservative." David Rock described how this conservative mentality, nourished by reactionary and proclerical European thinking, represented the philosophical beginnings of the Argentine right. Emerging from this worldview was the Liga Patriótica Argentina. As Deutsch pointed out, however, the Liga expressed and protected the interests of the establishment, and it barely criticized the liberalism that had justified its class position. In his essay, Dolkart depicted the Nacionalistas' ideological and political onslaught, influenced by European fascism, against liberal conservatism. The Nacionalistas blamed conservatives for having "sold" Argentina to foreign interests; for their part conservatives disliked the Nacionalistas' violent rhetoric and tactics. As their mutual distrust and antipathy grew, each group asserted its claim to being the authentic voice of the right. Nevertheless, the Nacionalistas and conservatives were forced to cooperate with each other in their struggle against the democratic center and, particularly, the left.

With some alterations, this pattern essentially has continued to the present. Richard J. Walter and Senkman showed in their essays how, during the first administration of Juan Perón and its immediate aftermath, some conservatives and some Nacionalistas alike joined Peronist forces, whereas others opposed them. Senkman sifted through the complicated events between the coups of 1955 and 1976 to trace rightist realignments, and he found that, with the addition of the Peronist right, the former rightist duo became a trio. United by their distaste for the left, the members of the trio disagreed on most other matters, and their infighting only exacerbated the political and economic disarray and the violence under the civilian governments of the era. Dissension between liberal and Nacionalista rightists among the military and its allies produced similar results during periods of military rule, as Paul Lewis amply demonstrated.

Thus, despite support from within the military and from other powerful elites, the right has been unable to create a strong, united movement. Following its general pattern in Latin America, and particularly in Argentine politics, the right has tended to atomize into a plethora of personalist and rigidly dogmatic groupings. The complex array of organizations that runs through this text, as well as the failed attempts to form a broad front with common goals and interests, attests to this problem. Division clearly has crippled the right's potential political strength.

The Argentine right also has displayed other weaknesses. Its much-vaunted nationalism notwithstanding, it was heavily influenced by European doctrine. Contemporary observers tended to exaggerate the ties between German National Socialists and Italian Fascists, on the one hand, and the Argentine right, on the other; the peak of such interaction, as the United States saw it, occurred during the 1940s. But the actual relationship was a more diffuse absorption of the reactionary thought that had crystallized at the turn of the century, especially in France. Although fascist ideology of the interwar period also found many supporters in Argentina, the Catholic authoritarianism of Francisco Franco in Spain best expressed the inspiration of the Argentine right. The Nacionalistas, especially, have viewed the concepts of religion, order, hierarchy, and corporativism as divinely inspired gifts from Europe to the Americas. They have never deviated from the hope that their compatriots would accept this vision as their own. Yet most Argentines have not embraced this Nacionalista vision, in part because they have considered it foreign, and the commonly used appellation *nazionalismo con zeta* expresses popular disgust with its exotic, proto-Nazi nature.

If Argentines have not identified the right with fascism, they have connected it, or at least its liberal and ultramontane factions, with the oligarchy, and this, too, has diminished its appeal. The right's inability to compromise or to act pragmatically when it did come close to attaining power, as happened in the early 1930s or in Perón's first presidency, also led to its failure, although these flaws were hardly unique in Argentine politics.

The right, especially its Nacionalista component, lacking able or charismatic political leaders, has relied heavily on intellectuals. Succeeding generations of essayists, largely centered in Buenos Aires but also found in the provinces of Mendoza, Córdoba, and Entre Ríos, have been responsible for disseminating rightist doctrine. Although many of these figures wrote for ephemeral journals, their output was consistent and influential.

For their leaders the various rightist factions also have turned to the military, thus contributing to political instability. Admiration for the armed forces and for the military's inherent sense of authority, hierarchy, discipline, and patriotism led rightists throughout the twentieth century to echo Leopoldo Lugones's famous call for "the hour of the sword." So, too, did their realization that infiltrating the military might be the quickest road to power for them, given their lack of success at the polls. Liberal and Nacionalista rightists viewed the presidency of General José F. Uriburu as the fulfillment of their desires; when he failed to meet their expectations, liberal rightists followed General Agustín P. Justo; then Nacionalistas favored Generals Arturo Rawson, Pedro Ramírez, and, at least for a time, Juan Perón. Each of the military officers who took over the government in an endless parade after Perón initially represented a new hope for different groups within the right. Yet despite this faith in military salvation, no general ever satisfied the right.

Perón came closest to fulfilling the Nacionalista right's ideological concerns, but he eventually provoked its wrath. The essays in this volume shed light on the ambiguous relationship between Peronism and Nacionalismo. The

Liga Patriótica Argentina's antileftist and social welfare interests, as described by Deutsch, resembled Peronist policies. Indeed, in an interview with Mark Falcoff, Perón admitted his association with the Liga.[2] Dolkart's depiction of Manuel Fresco revealed that there were also similarities between his governorship of Buenos Aires and the first Peronist presidency. Other authors examined the effect on Perón of Nacionalismo republicano, or so-called popular nationalism (itself influenced by Julio and Rudolfo Irazusta and other rightist figures), Social Catholicism, and Italian Fascist and Spanish corporativist labor doctrine. As Walter noted, the overlap between Peronism and Nacionalismo is evident.[3] Yet Walter also described how Perón alienated much of this support through, for example, his pragmatic policies on, among other matters, Jews. Senkman, however, demonstrated that, at least in his later years, Perón was not free of anti-Semitism, nor was his following.

If the relationship between Peronism and Nacionalismo remains controversial, the same is true of the ties between the latter and generic fascism. Historians have distinguished between Nacionalismo and fascism by citing the former's lack of interest in mobilizing or inability to mobilize a wide following, as well as the movement's religious and traditional character and the origins (upper to upper middle class) of most of its more visible members, at least before the 1940s. Yet, as the preceding essays demonstrated, not all Nacionalista groups shared these traits. Moreover, the Romanian Iron Guard, the Belgian Rex, and other European groups commonly considered fascist also were religious and traditional, and studies have shown that European fascists came from varied class backgrounds, including ones that resembled those of many Nacionalistas.[4] Cristián Buchrucker concluded that Nacionalismo of the pre-Peronist era was essentially a fascist movement,[5] although one could argue that it lacked the mass base. Senkman's treatment leads one to make similar judgments regarding the Nacionalista and Peronist right in the years from 1955 to 1976, but further study is needed.

This volume also contributes to the debate over whether or not Peronism was fascist during the 1940s and 1950s.[6] Noting Perón's working-class support, his nontotalitarian tendencies, and his disagreements with the Nacionalistas, Walter decided that Peronism was not. Yet some European fascist groups, such as the Hungarian Arrow Cross, recruited Argentine workers,[7] and Perón's differences with the extreme right over his pragmatism, his popular orientation, his treatment of the church, and the mobilization of women do not contradict a fascist bent. What emerges from this book is the striking ability of Peronism to make many of Nacionalismo's fascist traits, particularly its resolute opposition to the left, appealing to a wide spectrum of the Argentine population. In this sense, at least, Perón was more fascist than the Nacionalistas.

Whereas scholars continue to differ over the natures of Nacionalismo and Peronismo, the connection between the right and the Dirty War inspires no such dispute. Throughout its history the right has used violence against its opponents, beginning with the Liga Patriótica Argentina's suppression of unions and socialists in the post-World War I era and followed by Nacionalista attacks on leftists, students, and Jews thereafter. Senkman described how Jordán Bruno Genta's Nacionalista and ultramontane Catholic notions of counterrevolutionary war profoundly influenced national security doctrine, which in turn inspired the 1976 coup and the ensuing persecution of guerrillas and their suspected sympathizers.[8] Lewis further noted how the right, including the church hierarchy, supported the Dirty War. Clearly, from the Semana Trágica of 1919 onward, the right was laying the groundwork for the torture and disappearances that marked the late 1970s and early 1980s in Argentina.

What, then, is the ultimate significance of the Argentine right, especially of its extreme wing? The right's restless quest for power led it to promote military rule and instability from the late 1920s on. More importantly, the basis of its continuing hold over politics has been its appropriation of the image of Argentine nationalism. Rather than the left or the democratic center, the right put nationalist issues on the political agenda, and it rewrote Argentine history to suit its nationalist and authoritarian purposes. Furthermore, the right's nationalism, historical revisionism, and other features have had a powerful influence on other movements and regimes, from Peronism to the left-leaning Montoneros.[9]

Although Nacionalismo has not achieved power itself, it exerts a strong impact to this day, greater than that of its counterparts in neighboring countries. Brazil experienced the largest fascist movement in Latin America in the 1930s, the Ação Integralista Brasileira, but it was short-lived. Brazil's conservative elites found that their interests were better represented by Getúlio Vargas, who, with military backing, was able to suppress the Integralistas while co-opting some of their program. The Chilean Movimiento Nacional Socialista, or Nacistas, of the 1930s and early 1940s gained little success thanks to the strength of the Conservative party and its youth spin-off, the Falange Nacional, and to the strength of the traditional party system as a whole. Moreover, although both Brazil and Chile experienced rightist military dictatorships in recent years, there was no clear link between past and present, for example, between General Augusto Pinochet (1973–1990) and the Nacistas, as there had been between Nacionalismo and the corresponding tendency within the Proceso.

What emerges from this brief discussion of Brazil and Chile is the relative vigor of the moderate right in these countries; in Argentina, the weakness of the moderate right appears to have been decisive in propelling the Nacionalistas into action. Another factor that helps explain the Nacionalistas' relative prominence is the extreme factionalization of Argentine politics, permitting a minority, particularly an articulate one tied to powerful groups such as the military, to attain influence. Finally, Argentina's perennial economic and political crisis has stimulated the search for radical answers to the nation's problems, and the Nacionalistas' international conspiracy theories have won over many Argentines who feel resentful and victimized. Clearly, more comparative research is needed to establish the reasons for the importance of the Argentine right relative to that of rightist movements in other nations.

As a political and intellectual force in Argentina the right plays a central role in the country's historiography. This volume is the first narrative and analytical history of the right in its full spectrum. But clearly much remains to be studied. We have indicated already the need for research on the Nacionalista and Peronist right after 1955 and for comparative research; one could add to these areas the need to study the liberal right after the Década Infame.

Whereas this book has concentrated on local conditions motivating the Argentine right, such as immigration, the challenge from labor and the left, and the nation's economic dependency and perceived decline, the international context also deserves further attention. Rock, Deutsch, and Dolkart depicted the extensive European influence on Nacionalismo, particularly in the fascist heyday of the 1930s. More nebulous are the ties between the extreme right and European neofascist groups of the 1970s and 1980s, to which Senkman and Lewis alluded. It is also unclear whether national security doctrine and the models offered by the Brazilian (1964–1985) and Chilean (1973–1990) military regimes affected Argentina's civilian right as well as the military.

The social history of the right also contains gaps. One issue discussed in all the essays is the relationship between the Catholic church and Nacionalismo. The links between the two seem so important that one wonders to what extent Nacionalismo has taken over the church, although Dolkart described the church as more apolitical than activist. Much work is needed to clarify the exact nature of this relationship.[10]

Another significant topic in social history concerns the social origins of the members of the extreme right. According to Deutsch, the earliest groups were upper class in character. The strongest support for the right as a whole has come from the elite, which, after its failure to control the Radical party, viewed the right as most capable of protecting its class interests. Yet there was disagreement within the elite over whether to continue the facade of democratic rule combined with economic liberalism, under the Conservatives, or to opt for the Nacionalistas' blend of authoritarianism and economic nationalism. As gradually worsening economic conditions caused fear to spread among the formerly secure middle class, members of this group, especially its professionals, began to find Nacionalismo appealing, as Dolkart and Walter indicated. Nacionalismo first attempted to attract workers during the Década Infame. Senkman showed that this popularizing trend continued in the post-1955 era, as Peronists enrolled in the right. Lewis, however, pointed out the elitist origins of rightist intellectuals and officers in the same years; perhaps this was natural, given the recruitment patterns of the military governments. Thus, this book appears to dispel the widely accepted (although never proven) view of Nacionalismo as representing a downwardly mobile sector of the elite.

Nevertheless, additional research is required, particularly for the period since the late 1940s.

Gender represents still another area in social history that should be explored. Deutsch and Dolkart noted female participation in the Liga Patriótica Argentina of the 1920s and in Nacionalismo in the 1930s, respectively, and Senkman discussed Norma Kennedy's leadership in the Peronist right. Rock and Deutsch indicated the right's antifeminism, and Walter's description of Nacionalista opposition to Evita Perón also implied antifeminist feelings, as did his portrait of the Nacionalistas' puritanical, pro-family attitudes. To round out the picture of the Argentine right, however, scholars must direct more of their attention to the women within it and to its rhetoric related to gender.[11]

Argentine politics today make the study of the right more relevant than ever before. Public distaste for the military's human rights abuses and incompetence propelled Raúl Alfonsín into the presidency in 1983. In the early years of his term, additional information about the Dirty War further discredited the military and its allies on the right and led most Argentines to affirm their faith in democracy. A severe economic crisis, however, soon tested their faith. At the same time, the military demanded revindication; attempted coups led by Colonels Aldo Rico and Mohammed Alí Seineldín illustrated these demands and weakened Alfonsín's role. The church criticized the government for instituting divorce, permitting pornography, and otherwise undermining the family and morality. Rightist intellectuals warned of leftist plans to radicalize educational and other cultural institutions and, through them, to assert ideological control over society. Alfonsín handed the presidential sash to Carlos Saúl Menem in 1989, thus reestablishing the regular succession of elected civilian heads of state that was interrupted in 1930—a favorable sign for democracy. Nevertheless, there are constant reports of rightist destabilization efforts, and beneath its weak, besieged democracy seems always to lurk the specter of Argentina's century-long tradition of the right.

Notes

1. See, for example, Marysa Navarro Gerassi, *Los nacionalistas*, trans. Alberto Ciria (Buenos Aires, 1968), and Enrique Zuleta Alvarez, *El nacionalismo argentino*, 2 vols. (Buenos Aires, 1975).

2. Mark Falcoff, "Epilogue," in *Prologue to Perón: Argentina in Depression and War, 1930–1943*, ed. Mark Falcoff and Ronald Dolkart (Berkeley, 1975), 197. Also see Perón's imaginary musings on the Liga and its leaders in Tomás Eloy Martínez's perceptive *La novela de Perón* (Buenos Aires, 1985), 124–25, 138.

3. Cristián Buchrucker, *Nacionalismo y peronismo: La Argentina en la crisis ideológica mundial, 1927–1955* (Buenos Aires, 1987), 308–10; David Tamarin, *The Argentine Labor Movement, 1930–1945: A Study in the Origins of Peronism* (Albuquerque, 1985), 182–83; Paul H. Lewis, "Was Perón a Fascist? An Inquiry into the Nature of Fascism," *Journal of Politics* 42, no. 1 (February 1980): 246–50; José

Enrique Miguens, "The Presidential Elections of 1973 and the End of an Ideology," in *Juan Perón and the Reshaping of Argentina*, ed. Frederick Turner and José Enrique Miguens (Pittsburgh, 1983), 147–48.

4. On the Romanian Iron Guard and the Belgian Rex see, for example, Stanley G. Payne, *Fascism: Comparison and Definition* (Madison, WI, 1980), 115–18, 134–35; and Eugen Weber, *Varieties of Fascism* (Princeton, NJ, 1964), 96–105, 122–29, 165–69, 178–82. The varied class backgrounds of European fascism are exhaustively described in Stein Ugelvik Larsen, Bernt Hagtvet, and Jan Petter Myklebust, eds., *Who Were the Fascists? Social Roots of European Fascism* (Oslo, Norway, 1980).

5. Buchrucker, *Nacionalismo y peronismo*, 233.

6. The following authors, among others, do not consider Perón a fascist: Buchrucker, *Nacionalismo y peronismo*; various contributors to Turner and Miguens, *Juan Perón*; Gino Germani, *Authoritarianism, Fascism, and National Populism* (New Brunswick, NJ, 1978); Alberto Ciria, *Perón y el justicialismo* (Buenos Aires, 1971); and Eldon Kenworthy, "The Function of the Little Known Case in Theory Formation or What Peronism Wasn't," *Comparative Politics* 6 (October 1973): 17–45. The following do: Lewis, "Was Perón a Fascist?"; Sandra McGee Deutsch, *Counterrevolution in Argentina, 1900–1932: The Argentine Patriotic League* (Lincoln, NE, 1986); Charles Bergquist, *Labor in Latin America: Comparative Essays on Chile, Argentina, Venezuela, and Colombia* (Stanford, 1986); and Carlos H. Waisman, *Reversal of Development in Argentina: Postwar Counterrevolutionary Policies and Their Structural Consequences* (Princeton, NJ, 1987). In *Fascism*, p. 174, Payne concluded that "Peronism had most but not all the characteristics of European fascism."

7. On the Arrow Cross see Weber, *Varieties of Fascism*, 88–96, 157–64; István Deák, "Hungary," in *The European Right*, ed. Hans Rogger and Eugen Weber (Berkeley, 1966), 364–407. Given the economic and political similarities between these areas, it appears more fruitful to compare Latin American with East European movements than to compare, as most authors have done, the former with the West European movements.

8. Margaret E. Crahan noted the Catholic right's contribution to national security doctrine in "National Security Ideology and Human Rights," in *Human Rights and Basic Needs in the Americas*, ed. Margaret E. Crahan (Washington, DC, 1982), 105–7.

9. Rightist influences on the Montoneros are described in Richard Gillespie, *Soldiers of Perón: Argentina's Montoneros* (Oxford, England, 1982).

10. Fortunato Mallimaci, *El catolicismo integral en la Argentina, 1930–1946* (Buenos Aires, 1988), is a first step in this direction.

11. On gender and the Argentine right see Sandra F. McGee, "Female Right-Wing Activists in Buenos Aires, 1900–1932," in *Women and the Structure of Society*, ed. Barbara J. Harris and JoAnn K. McNamara (Durham, NC, 1984), 85–97; "The Visible and Invisible Liga Patriótica Argentina, 1919–1928: Gender Roles and the Right Wing," *Hispanic American Historical Review* 64, no. 2 (May 1984): 233–58.

Glossary

Argentinidad
  The nature of "Argentineness" in its authentic creole characteristics as a basis for nationalism and thus always a concern of the right.

Azules, Colorados
  Blues, Reds; factions of the military divided, respectively, between those who wanted an accommodation with civilian politicians and those who opposed it.

Concordancia
  The alliance of conservatives that governed Argentina during the Década Infame. Its mainstay was the Partido Demócrata Nacional.

Confederación General del Trabajo (CGT)
  An organization of trade unions formed in the 1930s. It became the foundation of Perón's power from 1943 to 1955 and remained the basis of Peronism thereafter.

Cordobazo
  In 1969 a student-worker uprising in the industrial city of Córdoba seized control of factories but was ruthlessly suppressed by the military. A second violent demonstration took place in the same city in 1971.

Corporate State
  A central tenet of the Nacionalistas and related to Italian Fascism. It posited replacement of representative democracy by an assembly of interest groups, including the church and the military. It also included the notion of organizing employers and workers in industrywide associations, thus repressing class conflict.

Década Infame
  Infamous Decade; the period from the revolution of 1930 to the revolution of 1943, two important military coups, and marked by strong right-wing domination.

Dirty War

The policy pursued during the military dictatorship from 1976 to 1983 aimed at suppressing "subversives" (all suspected leftists and leftist Peronists) through a state of siege, mass arrests, torture, and the disappearance of those secretly killed and buried (*desaparecidos*).

Estancia

Cattle ranch; in Argentina the system of latifundia that supported the wealthy elite (*estancieros*).

Frente Nacional

National Front; the proposed alliance of right-wing groups for electoral purposes in the 1930s and again in the 1960s.

Golpismo

A belief in the armed forces as the savior of Argentina from corrupt politicians that justifies the overthrow of civilian governments by a *golpe de estado* (coup d'état).

Gorillas

Extreme anti-Peronist officers, designated by their enemies as "apes," who favored military intervention to keep Peronism out of power.

GOU

Initials designating Grupo Organizador y Unificador, Grupo de Oficiales Unidos, or other titles; a secret army lodge of colonels with strongly nationalistic goals. It undertook the June 1943 military revolt with the participation of Juan Perón.

Integralismo

Rightist-nationalist doctrine in Portugal under Antonio Salazar in the 1920s and 1930s and the basis of Ação Integralista Brasileira under Plinio Salgado in 1930s Brazil.

Justicialismo

Doctrine, espoused by Juan Perón, that emphasized social justice from a balance of social and economic forces, elevated to the level of a political philosophy.

Liberalism

Historical usage in Argentina refers to nineteenth-century economic doctrine, especially free trade, adopted by the elite exporting class, whose policies dominated conservative parties during the twentieth century.

Lópezrreguismo

Policies of José López Rega, who as minister of social welfare was a major influence in the presidency of María Estela (Isabel) Martínez de Perón; doctrine meant support for the Peronist right.

Montoneros

Formed in the 1970s, a guerrilla group of radical Peronists involved in the violent activities that the military used to justify the Dirty War.

Partido Autonomista Nacional

The PAN was the political instrument of the *régimen* from 1880 to the rise of the Radicals; more than a political party, it was a system of elite control from Buenos Aires across the entire nation without any effective opposition.

Juan Domingo Perón

A career army officer, Perón became a colonel in 1941; joined the GOU; took part in the revolution of 1943; became minister of war, secretary of labor and welfare, and vice president; was elected president in 1946 and reelected in 1952; was overthrown in 1955; and returned to the presidency from exile in 1973. He died in office in 1974. Known as *El Líder*. Both his charisma and his prolabor policies are referred to as Peronismo.

Eva (Evita) Duarte de Perón

Juan Perón's second wife, an entertainer, who played an integral part in securing support for Perón among the working class through her welfare foundation until her death in 1952.

María Estela (Isabel) Martínez de Perón

Juan Perón's third wife, an entertainer as had been his second, who returned with her husband from exile and then became president herself after Perón's death in 1974; ousted in 1976.

Porteños

The people of the city of Buenos Aires—the port—who dominate Argentina.

Proceso

The Process of National Reorganization; the period of military dictatorship from 1976 to 1983, whose supposed mission of "reeducating" the Argentine people in Western values, capitalistic economics, and political stability, the military claimed, justified repression.

Régimen
> The regime; the liberal system supported by the elite, made up of *estancia* owners, bankers, and exporters, who dominated Argentina from 1880 to the Radical administrations after 1916. It served as a model for the conservatives during the Década Infame.

Revolución Libertadora
> The Liberating Revolution; a term used by the right to describe the uprising against Juan Perón, September 16–19, 1955.

Roca-Runciman Pact
> The generally used name of the Treaty of London, signed May 11, 1933, by Walter Runciman, head of the British Board of Trade, and Vice President Julio A. Roca, Jr., of Argentina; provided an Argentine beef quota in the British market in return for access for English manufactured goods in Argentina.

Semana Trágica
> The "Tragic Week" in January 1919 when a general strike resulted in attacks against Jews and suppression of workers.

Third Position
> That part of Justicialismo referring to a balance between extremes, notably between U.S. capitalism and Soviet communism.

Unión Cívica Radical
> The UCR, known as the "Radicals"; the party of the immigrant middle class, which, through revolutionary action, forced the *régimen* to allow the secret ballot. It came to power under its leader Hipólito Yrigoyen in 1916 and held the presidency until the revolution of 1930; over time it has split into various branches, including the Anti-Personalist Radicals.

Index

AAA. *See* Alianza Anticomunista
    Argentina
ACA. *See* Accion Católica Argentina
Ação Integralista Brasileira: fascist
    movement, 185
Acción Argentina, 92
Acción Católica, 12, 151
Acción Católica Argentina (ACA):
    Nacionalistas and, 81
Acción Nacionalista Argentina. *See*
    Nacionalistas
Achával Rodríguez, Tristán, 151
Action Française, 18–19
Adrogué, Carlos, 155, 157, 158
"Afirmación de Una Nueva Argentina"
    (ADUNA): Nacionalista
    manifesto, 72
Agrupación Monárquica: rightist
    group, 78
Agrupación Tradicionalista Española:
    rightist group, 78
Aguado, Jorge Rubén, 175
Aguilar, Francisco, 162
AJN. *See* Alianza de la Juventud
    Nacionalista
Alconada Aramburu, Carlos, 155
Alemán, Lucas, 19–20
Alemánn, Juan, 171, 174
Alemánn, Roberto, 175–76
Alende, Oscar, 169
Alfonsín, Raúl, 148, 187;
    characterized, 1
Alfonso XIII: abdication of, 77
El Aliancista: anti-Semitism and, 131–
    32
Alianza Anticomunista Argentina
    (AAA): death squad, 135, 138–39,
    141, 173
Alianza Civil: Revolution of 1930 and,
    69

Alianza de la Juventud Nacionalista
    (AJN), 71, 161, 165; agenda of,
    90–91
Alianza Libertadora Nacionalista
    (ALN, 109–10, 134, 161, 164;
    anti-Semitism and, 131–32;
    elections of 1948 and, 110–11;
    impact of, in 1940s, 100;
    reorganization of, 128
Alizón García, Fernando, 164
Alizón García, Julio, 153
Almirón, Rodolfo Eduardo, 134
ALN. *See* Alianza Libertadora
    Nacionalista
Alonso de Drysdale, Soledad, 78
Alsina, Cayo, 129; leads revolt,
    158–59
Alsogaray, Alvaro, 153, 157–59, 166;
    attacks Nacionalistas, 167
Alsogaray, Julio, 153, 158, 166–67
Alvear, Marcelo T. de, 41, 48–49, 57;
    candidacy of, 70–71
Amadeo, Mario, 124, 151, 153, 164–
    65; on Perón, 104, 115
Ameghino, César, 90
Anozateguí, Ignacio B., 165
Anti-Personalistas: anti-Yrigoyen
    faction, 39, 41, 69–70
Anti-Semitism, 24, 90–91, 140–41;
    ALN and, 110; Argentina right
    and, 9–12; Ezcurra Uriburu and,
    128; Gelbard and, 137; German
    and Argentine, 79–80; GRN and,
    130; Martínez Zuviría and, 103;
    Maurras and, 18; Meinvielle and,
    81; Nacionalistas and, 57;
    newspapers and, 131–32; Perón
    and, 112; Peronist right and, 135–
    40
Arab League, 128

Aramburu, Pedro, 124, 148, 150, 152–
  55, 157–58, 160, 163, 167, 170;
  administration of, 153–55;
  execution of, 169
Arana, Arturo Ossorio, 152, 154
Argentinidad: nationalist spirit, 39–40
Ariel (Rodó), 6, 16, 26
Aristotle, 6; on human social nature, 7
Asociación de Damas Argentinas:
  rightist group, 71
Asociación del Trabajo, 43; formation
  of, 37; Liga and, 42
Astigueta, José Mariano, 160, 165
Ateneo de la República: anti-Krieger
  Vasena organization, 163–66
Ateneo Social de la Juventud, 50
Augustine, Saint, 6
Avalos, Eduardo, 103
Avancismo: Nacionalista group, 74
Axis powers, 89; Perón and Argentina
  break with, 104–5
Azul y Blanco: Nacionalista party, 124
Azul y Blanco: Nacionalista organ, 124
Azules: army faction, 123, 125, 129,
  140, 158

Babbitt (Lewis), 6
Bakunin, Mikhail, 27
Balbín, Ricardo: liberal rightist, 121,
  140, 154–55
Balcón: Perón and, 112
Baldrich, Alberto, 105
Balmes, Jaime, 12; as ideologue, 14
Banco de Boulogne, 162
Bandera Argentina: rightist newspaper,
  73
Barceló, Alberto, 84, 90
Barrès, Maurice, 18, 24–25, 28;
  nationalism and, 17
Barrio Once: anti-Semitism and, 138
Barruel, Abbé Agustín: anti-Semitism
  and, 10
Bartfield, Federico, 174
Las Bases: Justicialista organ, 133
Baudelaire, Charles-Pierre, 25
Baxter, Joe: MNT leader, 127
Becher, Emilio: Gálvez on, 25
Beef: quota of, to Britain, 74–75
Belgian Rex: fascist group, 184
Belloc, Hilaire, 12
Bengoa, Justo León, 152, 153
Berdyayev, Nikolay, 12

Bignone, Reynaldo, 148, 176
Blanco, Eugenio, 153
Blue Book: Perón-Nazi connection and,
  109
Bolívar, Simón: on development of
  American states, 7
La Bolsa (Martell), 24
Bolsa de Comercio, 149, 153
Bonald, Vicomte Louis Gabriel
  Ambroise de, 12, 13
Borda, Guillermo Fals, 167, 169;
  "Fundamental Charter" and, 168;
  policies of, 163–64
Bordabehere, Enzo: assassination of,
  71
Borges, Jorge Luis, 80–81
Bourbons: Ibarguren on, 15
Braden, Spruille: opposition to Perón
  and, 108, 109
Bramuglia, Juan Atilio, 106
Britain: imperialism of, as political
  issue, 75–76
Bronner, Julio, 135; La Prensa on, 137
Buchrucker, Cristián: on fascism, 184;
  on right's influence, 94
Buenos Aires: Revolution of 1930 and,
  67–68
Buenos Aires Herald: anti-Semitism
  and, 11
Bulletin of the Red Cross, 77
Burge, César, 152
Burke, Edmund, 5
Busso, Eduardo, 152–53

Caballero, Carlos, 168; career sketch
  of, 164
Cabildo: Fresco newspaper, 1, 90, 138;
  impact of, 99–100
Cabot, John: on Perón, 108
Cabral, Angel, 155
CAC. See Cámara Argentina de
  Comercio
Cáceres Monie, José, 169
CACIP. See Confederación Argentina
  del Comercio, de la Industria, y de
  la Producción
Caliban (Renan), 6
Cámara Argentina de Comercio (CAC),
  149, 155, 156, 159
Cambaceres, Eugenio: on Italian
  immigrants, 24
Camillión, Oscar, 175

Cámpora, Héctor, 134, 148
Camps, Ramón J., 140; "subversives" and, 2
Cané, Miguel, 24
Capitalism: Argentine right and, 8–9
Caputo, Dante: characterized, 1
CARBAP: cattlemen's association, 175
Carlés, Manuel, 55, 57, 77; career of, 41; condemns Yrigoyen administration, 49; economic views of, 45–46; on "democracy," 48–49; on relationship of Liga to European rightist movements, 46; Patagonian labor movement and, 44–45
Carreras, Mario, 157
Carril, Bonifacio del: on Perón, 114, 115
Carulla, Juan E.: rightist journalist, 50, 53, 73
Casares, Tomás: Social Catholic movement and, 50
Castellani, Leonardo, 5, 12, 14
Castillo, Ramón S., 87, 90, 92–93, 101, 103; overthrow of, 99
Catalán, Juan José, 171
Catholic Church: anti-Semitism and, 80–82; Argentine right and, 15, 27, 36–37; Genta on role of, 129; increasing conservatism of, 21–23; Maurras and, 18–19; militancy in, 20–21; nationalism and, 16–17; Perón and, 108, 114; repression and, 173
El Católico, 20
El Caudillo, 135, 137–38
Centro de Acción Española: rightist group, 78
Centro Naval, 39, 41
Cerruti Costa, Luis B., 151–52
CGE. *See* Confederación General Económica
CGT. *See* Confederación General del Trabajo
Chapultepec, Treaty of: ratification of, 112
Christian Democratic League, 23
Christian Democrats, 125, 159
Círculo Militar, 41, 49
Círculos Obreros (Workers' Circles), 23, 37

Ciudad Católica, 161–62
Civilian authority: relationship to military rule, 148–50
Clement, Gastón, 156, 158
COARA. *See* Confederación de Organizaciones Anticomunistas de la República Argentina
Collins, Juan M., 127
Coloquios con Perón (Pavón Pereyra), 137
Colorados: army faction, 125, 129, 158–60
Comando de Organización: Peronist group, 134–35
Comando Superior Justicialista, 127
Combate: LNC newspaper, 131
Comisión Investigadora de Actividades Antiargentinas, 92
Comisión Pro-Defensa del Orden, 39, 41
Comité Antirracista: fights anti-Semitism, 80
Comité Nacional de la Juventud Argentina, 74
Communism, 129; Argentine right and, 9, 76–77
Compañero, 127
Concentración Nacional Universitaria: Peronist group, 134
Concepción católica de la política (Meinvielle), 81
Concordancia, 72; Justo and, 69–70, 74
Confederación Argentina del Comercio, de la Industria, y de la Producción (CACIP): business lobby, 45
Confederación de Organizaciones Anticomunistas de la República Argentina (COARA), 131
Confederación General del Trabajo (CGT), 82, 132–33, 136–37, 139–40; liberal right and, 122
Confederación General Económica (CGE), 132–35, 137
Consejo Ejecutivo, 41–42
Consejo Nacional de Desarrollo, 169
Consejo Superior del Nacionalismo, 91
Conservative party, 36
Consigna, 135
Consigna Nacional, 138
Cooke, Juan I., 106
Córdoba: violence at, 71, 168

Cornejo Linares, J. C., 128
Cornejo Sarávia, José Octavio, 158
Costa Méndez, Nicanor, 164, 175
Costas, Robustiano Patrón, 92–93, 101
Counterrevolution: Genta on, 29;
    ideology of, 6–12
Creoles: in Villaguay conflicts, 43
Crisol: rightist newspaper, 73, 100,
    153; on link between Liga and
    Nacionalistas, 58
Criterio: Catholic journal, 50, 52, 80–
    81, 151
El Cronista: on López Rega, 139
Cuadernos del Sur: Opus Dei journal,
    163
Cueto Rua, Julio César, 153
Cursos de Cultura Católica: Social
    Catholic movement and, 50
Curutchet, Ricardo, 124

Dahau, Luis F., 71
DAIA. *See* Delegación de Asociaciones
    Israelitas Argentinas
Damiano, Manuel, 134
D'Andrea, Héctor, 164
Danzey, Alberto, 43
Darío, Rubén, 27
Daudet, Léon: on capitalism, 8
Década Infame (1930–1943), 101, 103,
    154, 186; Argentine right during,
    65–94
Defensa de la Hispanidad (Maeztu),
    52
Delegación de Asociaciones Israelitas
    Argentinas (DAIA): Jewish group,
    136, 138–39
Dellepiane, Luis J.: Semana Trágica
    and, 38
Dell'Oro Maini, Atilio, 151, 153, 165;
    Social Catholic movement and, 50
Democracy: Argentine right and
    movements toward, 121–32
Desarrollismo: industrialization policy,
    121
Descartes, René, 6, 9
Deutsch, Sandra McGee, 181, 184,
    186–87
El Diario de Gabriel Quiroga
    (Gálvez), 28
Díaz Bessone, Ramón Genaro, 172–73
Díaz Colodero, Mario, 163–64, 168,
    171

Dickmann, Enrique, 79, 88
Dirty War: repression and, 93, 173,
    184–85, 187
Dolkart, Ronald H., 55, 181, 184, 186
Doll, Ramón, 76
Domecq García, Manuel, 41; Semana
    Trágica and, 39
Donoso Cortés, Juan, 12, 52; as
    ideologue, 13–14
Drago, Mariano, 158
Dreyfus affair, 6
Drumont, Edouard: anti-Semitism and,
    24
Duarte, Eva ("Evita"). *See* Perón, Eva
    Duarte

Echeverrigaray, Miguel Angel, 165
Education: Ibarguren on, 15
Ejército Revolucionario del Pueblo
    (ERP), 171
Elections of 1948 (Argentine
    congress): ALN and, 110–11
En la sangre (Cambaceres), 24
ERP. *See* Ejército Revolucionario del
    Pueblo
Estancias: feudal democracy of, 26–27
Estrada, José Manuel: on liberalism,
    21–23
Estrada, Santiago de, 124
Estrada, Santiago de, Jr., 165
Etchecopar, Gastón Terán, 165
Etchecopar, Máximo, 124, 163; on
    declaration of war against Axis
    powers, 107; Perón and, 113
Europe: effect of rightist movements
    in, on Argentine right, 2–6
Ezcurra Uriburu, Alberto, 126–28
Ezeiza Airport massacre (1973), 134–
    35
Ezpezel, Alberto, 165

FAL. *See* Fuerzas Armadas de
    Liberación
Falange Española de Buenos Aires:
    rightist group, 78
Falcoff, Mark, 184
Falkland Islands, 176. *See also* Islas
    Malvinas
Farrell, Edelmiro, 103–4, 107, 160
Fascism, 46; defined, 3–4; European
    rise of, contrasted with rise of
    Argentine right, 65–66; impact of,

on Argentine right, 182–83; Nacionalistas and, 77; Perón and, 115; relationship to Nacionalistas and Peronism, 184–85; rise of Argentine, 86–94
Federación de Organismos de Ayuda a la República Española, 78
Federación Obrera Comarcal: Villaguay conflicts and, 43
Federación Obrera Nacionalista Argentina (FONA): rightist group, 71, 82
El Federal: anti-Semitism and, 131–32
Feminism: Argentine right and, 8
Ferrer, Aldo, 169–70
Fichte, Johann Gottlieb, 16
Fidanza, Amílcar, 127
Filippo, Virgilio: anti-Semitism and, 81
Finer, Samuel: on military political rule, 147
First Argentine Soviet, 38
Florit, Carlos, 124
FONA. *See* Federación Obrera Nacionalista Argentina
FORJA. *See* Fuerza de Orientación Radical de la Joven Argentina
El Fortín, 100, 138
France, Anatole, 25
Franceschi, Gustavo, 5; on failure of Christian Democratic League, 23; rightist movement and, 81; on Spanish philosophy, 13–14
Franco, Francisco, 87, 151, 183; Argentine right and, 2; Perón and, 111; Sánchez Sorondo and, 84; Spanish Civil War and, 77–78
Frank, Waldo: on *El Pampero*, 91
Freemasonry (Masons), 2, 8, 129, 137, 173; Argentine right and, 10–11
French Revolution: Balmes and, 14; conservative attacks on, 7; de Maistre on, 12–13; Maurras on, 51
Frente Nacional (National Front): rightist group, 72
Fresco, Manuel A., 73, 83, 89, 184; *Cabildo* and, 100; conservative-Nacionalismo alliance and, 84–86; Ortiz on government of, 89–90
Frigerio, Rogelio, 128

Frigoli, Amadeo, 175–76
Frischknecht, Federico, 166–67
La Fronda, 55, 73, 99; attack on offices of, 70–71
Frondizi, Arturo, 148, 155, 157–60, 163, 165–66, 169, 175; liberal right and, 121–22, 140; UCRI and, 154
Fuente, Ramiro de la, 165
Fuerza de Orientación Radical de la Joven Argentina (FORJA), 103
Fuerzas Armadas de Liberación (FAL), 134
"Fundamental Charter" (1969), 168
Fustel de Coulanges, N. D.: nationalism and, 17

Gallardo, Guillermo, 165
Galtieri, Leopoldo Fortunato, 148, 175–76; on fascist tendencies of junta, 2
Gálvez, Manuel, 28, 52; Barrès's impact on, 17; novels of, characterized, 27; on Becher, 25; on materialism, 26; on radicalism, 4; Spanish influence on, 24
Ganivet, Angel, 5, 16, 24, 28
García Belsunce, Horacio, 159
García Martínez, Carlos, 175
García Mata, Rafael, 165
Garibaldi, Giuseppe, 16
The Gastronomic Sentinel, 77
Gelbard, José Ber, 133, 135–37, 140
Gelli, Licio, 173–74
Genta, Jordán Bruno, 15, 185; counterrevolution and, 6, 29, 128–29; on Communist theory and practice, 9
German Workers' party, 46
González, Enrique P., 103
Gorillas: extreme anti-Peronist faction, 121
Gorostiaga, Roberto, 162
Gorrit, Juan Ignacio, 20
GOU. *See* Grupo Organizador y Unificador
Goyena, Pedro: on role of Catholic Church in education, 20
Goyeneche, Juan Carlos, 151
Graiver, David, 135, 140
Gran Acuerdo Nacional, 170

Gran Colecta Nacional: Social Catholic
fund-raising movement, 50
La Grande Argentina: Nacionalista
newspaper, 125
Great Depression: hits Argentina, 49–
50
Green, Guillermo Mac: MNT and, 130
Grinblack, Daniel, 130
GRN. *See* Guardia Restauradora
Nacionalista
Grondona, Mariano, 157–58
Grupo de Oficiales Unidos, 93
Grupo Organizador y Unificador
(GOU): rightist military group,
101–4, 106
Guardia Restauradora Nacionalista
(GRN): paramilitary group, 127,
129–31
Guevara, Juan, 152, 161–62, 169
Guevara, Tristán, 155
Guglialmelli, Aquiles: fascism and,
89
Guglialmelli, Juan, 169–70
Guido, José María, 148–49, 166, 175;
administration of, 156–60; interim
presidency of, 125
Guzzetti, César, 1–2

Halperín, Tulio: on liberalism, 1
Harguindeguy, Albano Eduardo, 172
Hartung, Teodoro, 152
Herder, Johann Gottfried von, 16
Historiography: of Argentine right,
181–87
Hitler, Adolf, 2, 4, 87–88; Argentine
right and, 78–79; nonaggression
pact with Soviets and, 89
Hobbes, Thomas, 2
Holmberg, Elena, 174
Holmberg, Enrique, 174
Huella, 126, 131
Hull, Cordell, 103
Hungarian Arrow Cross: fascist group,
184

IAPI. *See* Instituto Argentino para la
Promoción del Intercambio
Ibarguren, Carlos, 50
Ibarguren, Federico, 12, 124; on
Bourbons, 15
Idearium Español (Ganivet), 16
Ideology: European origins of
Argentine right's, 12–19

Illia, Arturo, 122, 125, 130–32, 148,
160, 163; overthrow of, 161
Il Mattino d'Italia, 79
Imaz, Francisco Antonio, 161–62, 169
Instituto Argentino para la Promoción
del Intercambio (IAPI), 155
Integralismo, 5; Argentine right and, 2
La Internacional: Communist publication, 77
International Eucharistic Congress
(1934), 81
Irazusta, Julio, 26, 52–53, 138, 165,
184; ideology of, 4–5; on British
imperialism, 75; on Lugones, 52–
53; on Maurras, 50–51; on Perón,
113
Irazusta, Rudolfo, 52, 184; on British
imperialism, 75; on democracy, 53
Islas Malvinas (Falkland Islands), 1,
75-76, 176

Jassem, Raúl, 128, 131
Jews: Argentine right and, 9–12;
blamed for radicalism, 38–39;
persecution of, 79–80. *See also*
Anti-Semitism
Jockey Club, 149, 156, 162
Journalism: Década Infame and, 73–74
Juan Manuel de Rosas Institute:
establishment of, 76
Juárez Celman, Miguel: overthrow of,
22
Junta Central, 41–42
Justicialista movement, 131
Justo, Agustín P., 10, 56, 91, 183;
administration of, 70–71, 74–86;
plans coup, 67; presidential
candidacy of, 69–70
Juventud Autonomista: anti-Semitism
and, 24
Juventud Peronista, 126–27, 134–35
Juventud Sindical: Peronist group,
134
Juventud Trabajadora Peronista:
Peronist group, 135
Juventud Universitaria Peronista:
Peronist group, 135

"El Kahal" (Wast), 10
Kant, Immanuel, 6–7, 16
Kelly, Patricio Guillermo, 128
Kennedy, Norma, 134–35, 187; anti-
Semitism and, 138–39

Krause, Julio César, 153
Krieger Vasena, Adalbert, 153, 166–
67, 170; falls from power, 168;
financial policies of, 162–63, 167–
68
Kropotkin, Pyotr Alekseyevich, 27
Kuhl, Livio Guillermo, 175

Labayrú, Bernardino, 152, 158
Labor Code (1937): Fresco and, 86
Labor unions: rightist movements and,
36–37, 82–83; under Perón, 122–
23
Laferrère, Roberto de: on Rosas, 76
La France Juive (Drumont), 24
Lanari, Juan Aguirre, 176
Landaburu, Jorge, 153
Landaburu, Laureano, 153
Lanús, Adolfo, 153, 158
Lanusse, Alejandro, 132, 148, 150,
166–67, 169–70; purge by, 169
Lanusse, Antonio, 167
Las Palmas del Chaco Austral: labor
conflict at, 42–43
Lastra, Bonifacio, 165
Law of Professional Associations, 122;
labor contracts and, 154–55
LCA. *See* Legión Cívica Argentina
Le Bon, Gustave: as ideologue, 17
Legionarios Civiles de Franco: rightist
group, 78
Legión Cívica, 165
Legión Cívica Argentina (LCA), 88,
100; Uriburu and, 68–69
Legión de Mayo, 55–56
Legión Nacionalista
Contrarrevolucionaria (LNC):
paramilitary group, 128–31
Lenin, Vladimir I.: on Marxism, 9
Lennon, Lucas Jaime, 176
Levingston, Roberto M., 148–50, 169–
70, 175
Lewis, Paul, 141, 182, 186
Lewis, Sinclair, 6
Liberal right: activities of (1955–1966),
121–22
Liccardo, Cayetano, 176
Liendo, Horacio, 172, 175
Liga. *See* Liga Patriótica Argentina
Liga Patriótica Argentina, 35, 151,
181–82, 184–85, 187; Barceló
and, 85; components of, 42;
contrasted with Nacionalistas, 56–

58; Semana Trágica and rise of,
39–47
Liga Patriótica Militar (LPM), 47
Liga Republicana, 19, 55–56, 80
Liga Social Argentina, 23
Ligue Civique: Liga and, 47
Liguistas. *See* Liga Patriótica
Argentina
Lima, Alberto Brito, 134
Llamazares, Juan, 153
Llambías, Héctor, 165
Llerena Amadeo, Juan Rafael, 171
LNC. *See* Legión Nacionalista
Contrarrevolucionaria
Locke, John, 3, 21
Lojendio, Juan Pablo de, 78
Lonardi, Eduardo, 121, 124, 148–50,
158, 163–64, 166–67; administra-
tion of, 150–54
López, Adolfo, 166
López Rega, José, 133–35, 138; Isabel
Perón and, 138; Pro-Patria and,
173–74
López Saubidat, Carlos A., 160
Loza, Juan Bautista, 157
LPM. *See* Liga Patriótica Militar
Lugones, Leopoldo, 27, 28, 50, 53,
183; as ideologue, 25–26; as
literary icon, 73; democracy
and, 52; "Hour of the Sword"
speech, 49; on effect of
World War I on Argentine right,
28–29; on pre-World War I
liberalism, 3; repudiates youthful
radicalism, 49; xenophobia of,
10–11
Lutzky, Daniel: on repression, 172

Maeztu, Ramiro de, 52
Maistre, Joseph de, 5, 28; on
constitutionalism, 12–13
Malbrán, Manuel, 164
Mallea, Eduardo, 80
Malón: anti-Semitism and, 131–32
The Man on Horseback (Finer), 147
Manrique, Francisco, 170
Martel, Julián: anti-Semitism and, 24
Martelli, Rodolfo G., 160
Martínez, Francisco, 155
Martínez, Rodolfo, 158–59;
characteristics of, 157
Martínez de Hoz, José Alfredo, 85,
159–60, 171–76

Martínez Paz, Enrique, 164, 166; policies of, 161
Martínez Vivot, Julio, 176
Martínez Zuviría, Gustavo (author), 103, 166
Martínez Zuviría, Gustavo (general), 166
Martínez Zuviría, Jorge, 166
Marx, Karl, 9, 81
Marxism: GRN and, 130; Sánchez Sorondo and, 84
Masons and Masonry. See Freemasonry
Massera, Emilio, 172–74
Materialism: Galvez on, 26; Oliver on, 26
Maurras, Charles, 5–6, 12, 28, 46; as ideologue, 17–19, 53; concept of monarchy, 51–52; Irazusta on, 50–51; Social Catholic movement and, 50
Mazzinghi, Jorge, 164
Mazzini, Giuseppe, 16
McLoughlin, Eduardo, 153, 170
Medrano, Samuel, 165
Meinvielle, Julio, 5, 125, 153, 164–65, 169; GRN and, 130; on Perón, 112–14; rightist movement and, 81
Méndez Delfino, Eustaquio, 159–60
Mendiondo, Pedro, 153
Mendióroz, Carlos, 165
Mendióroz, Mario, 165
Menem, Carlos Saúl, 187
Menéndez, Benjamín, 114, 159
Menéndez, Luciano Benjamín, 172, 174
Menéndez Pelayo, Marcelino, 12, 17, 28; as religionist, 14; Catholic Church and, 15
Mercier, Alberto, 153
Metallurgical Workers' Union, 151. See also Unión Obrera Metalúrgica
Michelini, Pedro, 131
Migone, Raúl, 153
Miguel, Lorenzo, 137, 173
Milicia Cívica Nacionalista: rightist group, 71, 82
Military rule: Argentine right and, 147–48; relationship to civilian rule, 148–50
Miranda-Eady Agreement (1946), 112
MNRT. See Movimiento Nacionalista Revolucionario Tacuara

MNT. See Movimiento Nacionalista Tacuara
Moderate right: weakness of, in Argentina, 185–86
Molina, Juan Bautista: policies of, 91
Monarchy: Maurras concept of, 51–52
Montemayor, Mariano, 124
Montesquieu, Baron de, 17
Montoneros: leftist Peronist guerrillas, 134–35, 171, 185
Morales, Juan Ramón, 134
Morir en Madrid (film), 165
Moscoso, Augusto: GRN and, 129–30
Movement for Integration and Development: Frondizi project, 175
Movimiento Nacionalista Revolucionario Tacuara (MNRT): paramilitary group, 127–28
Movimiento Nacionalista Tacuara (MNT): paramilitary group, 126–28
Movimiento Nacional Socialista (Nacistas) (Chile), 185
Moyano Llerena, Carlos María, 169–70
Muñiz, Carlos, 152, 158–60
Munzer, Thomas, 9
Mussolini, Benito, 4, 87; Argentine right and, 2, 78–79, 91; Nacionalistas and, 52; Sánchez Sorondo and, 84, 88–89

La Nación: on rise of radical movements, 38; Villaguay conflicts and, 43–44
Nacional, 135
Nacionalismo: anti-Semitism of, 11; as counterrevolutionary movement, 3. See also Nacionalistas
El nacionalismo de Rosas (Laferrère), 76
Nacionalistas, 35, 50, 56–58, 132, 138, 140, 148–49, 159, 170, 181, 187; activities of, 47–58, 124–25; Alsogaray attacks, 167; anti-Semitism of, 57; assessment of, 176–78; contrasted with Liga Patriótica Argentina, 56–57; division within, 101; fascism and, 89; Maurras and, 51–52; Mussolini and, 52; paramilitary bands within, 126–30; Perón and, 99–116, 183–84; philosophy of, 183; ratio of, to

right-liberals in military cabinets, 150; relationship to Peronism, 184–85; role of, during Década Infame, 65–69, 71–77, 81–94; ties with rightist organizations, 130–32

Nación Arabe, 131

Nacistas. *See* Movimiento Nacional Socialista

National Consultative Council: Lonardi organization, 152

National Front: rightist groups and, 130–32

Nationalism: Catholic Church and, 16–17

National Propaganda (British antiradical group): Liga and, 47

Nativism: role in, in Argentine right, 28

Navarro Gerassi, Marysa, 109

Nazi party: role of, in Argentina, 88, 91–92, 182–83; nazism contrasted with Argentine right, 4

The New Middle Ages (Berdyayev), 12

"Night of the Long Clubs," 161

Níklison, José E., 23

Noble, Roberto J., 90

La Nueva República: Nacionalista organ, 8, 12, 19, 53–58

Nuevo Orden, 87, 131

Número: Catholic journal, 50

Obligado, Héctor, 164

Oliva, Gilberto, 129

Oliver, Ricardo: on materialism, 26

Olmedo, Ernesto, 164

Oneto Gaona, Juan Martín, 164

Onganía, Juan Carlos, 122, 148–50, 158–60, 169, 171, 175; presidency of, 161–69

Opus Dei: Catholic lay society, 163–65

La organización de la paz (Lugones), 52

Organización Popular Contra el Facismo y el Antisemitismo: fights anti-Semitism, 88

Oroño, Nicasio: repression by, 20

Ortega y Gasset, José, 52

Ortiz, Raúl Scalabrini: on British influences, 11–12

Ortiz, Roberto M., 91; administration of, 86–87, 89; illness of, 90; on Fresco, 89–90

Osés, Enrique P., 73, 81; Nazi propaganda and, 91–92; on liberalism, 8

Osinde, Jorge, 134–35

Ottalagano, Alberto, 138

Oxenford, Eduardo, 175

P-2. *See* Propaganda-Due

Pablo Pardo, Luis María de, 153, 169

Pacto Social. *See* Social Pact

Page, Joseph: on Perón's "expediency," 107

Palacio, Ernesto, 81, 109, 165; on Lugones, 53; Perón and, 114

Palmer, A. Mitchell: Carlés and, 46–47

El Pampero: Argentine Nazi newspaper, 91, 99–100

PAN. *See* Partido Autonomista Nacional

Paramilitary bands: within Nacionalistas, 126–30

Partido Autonomista Nacional (PAN): splintering of, 36

Partido Demócrata Nacional (PDN): role of, during Década Infame, 65, 69–71, 85, 89–90, 92

Partido Demócrata Progresista (PDP): founding of, 36

Partido Fascista Argentina (PFA), 79

Partido Laborista, 108

Partido Nacional Fascista: formation of, 79

Pastor, Carlos Washington, 173

Pastore, José María Dagnino, 168–69, 170

Patagonia: labor movement in, 44–45

Patria Bárbara, 128, 131

Patria Peronista, 135, 138

Pavón Pereyra, Enrique: Perón on, 137

PDN. *See* Partido Demócrata Nacional

PDP. *See* Partido Demócrata Progresista

Pearson, Enrique, 164

Pelltzer, Enrique, 164

Peluffo, Orlando, 105–6

Perkins, Jorge Walter, 157

Perlinger, Luis, 103; conflict with Perón, 105–6; Nacionalistas and, 105

Perón, Eva Duarte ("Evita"), 109, 150, 187; death of, 114; influence of, 111–12

Perón, Isabel, 133, 148, 171–72

Perón, Juan Domingo, 4, 94, 128,
131, 148–51, 153, 155, 157, 163,
166, 169–70, 182; assessment of,
115–16; attacks Catholic
Church, 152; DAIA and, 136;
demagoguery of, 151; effect of
his death on domestic policy,
133, 137–38; Ezeiza Airport
massacre and, 134–35; Fresco
and, 90; friction with
Nacionalistas, 111–12; labor right
and, 122–23; Liga and, 184;
Nacionalista ideology and, 183–
84; overthrow of, 119, 121, 132;
rightists and, 99–116; rise of, 93;
Social Pact and, 135; United
States and, 106–7
Peronist right: activities of, 134–40;
anti-Semitism of, 135–40
Pétain, Henri, 18
PFA. *See* Partido Fascista Argentina
Pico, César, 52, 81
Pinedo, Federico, 71, 156; resignation
of, 157
Pinochet, Augusto, 185
Piñon Figueiras, Evaristo, 162
Pistarini, Pascual, 161, 166
Plan Andinia: alleged Zionist plot,
138
Plato, 12
Podestá Costa, Luis, 153
Poggi, Raúl, 156–57
Policlínico Bancario de Buenos Aires:
robbery of, 127
Pomar, Gregorio, 43
Popular Conservatives, 125, 159
Poujada family: assassination of, 139
Prebisch Report: economic study, 154–
55
La Prenza, 89, 150–51, 153, 155; on
Bronner and Social Pact, 137
Presencia: Perón and, 112–13
Primera Plana, 136
Primicia Argentina, 137
Primo de Rivera, José Antonio, 131
Primo de Rivera, Miguel, 46, 52
Proceso de Reorganización Nacional:
government during, 171–76;
repression of, 141
Progressive Democratic party, 155
Propaganda-Due (P-2), 173
Pro-Patria (Masonic lodge): activities
of, 173–74

La Protesta: on Liga, 40
Protocols of the Elders of Zion: anti-
Semitism and, 10
Pueyrredón, Ernesto, 163–64
Puigbó, Raúl, 165

QB VII (movie): rightist objections to,
138
Que quieren los Nacionalistas?
(Valenti Ferro), 72
Queraltó, Juan, 110
Quincena: Perón and, 113

Radical party: Argentine right under
rule of, 35–58
Ramírez, Emilio, 103
Ramírez, Pedro, 151, 183; government
of, 102–4
Ramos Mejía, José M.: on immigrants,
24
Rattenbach, Benjamin, 158–59
Rauch, Enrique, 125, 157, 160, 166
Rawson, Arturo, 183; government of,
102
Real, Pedro, 165
Redemocratization: Argentine right
and, 132–40
Red Scare: Palmer and, 47
Reed, Edward: Perón and, 106–7
Renan, Ernest, 5, 25–26; as ideologue,
16
Repetto, Héctor, 165–66
Repetto, Nicolás, 69
Rerum Novarum: church-state relations
and, 22–23
Resnitzky, Nehemías, 139
La Restauración Nacionalista (Rojas),
26, 28
Retorno, 131
Revisionism: Rosa and, 15–16
Revolución Libertadora, 119, 124;
overthrow of Perón and, 121
Revolution of 1930: discussion of, 67–
74
Rial, Arturo, 152
Rico, Aldo, 187
Right: defined, 3
Right-liberals, 159; assessment of,
177–78; characteristics of, 147,
149; ratio of, to Nacionalistas in
military cabinets, 150
Rivadavia, Bernardino, 165
Roca, Eduardo, 164

Roca, Julio A., 36, 76; as nationalist, 55

Roca, Julio A., Jr., 70, 76; beef quota and, 74–75

Roca-Runciman Pact: Nacionalistas and, 74–76

Rock, David, 182, 186–87

Rodó, José Enrique, 5–6, 16, 26

Rodrigo, Celestino, 138–39

Rodríguez Galán, Alberto, 160

Rodríguez Varela, Alberto, 171

Rojas, Isaac, 152, 154, 160

Rojas, Ricardo, 26–28; on value of language, 25

Romanian Iron Guard: fascist group, 185

Roosevelt, Franklin D., 5

Rosa, José M.: revisionism and, 15–16

Rosas, Juan Manuel de, 15, 109, 128; as clerical leader, 19; characterization of, 76

Roth, Roberto ("Bobby"), 166, 169

Rousseau, Jean-Jacques, 3, 7, 9, 16, 20–21; de Maistre on, 13

Ruiz de los Llanos, Gabriel, 138

Ruiz-Guiñazú, Alejandro: rightist coalition and, 89

Runciman, Walter: beef quota and, 75

Russian Revolution (1917): effect of, on Argentine right, 28–29

Sabbatini, Amadeo, 71

Sáenz Peña, Roque, 27, 41

Sáenz Peña Law (1912): passage of, 36

Saint-Jean, Alfredo Oscar, 176

Salas, Acdeel, 155

Salimei, Jorge: policies of, 162

Samuel, Arthur, 11

Sánchez Sorondo, Marcelo, 124–25; on Maurras, 17–18

Sánchez Sorondo, Matías G., 93; anticommunism and, 77; conservatism-Nacionalismo alliance and, 83–85; on Mussolini, 88–89

Sanguinetti, Juan Carlos, 93, 106

San Martín, José de, 74

Sarávia, José María, 161

Sasetrú: industrial conglomerate, 162

Segunda República: Nacionalista organ, 124; policies of, 125

Seineldín, Mohammed Alí, 187

Semana Política, 138

Semana Trágica (1919): workers' revolt, 37–47, 50, 79, 185

Senkman, Leonardo, 181–82, 184–87

Señorans, Eduardo, 157, 161–62

Sepich, Juan: Freemasonry and, 10

Serrano, Basílio, 164

Servicio de Información del Estado, 162

Sigaut, Lorenzo: economic policies of, 174–75

Sindicato de Mecánicos y Afines del Transporte Automotor (SMATA): mechanics' union, 134

Sindicato Obrero de Diques y Darsenas Puerto de la Capital: dockworkers' union, 82

Sirota, Graciela, 126

Sixty-two Organizations, 137

SMATA. *See* Sindicato de Mecánicos y Afines del Transporte Automotor

Smith, Adam, 3

Social Catholic movement, 23, 36–37, 42, 50

Socialistas Independientes, 69

Social Pact, 135, 137; Gelbard and, 133–34; *La Prensa* on, 137

Sociedad Mixta Siderúrgica Argentina (SOMISA), 175

Sociedad Rural Argentina (SRA), 149, 155, 156, 159, 164

Solá, Hidalgo, 174

Solano Lima, Vicente, 120, 125

Solari, Juan Antonio, 92

Sol y Luna, 100, 151

SOMISA. *See* Sociedad Mixta Siderúrgica Argentina

Spanish Civil War: Argentine right and, 77–78

Spanish Inquisition: Menéndez Pelayo on, 14

SRA. *See* Sociedad Rural Argentina

Stalin, Joseph: nonaggression pact with Germany and, 89

Stimson, Frederic J.: Carlés and, 46

Storni, Segundo, 103

Strikes: rise of Argentine right and, 37

Suárez Mason, Carlos, 172–74

Syllabus, 20

Synarchy, 136–38

Tacuara: terrorist group, 161

Taine, Hippolyte-Adolphe, 5, 24–25; as ideologue, 16–17

Tamborini, José: presidential candidacy of, 109
Tami, Felipe, 162
Terrorism: Videla on, 1
Thermann, Edmund von, 87
Thomas Aquinas, Saint, 6
Thucydides, 12
Timerman, Jacobo, 135, 140, 174
Toledo, Pedro de, 46
Toranzo Montero, Federico, 157–60
Torre, Alberto R., 131
Torre, Lisandro de la, 36, 69, 71
Transoceanic News Service, 88
Treitschke, Heinrich von, 2
Trevor-Roper, Hugh, 2
Tricki, Hussein, 128
Túrolo, José María, 158

UCR. *See* Unión Cívica Radical
UCRI. *See* Unión Cívica Radical Intransigente
UCRP. *See* Unión Cívica Radical del Pueblo
UIA. *See* Unión Industrial Argentina
UNA. *See* Unión Nacional Argentina
Unamuno, Miguel, 24–25
Unión Cívica Nacionalista, 126
Unión Cívica Radical (UCR): liberal right organization, 35, 67, 121, 153–54. *See also* Radical party
Unión Cívica Radical del Pueblo (UCRP): liberal right organization, 121–22, 125, 154
Unión Cívica Radical Intransigente (UCRI): liberal right organization, 121–22, 154
Unión Democrática: anti-Peronist coalition, 108
Unión Federal: Nacionalista party, 124, 153
Unión Industrial Argentina (UIA), 149, 153, 155, 159, 164
Unión Nacional Argentina (UNA), 90
Unión Nacionalista Universitaria: rightist group, 71
Unión Obrera Metalúrgica (UOM), 123
Unión Popular: neo-Peronist group, 125, 159
United States: Perón, relations with, 106–7
UOM. *See* Unión Obrera Metalúrgica

Uranga, Juan José, 152
Uriburu, José F., 53, 55–57, 73, 82–83, 86, 91, 151; plans coup, 67; Revolution of 1930 and, 67–70

Valdez Cora, Ramón, 71
Valenti Ferro, Enzo: proposals of, 72–73
Vandor, Augusto T., 131; assassination of, 169; labor right and, 123
La Vanguardia: on Liga, 40
Vargas, Getúlio, 185
Vásquez de Mella, Juan, 52
Vega, Agustín H. de la: LNC and, 128–29
Verlaine, Paul, 25
Verrier, Roberto, 153
Vestre, Juan C., 131
Videla, Jorge Rafael, 148, 150, 174–76; guerrilla tactics and, 172–73; on terrorism, 1; Proceso and, 171
Vidueiro, Carlos, 166, 168
Villada Achával, Clemente, 151
Villada Achával, Manuel, 151–52
Villaguay: worker conflicts at, 43–44
Villalón, Héctor, 127
Villegas, Osiris, 160, 166
Viñas, Alberto, 55
Viola, Roberto, 148–49, 172, 174–75
Vivar, Joaquín Díaz de, 109
Voltaire, François-Marie Arouet, 17
La Voz del Plata, 100
La Voz Nacional, 53, 131

Waisman, Carlos, 2
Walter, Richard J., 182, 184, 186
Wast, Hugo: as pseudonym of Martínez Zuviría, 10, 103, 166
Wehbe, Jorge, 176
Weisbrot, Robert: on Perón's anti-Semitism, 112
Women: Catholic view of, 23; Liga and, 41, 44–45, Nacionalistas and, 56
Workers' Circles (Círculos Obreros), 37; as rightist vehicle, 23
World War I: effect of, on Argentine right, 28–29

Yacimientos Petrolíferos Fiscales, 48
Ygartua, Luis María, 153

Yrigoyen, Hipólito, 35, 38, 41–42, 53, 55, 83, 87, 103, 157; Argentine right and, 48, 67; deposition of, 67; election of, 36; Great Depression and, 49–50; labor policies of, 37; newspaper attacks on, 73; reelection of, 49

Zavala Ortiz, Miguel Angel, 159
Zionism, 129; Perón on, 136–37
Zola, Emile, 27, 28
Zorraquín Becú, Ricardo, 165
Zuberbühler, Luis, 45
Zuleta Alvarez, Enrique, 12; on Maurras, 17

Latin American Silhouettes
Studies in History and Culture

William H. Beezley and
Judith Ewell
Editors

Volumes Published

William H. Beezley and Judith Ewell, eds., *The Human Tradition in Latin America: The Twentieth Century* (1987). Cloth ISBN 0-8420-2283-X Paper ISBN 0-8420-2284-8

Judith Ewell and William H. Beezley, eds., *The Human Tradition in Latin America: The Nineteenth Century* (1989). Cloth ISBN 0-8420-2331-3 Paper ISBN 0-8420-2332-1

David G. LaFrance, *The Mexican Revolution in Puebla, 1908–1913: The Maderista Movement and the Failure of Liberal Reform* (1989). ISBN 0-8420-2293-7

Mark A. Burkholder, *Politics of a Colonial Career: José Baquíjano and the Audiencia of Lima* (1990). Cloth ISBN 0-8420-2353-4 Paper ISBN 0-8420-2352-6

Kenneth M. Coleman and George C. Herring, eds. (with Foreword by Daniel Oduber), *Understanding the Central American Crisis: Sources of Conflict, U.S. Policy, and Options for Peace* (1991). Cloth ISBN 0-8420-2382-8 Paper ISBN 0-8420-2383-6

Carlos B. Gil, ed., *Hope and Frustration: Interviews with Leaders of Mexico's Political Opposition* (1992). Cloth ISBN 0-8420-2395-X Paper ISBN 0-8420-2396-8

Charles Bergquist, Ricardo Peñaranda, and Gonzalo Sánchez, eds., *Violence in Colombia: The Contemporary Crisis in Historical Perspective* (1992). Cloth ISBN 0-8420-2369-0   Paper ISBN 0-8420-2376-3

Heidi Zogbaum, *B. Traven: A Vision of Mexico* (1992). ISBN 0-8420-2392-5

Jaime E. Rodríguez O., ed., *Patterns of Contention in Mexican History* (1992). ISBN 0-8420-2399-2

Louis A. Pérez, Jr., ed., *Slaves, Sugar, and Colonial Society: Travel Accounts of Cuba, 1801–1899* (1992). Cloth ISBN 0-8420-2354-2   Paper ISBN 0-8420-2415-8

Peter Blanchard, *Slavery and Abolition in Early Republican Peru* (1992). Cloth ISBN 0-8420-2400-X   Paper ISBN 0-8420-2429-8

Paul J. Vanderwood, *Disorder and Progress: Bandits, Police, and Mexican Development.* Revised and Enlarged Edition (1992). Cloth ISBN 0-8420-2438-7   Paper ISBN 0-8420-2439-5

Sandra McGee Deutsch and Ronald H. Dolkart, eds., *The Argentine Right: Its History and Intellectual Origins, 1910 to the Present* (1993). Cloth ISBN 0-8420-2418-2   Paper ISBN 0-8420-2419-0

Jaime E. Rodríguez O., ed., *The Evolution of the Mexican Political System* (1993). ISBN 0-8420-2448-4

Steve Ellner, *Organized Labor in Venezuela, 1958–1991: Behavior and Concerns in a Democratic Setting* (1993). ISBN 0-8420-2443-3